THE MISSING LINK
BETWEEN
THE GENESIS CREATION
AND
SCIENTIFIC FINDINGS

B. R. Hicks

P.O. Box 786
Jeffersonville, Indiana 47131-0786

Publisher: Christ Gospel Press
P. O Box 786
Jeffersonville, Indiana 47131-0786

© Christ Gospel Churches Int'l., Inc., 1988

ISBN 1-58363-059-7

Printed in the United States of America.

Table of Contents

Foreword

THE origin of mankind has been one of the most perplexing questions with which mankind has contended. The desire for intrinsic understanding of the genesis of the species has established the premise for scientific research and theological debate. Two diametrically opposing contentions have emerged, evolution and creation.

The theory of evolution is recognized and more widely accepted as the progenitor of mankind. The theory of the origin and the perpetuation of the species by the means of evolution is proclaimed by the majority of the scientific community as the most logical and feasible of the two contentions. Education has promoted the evolutionary theory as the principle ideological basis for the origin of mankind. The debate over the issue has reached into the minds of individuals, families, and the nations of the world.

The debate continues because conclusive scientific proof of linkage between identified species has never been found. One finds that the theory of evolution has gendered more questions than solutions with regard to the ultimate answer to the origin of mankind. Neither have the traditionally held views of the creationists supplied all the answers. Here, in this book, Rev. B. R. Hicks introduces a new and revolutionary concept which bridges the gap between the opposing contentions of the evolutionists and the creationists.

Reverend Hicks, a proponent of the Scriptures as the divinely inspired Word of God, has taken the controversial subject of the origin of mankind and has diligently prayed and searched the Scriptures for the truth. In her search for an answer, she has found conclusive proof for the theory of creation which agrees with scientific findings.

This book shows the unique harmony between the Scriptures and scientific discoveries. By answering the profound question of why and how there have been times of massive disappearances of life on the earth, Reverend Hicks has shown that the links missing in the minds of scientists, with which they hope to establish the theory of evolution as fact, will never be found. Her documentation of the weaknesses found in the theory of evolution and in the views traditionally held by creationists should set to rest the "argument of the ages" for any reader who has a mind open to the truth.

L. D. McClellan
Associate Professor, BS, MA, EdD
University of Louisville

Acknowledgments

I would like to express my sincere appreciation to everyone who has helped in the preparation of the manuscript: to Betty Conway and Martha Anderson for editing and proofreading; to Lois Murry for layout and diagrams; to Dorothea Wright for layout; to Renee Sandusky for typing; and to Mel Jacobsen for typesetting. My special thanks go to Ron Grunder for much of the art work.

Producing a book requires dedication and cooperation on the part of everyone who handles the material, from the author until the finished book is offered to the reader. Many people who encouraged me to write this book offered suggestions and helped in gathering scientific information for my use. However, I take full responsibility for the entire content of the book—both Biblical and scientific.

I am grateful to have people helping prepare my books for print who have a sincere love for God's Word and a desire to see the truth upheld.

Introduction

SCIENTIFIC evidence proves that the earth has been in existence for billions of years. Scientific evidence also indicates that man lived upon this prehistoric earth millions of years ago.

These discoveries actually confirm the teachings of God's Word which record the existence of a prehistoric earth and prehistoric creatures living upon the earth!

Yes, it is true! There is *no disagreement between true science and God's Word.* Lack of knowledge of the truth that is in the Bible has kept both the religious world and the scientific world from finding answers to many of the most perplexing questions man has pondered.

From a scientific and a philosophical viewpoint man has asked the following questions:

- Do the Bible and science agree?
- How were all things brought into existence?
- Are living and nonliving matter the results of scientific laws which operated to form matter into precise order and functions, or is there a self-existent Master Designer Who instituted the laws that govern all things?
- What has caused the episodic, massive extinctions of life on earth?
- Has the theory of evolution rendered the Bible obsolete?
- Can science furnish all the answers we need about the origin of life?

Scientists feel they have answered most of these questions to their satisfaction. Yet, in his book, *Space Time Infinity*, Dr. James S. Trefil, professor of physics at the University of Virginia, says there remain three profound questions still unanswered by science: Where did the moon come from? What exactly are the fusion reactions that drive the sun? Why does life on earth suffer episodic massive extinctions?

It is to this last profound question that this book mainly addresses itself. God's Word gives clear answers to all of our questions.

To the first and most basic question—how was all creation brought into existence—we have two viewpoints: one comes from the believers in God, and one comes from the nonbelievers in God.

The believers base their explanations on the truth of God's Word, while the nonbelievers base their answers on their own hypotheses. Believers know and believe that God created all things from His eternal master plan by His almighty divine power and that He has assigned a purpose to all life. The believer ascribes the cause of all matter, both nonliving and living, to the LORD God and recognizes that He is the Creator of all species of plants and animals, and that He is the Creator of mankind. To the believer, God is the One Who created everything out of nothing but His invisible Word. The believer attributes God with the work, composition, and production of all creation and believes that God brought all things from nothing to something. That man can discover the chemical ingredients and laws which God used in His creation is possible, but the secret of how He united inorganic and organic materials in various, visible, living forms is still a mystery. At some point, man in his search has to get back to the realm where there was no visible thing. At that point he is stymied unless he acknowledges that a power beyond finiteness exists.

Creation is the first realm of four great operations attributed to God. The second realm of God's operations is that of *Owner* and *Master*. The third realm of His operations is that of *providence*, and the fourth realm is that of His *redemption*.

The second explanation for the existence of creation comes from the nonbeliever who presents his hypothesis as though it were a proven fact; therefore, he thinks everyone should take his mere supposition for granted. The nonbeliever never deals in his hypothesis with the facts of the true beginning of matter. He supposes that nonliving matter came into existence by itself and eventually turned into living matter. Then the little original speck of living matter moved upward in its evolutionary development until it reached the epitome of a perfect machine called a human being. He refuses to acknowledge the source of energy that has the power to transform nonliving matter into living matter, and he bypasses the question of how life could have arranged itself into multiplied millions of complex forms without a mastermind.

Faced with finding the origin of life from a natural standpoint, scientists call it an unsolved problem. Just how all the necessary ingredients arranged themselves into a functioning cell capable of reproducing itself is, according to one scientist, "the central question faced today by researchers who probe the origins of life." He also stated, "About the moment of creation itself, we can only wonder."*

For centuries a battle has raged between the believer and the nonbeliever over the answer to the origin of the earth and its world of inhabitants. Who is right?

*Trefil, James S. *Space Time Infinity* (Smithsonian Institution, Washington, D.C., 1985).

The very best place to go in order to find the answer to the origin of the earth and its inhabitants is to search the divine Word of God, the Book given to man by the *Creator*. The Bible is the instrument through which God reveals Himself to man and tells of man's origin and the origin of the earth on which he lives.

In both the natural world and in the spiritual world, knowledge is not easily gained. In the spiritual world, one must apply himself to diligent study, praying for understanding and the wisdom to recognize truth. In my years of being a believer, as I have prayed and studied God's Word, many Scriptures have been opened to me through God's Spirit, and I have been able to find the answers that to me have supplied the link between what believers uphold as the truth and what scientists have discovered as truth, which has appeared to both groups to be contradictory.

God's Word does have the answers.

The purpose of this book is threefold: 1) to strengthen the faith of those who believe that God is their supreme Creator; 2) to help those who have lost their confidence in God to recover their faith in their divine Creator; and 3) to help those find faith in their Creator who have never experienced the great joy and peace that come to the heart and soul that trust in God.

As, together, we look into the Word of God, I trust that each mind and heart will be enlightened by God's illuminating truth. Then, perhaps every reader will choose to stand with the believers in God, not with the nonbelievers.

— The Author

Prologue

Chapter One

The Bible, the Divine Word of God, and Science

CERTAIN facts and spiritual principles need to be established before getting into the main portion of our book so that no confusion arises over what we hold to be the truth. These principles are also the answers to many of man's questions. So, although it may not be exactly proper procedure, the Prologue will be quite lengthy and will be divided into two chapters which will cover two essential points: first, that the LORD God is the Author or the Originator of the Bible, and He also is the Creator or the Originator of science, the laws of nature; and second, that God, the CREATOR, is the CAUSE of ALL things.

The first spiritual principle of truth that we must learn in order to understand all other spiritual truth is that the LORD God is the Author or the Originator of the Bible; and He *is* the Creator or the Originator of science or the laws of nature.

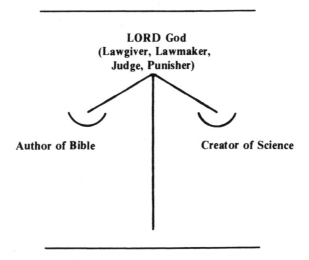

Since God is the Originator of both the Bible and science, there is perfect harmony of truth and knowledge between His spiritual world and His natural world.

The principles of truth or the laws of nature that govern His natural world are visible pictures of His infinite, divine principles of truth that govern His spiritual world.

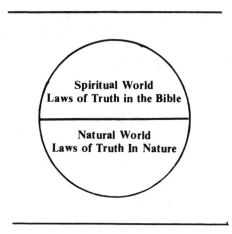

Thus, the knowledge of truth to be found in the Bible and the knowledge to be found in the laws of nature make one complete wheel of unity and harmony which encompasses all truth in the natural and the spiritual realms.

The meanings of the words *Bible* and *science* help us comprehend their application. The term *Bible* is employed to describe the Holy Scriptures of the Old Testament and the New Testament which together form the "Book of books." The word *Bible* was first instituted by Chrysostom, who lived in the fifth century. The word *Scripture* comes from the Latin word *scriptura*, meaning writing, and conveys the analogous idea that the "Scriptures" alone are worthy of being called writings. People's high esteem for the Bible arises from the fact that it is the divine, inspired Word of God.

The revelation of God's master plan for creation is in complete harmony with true science or the laws of nature which are the implementation of God's master plan in His wondrous works of creation. The authority of the Holy Scriptures, the Bible, does not depend upon the testimony of any man or any church, but is wholly dependent upon God Who is truth Himself and Who is the Author of all truth. The Holy Scriptures contain all truth necessary for the salvation of man and for his striding forward and upward in his spiritual education and his moral development, according to God's high, moral calling for him. The Scriptures contain all the wisdom, understanding, and knowledge necessary for the completion of man's spiritual education and moral development.

The Bible consists of sixty-six books which constitute an organic whole. It is divided into two parts: the Old Testament or covenant and the New Testament or covenant. The former contains thirty-nine books; the latter contains twenty-seven books. The word *testament* signifies the will or covenant of God. The Old Testament is the covenant and will of God that He first made with Adam; then later He led Abraham deeper into the Old Testament covenant in a more special way. God subsequently unveiled His covenant and His will more fully to Moses and to the nation of Israel at Mount Sinai. The New Testament or covenant was formed in connection with the advent of the life and death of Jesus Christ. The Old Testament originally was written in Hebrew (except Jeremiah 10:11; Ezra 4:8 to 6:18, 7:12-16; and Daniel, chapter two, from the middle of verse four to 7:28, which are East Aramaean [Chaldean]). According to Dr. Lamsa and the Eastern Catholic Church,* the New Testament was originally written in Aramaic.

God's Word, the Bible, contains knowledge of the LORD God as the Creator of both the spiritual and the natural worlds. Within God's creative works is the scientific knowledge of God's wonderful governmental laws that control and guide nature into fulfilling His divine will. Thus true science is a revelation of the knowledge of God's laws of nature.

The word *science* means to know or to have knowledge. True science is knowledge that has been amassed, severely tested, coordinated, and systematized, especially regarding those wide generalizations called the "laws of nature."

The Universal Dictionary of the English Language gives Herbert Spencer's description of the word *science* in a threefold manner. Herbert Spencer, the philosopher who lived in 1820 and devoted his works to the application of the principles of evolution, to the phenomena of mind and of society, clarifies the sciences as follows:

- **Abstract Sciences:** logic and mathematics
- **Abstract-concrete Sciences:** physics and mechanics
- **Concrete Sciences:** geology, biology, and sociology

No science rests on a firmer base than mathematics, which being founded on demonstrative evidence, may be accepted as absolutely true. The results of logic, which is a deductive science, are much less certain, for error may creep into the premise, with the results of vitiating the conclusion.

---

*Dr. George M. Lamsa, *Holy Bible, From Ancient Eastern Manuscripts* (Philadelphia, PA: A. J. Holman Co., 1957, 19th printing).

All other sciences are to a large extent inductive. Those resting on the "probable evidence" are not really science or knowledge in the strict sense of the word, but continually may approach nearer and nearer to it as scientific methods improve. The sciences, as man knows them, vary in the distance they have moved toward perfection, astronomy and therapeutics having gone far forward. The inductive sciences dealing with humans and animals may be divided into the mental and the physical. The former can be studied largely by reflection on our own mental operations, inductive and deductive reasoning, the whole ending in as wide a generalization as the ascertained facts will permit.

No one can be a truly scientific student unless he considers truth of priceless importance and is prepared to sacrifice all preconceived notions and carefully elaborated opinions whenever he discovers them to be erroneous. No expenditure of money, time, or even life is considered extravagant if the sacrifice be made for the discovery of fresh truth. The initial stages of man's progress in the knowledge of the different sciences are to be sought in a remote period of antiquity.

Moral science came first and reached some degree of progress in knowledge and enlightenment when, at Sinai, God gave man His commandments about the right conduct man should have toward God and toward his fellows.

Mental science, or the investigation of the thinkings and feelings of the mind, came next. However, to this day, this science has made only slow progress because of lack of acquaintance with God's Word and God's Spirit.

Physical science really was commenced, though it was in its infancy, when ancient myths of observation were formed, many of which were hypotheses to account for natural phenomena. Its progress was very slow until the eighteenth century. However, its progress since then has been increasingly rapid.

Prior to this, the greatest advances were made in astronomy and in physics, then in chemistry and botany. Geology did not attract much notice until the beginning of the nineteenth century, and anthropology not until its second half.

True science often has been persecuted by its own most earnest cultivators. Fellow scientists have been known to ridicule the work of other scientists because they were ignorant of the beneficial effects which their discoveries would have for mankind.

Scientists' discoveries of physical laws have made modern inventions possible which have helped mankind incalculably. With the invention of the steam engine came trains and ocean steamers, making mass transportation faster. The internal combustion engine put the world on wheels and in the air. The invention of telegraphy and telephones made worldwide communication possible. And now, computers work with fantastic speed to aid communication, the compilation of data, and numerous other functions which make our modern world a marvel of science and industry. All these modern conveniences have been a result of men's faithful scientific inquiries into God's practical laws of nature. Therefore, we owe an immense debt of gratitude to God and to the many dedicated, true scientists who have sacrificed their lives upon the altar of unending toil and labour to give us the many modern conveniences that we enjoy daily.

True science is coordinated knowledge, arranged and systematized regarding mind or matter. True science is knowledge derived or resulting from obtaining precepts and the principles of the general laws of nature which are called "theories" as correlative with art. The art of science is the application of theoretical knowledge in practice. Thus, true science discovers theoretical knowledge and joins it to practical empirical knowledge.

Consequently, science can be regarded only as true science after its theories have been tested and proven through union with experiential knowledge. Theory cannot be considered a true theory until it has been tested and proven by being able to be joined to the practical working of the laws of nature. Hence, when the theoretical knowledge of science is joined to the empirical knowledge of science, it can be said to be true science. Applied science is a science whose laws are employed and exemplified in dealing with concrete phenomena. The Bible reveals the governmental laws of nature; and true science is a discovery of the practical operation of God's laws which He instituted to control nature.

The knowledge of the Bible and the knowledge of true science are in agreement and harmony. A scientist can discover and learn about God's creation and His divine laws of nature because God has instituted them from the beginning to govern His creation. Man is a discoverer, not a Creator.

Chapter Two

God, the Creator, the Cause of All Things

THE second spiritual truth that we must learn is the eternal principle called "cause and effect" that is seen in both the natural realm and the spiritual realm. This eternal universal Cause is the Almighty God Who has exerted His omnipotent power into acts and has brought the invisible substance of His thoughts and will into visible forms of creation. The LORD God, the eternal universal Cause of all things, has created all things and placed them under the control of His fixed laws of nature.

Cause is that which produces a thing or an effect. Cause is the source from which anything proceeds or arises. Cause is the reason, ground, or motive of action. Almighty God is the eternal Cause from Whom all things have proceeded and by Whom all things have been produced.

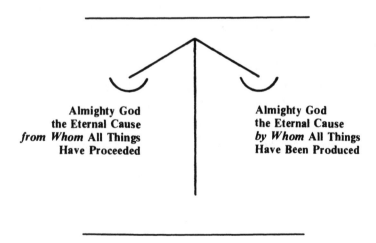

Almighty God
the Eternal Cause
from Whom All Things
Have Proceeded

Almighty God
the Eternal Cause
by Whom All Things
Have Been Produced

Almighty God is the eternal universal Cause, order, and connection of all things. He is the eternal reason for the movements and operations of the mind, which in turn control the movements of the body. Almighty God is the Cause of all animate and inanimate things. He is the primary Cause or the first Cause of all things. It is the first

Cause that gives birth to the effect. Almighty God is the first Cause that produced and brought into existence all things. The Bible reveals God as the Cause of all existence and the Creator of all life and the Maintainer of it in all the universes.

The Bible reveals Jesus Christ as the Son of God and the Creator of all creation. The Bible is our only infallible guide to the prophetic past, the present, and the prophetic future.

The Bible gives us the most accurate, the most sensible, the most believable explanation, and the most truthful explanation about the creation of all things.

The Bible takes us back to the prophetic past, to God—the beginning Cause of all things. "In the beginning God . . ." (Genesis 1:1).

The Hebrew word for *beginning* is *ray-sheeth*, meaning to be first in place, time, order, or rank, the first cause or principal thing. *Ray-sheeth* signifies the seat of movement, as the divine organ from which all external and internal movement has its origin. Hence, in the beginning of all movement is God. In the very beginning of all things coming into existence, it was God, the eternal universal Cause, Who through His internal movement conceived His master plan for all creation, and Who through His external movement gave His master plan to His Son Who created all things. The Hebrew word *ray-sheeth* expresses the fact that the heavens and the earth came into existence in the beginning solely by the creative movements of God.

Before all creation, the infinite unbegotten God existed with neither beginning nor end. Then, He begot His only begotten Son, Christ, Who is called Wisdom, the *Torah* or the Word of God, Who in turn created all finite creation according to the master plan of the infinite God.

Therefore, infinite existence is a description of the state of independent being and the continuance of the independent being of the supreme Sovereign God. The infinite God is independently self-existent. His existence is not dependent on anyone or anything. Even the Christ, the Son of God, acknowledged that God, His Father, was the Cause of His existence and the Maintainer of His existence.

> Jesus said unto them, If God were your Father, ye would love me: for *I proceeded forth and came from God*; neither came I of myself, but he sent me (John 8:42).

Christ witnessed that He had His origin from God, the Father, and that He had proceeded forth from Him. He also testified that He owed the maintenance of His existence or His life to God the Father.

> As the living Father hath sent me, and *I live by the Father*; so he that eateth me, even he shall live by me (John 6:57).

God the Father is the first Cause of all existence including that of His Son, the Christ, the Word of God. As the Son lives by God the Father, all finite creation in turn exists and lives by the Son. The finite existence of all things in the universes, both living and nonliving, is completely dependent on God; not only every thing's existence, but the maintenance of its existence totally depends on the Creator-God.

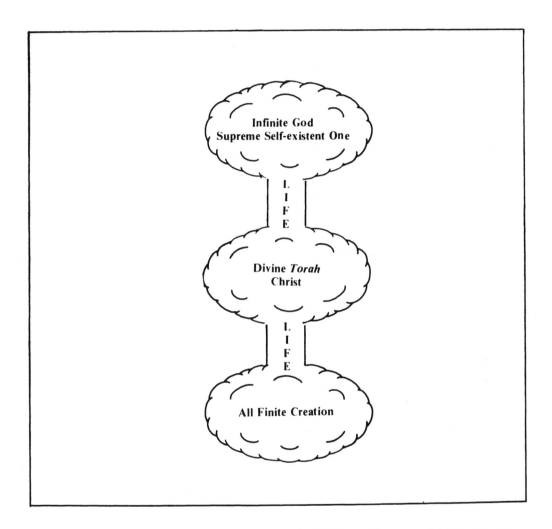

God, the unbegotten Father, through His infinite existence which had neither beginning nor end, begat His only begotten Son, the divine *Torah*, the divine Word, the LORD Jesus Christ, Who created all things. The infinite God, through His Son, has given life or inherent power of motion and the ability to reproduce itself to all living matter.

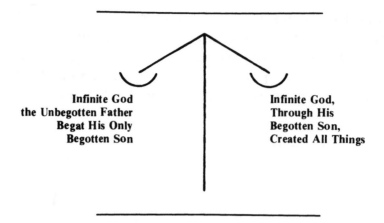

Infinite God
the Unbegotten Father
Begat His Only
Begotten Son

Infinite God,
Through His
Begotten Son,
Created All Things

The wise man in the Book of Proverbs gives an account of the Son or Wisdom, Who was *brought forth* into existence before any and all creation.

> LORD possessed me *in the beginning* of his way, before his works of old. I was set up from everlasting, *from the beginning*, or ever the earth was. When there were no depths, I was brought forth: when there were no fountains abounding with water. Before the mountains were settled, *before the hills was I brought forth: While as yet he had not made the earth, nor the fields, nor the highest part of the dust of the world.* When he prepared the heavens, I was there: when he set a compass upon the face of the depth: When he established the clouds above: when he strengthened the fountains of the deep: When he gave to the sea his decree, that the waters should not pass his commandment: when he appointed the foundations of the earth: *Then I was by him, as one brought up with him*: and *I was daily his delight*, rejoicing always before him: (Proverbs 8:22-30).

The Bible gives a clear and concise account of the *beginning*, which no finite creature could do apart from the divine inspiration of God. The Bible helps one understand something about the beginning (the prophetic past), about the infinity of God and His Son, and about the origin of all life or existence.

God begat His Son or He brought Wisdom to birth before the creation of the universe because He ordained that His Son have a part in His creative work. God filled His Son with His all-encompassing intelligent will, which manifested itself in the creation of the universes and the maintenance of them.

God's Son, the Wisdom of God, presided over the birth of matter, both nonliving and living. God's infinite Wisdom, Word, or Son is the eternal and unerring Ruler and Guide over all finite creation.

The Psalmist confirmed in his writings in the Old Testament dispensation that the work of the Father and the Son in creation was a unified work.

> Let them praise the name of the LORD: *for he commanded*, and
> *they were created* (Psalm 148:5).

The infinite unbegotten Father commanded His only begotten Son to create all things according to His master plan, and the Son passively and actively obeyed, creating all things, assigning them their place and their power to be and to do according to the divine will of God.

In the New Testament dispensation, the Apostle John also confirmed the same principle of truth about the unified work of the Father and the Son in creation.

> *In the beginning was the Word*, and the Word was with God, and
> the Word was God. The same was *in the beginning with God*. All
> things were made by him; and without him was not any thing
> made that was made (John 1:1-3).

The apostle asserted the divinity of God's Word, Wisdom, the Christ, Who was present with the Father in eternity past. God brought His Word to birth in the beginning, and He is the Truth, the Amen, and the Faithful Witness of the mind of God that was manifested through His master plan in creation. The Word is also the One Who brings the truth from God, and He is the One Who speaks to God for us. God's eternal Word existed in the bosom of God in the beginning before time and before creation. The eternal Word, the Christ, was in the beginning, and all creations were produced and brought into being by Him.

The Word of God had an infinite beginning before the world had a finite beginning. The Word of God has the same infinite divine essence and substance as God. Therefore, the Word was with God, and the Word was God. God, the Word, was the Creator of all things, and He is the Redeemer of all things, and He is the Judge of all things.

Creation was and is the unified work of God the Father and God the Son. God the Father began His master plan for all creation. Then He gave His master plan to His Son Who implemented the master plan by creating all things. God's Word began all the creation; furthermore, God's Word finished all the creation, and God's Word preserves and maintains all creation. If God's Word did not preserve and maintain His creation, it would not long endure.

The Apostle Paul, in the New Testament dispensation, also bore witness to the creative works that were done by the Son of God.

> *For by Him were all things created*, that are in heaven, and that are in earth, visible and invisible, whether they be thrones, or dominions or principalities, or powers: *all things were created by him*, and for him: And *he is before all things*, and *by him all things consist* (Colossians 1:16,17).

All things not only were created by the Son of God, but they also consist in their order by Him. ALL things consist or remain fixed, held together, and have a concurrent existence because of the power and dominion of the Word of God. All things are fixed in harmony, agreement, and accord with the divine will of God the Father, Who is the first Cause of all things. All things exist in congruous dependence upon the power of God's Word.

> Who being the brightness of his glory, and the express image of his person, *and upholding all things by the word of his power*, when he had by himself purged our sins, sat down on the right hand of the Majesty on high: (Hebrews 1:3).

All creation is supported and held together by the power of God's Word, the Son of God; it is preserved from disbanding and running into confusion by the infinite, divine power of God's Word.

Sir Isaac Newton confirmed this spiritual principle of God's divine upholding power when he discovered the *scientific law of gravitation*. He realized from his study of the science of mechanics and the science of astronomy that one law could govern the entire universe. To quote from Dr. James Trefil's book, *Space Time Infinity*, where he is writing about Newton's discoveries, he says, "There seemed to be no connection at all between the stately turning of the planets and the fall of an apple. It was Newton's gift to humanity to realize that such artificial distinctions do not really hold in nature—that the universe is a single seamless web, and the force that guides the moon also causes the apple to fall."

Christ is the universal upholder of all things. Christ made the worlds, and He bears up the worlds, preventing them from falling apart.

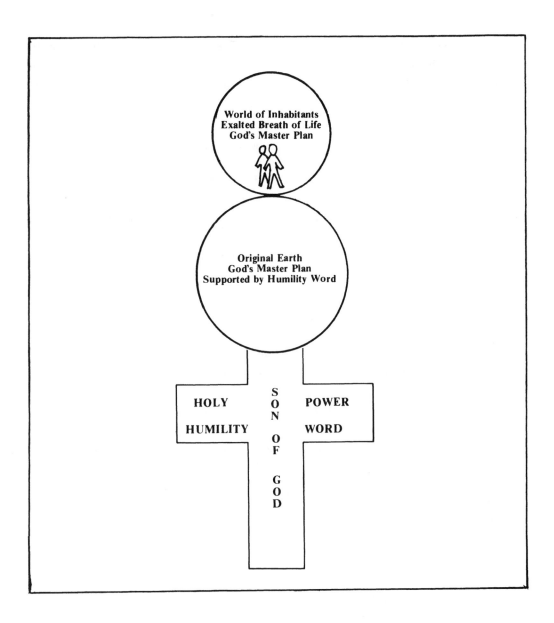

If it were not for the invisible power and dominion of the Word of God, the sun, moon, and stars, and all the host of heaven, would fall out of their orbits. If it were not for the power of the infinite, divine Word of God, the earth again would be submerged in a watery grave because the seas would overflow their banks, drowning everyone.

All things live, breathe, and have their being because of the divine Word of God. So why do atheistic scientists try to discard and negate the very One Who is giving them life and breath? It would be an unwise move for one to try to cut down the pillars of the house in which he dwells. It would be an unwise move for one to try to bore holes in the ship that bears him up above the water. Likewise, it is unwise to fill one's mind with thoughts that destroy the pillars of power and truth which are upholding him, giving him the very breath of life.

> And to make all men see what is the fellowship of the mystery, which *from the beginning of the world hath been hid in God, who created all things by Jesus Christ*: (Ephesians 3:9).

Nothing is more conclusive in the Bible than the truth that the infinite God, the first Cause, created all things by His Son, Jesus Christ. The divine Word was God, and as such He was "in" the beginning with God. But the created worlds were and are only "from" the beginning.

> Thus saith God the LORD, *he that created the heavens, and stretched them out; he that spread forth the earth*, and that which cometh out of it; he that giveth breath unto the people upon it, and spirit to them that walk therein: (Isaiah 42:5).

The LORD God created the heavens, or as the Hebrew reads, He "beat" them out, implying extension and firmness. He gives the breath of life to the people upon the earth, His divine Spirit to them that walk therein. Because the LORD God is the first Cause of all creation, He is the Fountainhead of all power.

The LORD God stretched out the upper world and spread forth the lower world.

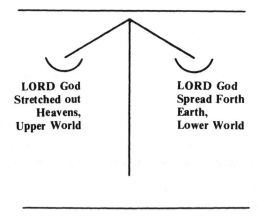

LORD God	**LORD God**
Stretched out	**Spread Forth**
Heavens,	**Earth,**
Upper World	**Lower World**

God stretched out the heavens, meaning that He drew them out, extending them in length. God made the heavens strong by drawing them tight, by twisting them tight. He drew them out to greater length and greater breadth until they reached the ultimate of His satisfaction and His pleasure, according to His holy purposive will. God stretched out the heavens as a canopy for the lower world. God spread out (extended) the earth without the least separation. He extended the earth within a circular form. God spread out the earth in all directions; therefore, it was expanded to a broader surface.

> Even every one that is called by my name: *for I have created him for my glory, I have formed him*; yea, *I have made him* (Isaiah 43:7).

Everyone is called by the Name of the LORD, his Creator; therefore, God will not cease working His mysterious master plan until ALL creatures acknowledge Him as the supreme, Sovereign God. The LORD has created man for His glory so that man might not cease to praise Him and spread the wonderful knowledge of light and truth of His Holy Word abroad in the earth. God personally formed and made man for His honour and glory. Hence it is the most reasonable thing for man to glorify his Creator. If God stretched out the heavens above to declare His glory, and if He spread forth the earth for a home for man, surely man ought to spread out God's glory and fame "below" upon the earth by declaring that God is the first Cause and Creator of all things!

> I have made the earth, and created man upon it: *I, even my hands, have stretched out the heavens*, and all their host have I commanded . . . For thus saith the *LORD that created the heavens; God himself that formed the earth and made it;* he hath established it, he created it not in vain, he formed it to be inhabited: I am the LORD; and there is none else (Isaiah 45:12-18).

God created and stretched out the heavens and commanded or ordained that the host of the heavens give honour to Him by doing His will. God also created, formed, and established the earth and ordained that the host of earth give Him honour by doing His will and glorifying His Name. The Creator-God is the sole, supreme power over His creation. As such, He has a right to make laws for it, give laws to it, and expect obedience from it. God did not create the earth in vain; He formed it to be inhabited by man. He desired man to dwell upon it in righteousness and to walk in His moral light

21

of truth and justice. The discarding of God as the Creator is sheer folly and is a sure sign of the depths of diseased perception of reality in man's mind.

> *Have we not all one father? hath not one God created us?* why
> do we deal treacherously every man against his brother, by
> profaning the covenant of our fathers? (Malachi 2:10).

This verse establishes the Fatherhood of God and the brotherhood of man, according to God the Creator of all.

When man fills his heart with atheistic notions about God, his heart also becomes filled with corrupt, lawless principles of wickedness. Hence, he becomes a doer of corrupt, lawless practices against God his Creator and against his created brothers by dealing treacherously with them. If the creature falsely denies any responsibility toward his Creator as the Owner and Master, he cannot be expected to accept his responsibility for being true, honest, and just toward his fellow brother-creatures. God did not intend for man to dwell in darkness and confusion about Who His Creator is. So, He has given man the light of truth through the Holy Scriptures concerning Himself as the first Cause and as the Creator. Through His Holy Word, He also has revealed His Sovereign master plan for man and His powerful working ability to implement His plan.

The Scriptures that we have noted all agree in their revelation about Who created the heavens and the earth and all that dwell therein.

The "Who" of creation is the one eternal God, the Father, the first Cause, and His Son, the Christ, the Word of God.

Before the beginning, the only omniscient, omnipotent, and omnipresent God existed without beginning and without end. Then, God begat His Son Who created celestial worlds with angelic life and terrestrial worlds with human life because He desired to share with others the divine perfection of His glory and the infinitude of His goodness.

God's purposive will in the beginning was to build celestial worlds and terrestrial worlds for His creatures to dwell in, places in which they could share the goodness and glory of the holy nature of His Name. The infinite God, the first Cause, is the Master Architect Who conceived the thoughts of His master plan or the blueprints for these celestial and terrestrial houses. God brought His master plan to birth and revealed it to His Son, the Builder, Who built all the edifices of creation. The Son built all things according to the exact dimensions, forms, and arrangements of God's blueprint. Furthermore, the grand edifices of creation were built precisely according to the plans of the Master Architect. The Word of God, the Christ, under the supervision and superintendence of God the Father, created, made, and erected all the great celestial and terrestrial edifices. God, as the first Cause, is the wise Designer of everything that has been created and that will be created. God is the divine Sovereign Architect Who, through His Son, has fashioned and framed the worlds.

Any well-planned building in the natural realm begins in the mind of the architect with a thought which increases into a master plan or blueprint. However, when the building is finished, very few will recognize the parental idea from which the whole plan was brought to birth. Very few are interested in the foundational pillars of a structure, whether it be a building or a bridge that may support thousands of tons of wood, concrete, and steel. Everyone knows that an architect in the natural realm has a purpose for a building that has originated from his master plan.

Buildings in the natural realm are built with specific designs in order to serve the purpose of the owner. Likewise, God also created the heavens and the earth from His master plan according to his specific designs to serve His purposive will as the Owner and the Master. God's design for His creation is that it should seek and find His goal and objective for it, while it is serving and worshipping Him as the Creator and sharing in the goodness and glory of His Name.

As the first Cause, God encompasses all the objects of His creation together in unity by His eternal power and Godhead. God is the Ruler, the Lawmaker, the Lawgiver, and the Judge of all His creation.

The LORD God, as the Ruler and Regulator over His creation, has made laws for its benefit and has given laws to govern it, both naturally and spiritually. God, as the Judge, decides and determines the offenses of His creation and dispenses His punishments in proportion to the offenses. God has a pattern and plan for His creation; therefore, He has a purpose and reason for His creation.

This, then—that God is the Creator of all things—is an essential spiritual principle that we must know if we are to understand the earth's and man's origin.

In the remaining chapters of this book, we will be presenting the four schools of thought concerning the origin and history of the earth and its world of inhabitants.

Then from the Scriptures, we will show how the original, created earth underwent three catastrophic judgments and restorations. After each judgment, the earth was restored. The original earth and two of its restorations existed in the prehistoric aeons of the past. The present earth is the third restoration of the earth. Each time God judged the earth, its world of inhabitants was destroyed. The account of man's creation in the Book of Genesis is the record of the previous creation of man and the creation of present-day man, who was created to inhabit the recreated earth after it had been judged for the third time. **This truth forms the missing link between the ideas creationists have purported in their interpretation of the Genesis creation and what scientists have uncovered in their search for answers to man's origin.** It is an answer to the scientific world's question about the periodic massive extinctions of life on the earth, which they have indisputable evidence of having happened—but which they cannot explain. This truth is also the reason scientists never will be able to establish a link between all the fossils, nor ever find the mechanism that will turn evolution into a scientific fact.

Because God's catastrophic and cataclysmic judgments were so complete, man is left with gaps in his information of the history of the earth and its world of inhabitants. Therefore, it is impossible for anyone to piece together a true and complete picture apart from the Holy Scriptures. No written records were left by prehistoric man; only a small witness in the earth's crust and a few fragmental fossils leave evidence of ancient by-gone days. However, God's prophetic Word discloses the truth about man's past history.

In the September, 1983, issue of *Science Digest*, there is an article entitled "The Dinosaur Massacre, a Double-Barrelled Mystery" by Robert Jastrow. In the article he says, "Everyone knows the dinosaurs vanished 65 million years ago. The suddenness of their disappearance suggests that they were wiped out by some natural disaster. What was this catastrophe?" The Bible answers this question.

Many facts and laws of nature that scientists have discovered are referred to in the Bible; some of these will be noted in this book. The discovery of these facts and laws substantiate the truth of the record God has given man about his home, the earth, and about the universe.

Finally, we will give a brief history of evolution and examine some of its paradoxical theories. We trust everyone's faith in His Creator will be strengthened by the time he has read this book.

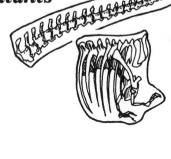

Part One

The Four Schools of Thought Concerning the Origin and History of the Earth and Its World of Inhabitants

The Four Schools of Thought

ALEX Haley's much publicized book, *Roots*, opened the floodgate to a new wave of interest in the study of genealogy. Since the publication of Mr. Haley's book, untold volumes have been printed to explain how to trace a family tree to its roots. A search for one's beginning may unearth many interesting facts and even much beneficial knowledge about the roots of a natural family tree; however, it is not possible for man to discover his true roots, either spiritually or naturally, unless he turns to the Word of God. From the Bible we learn that the Creator-God is the Source of all forms of life, including mankind.

Certainly the God Who made us did not intend that we live our lives in a state of mental confusion about such an important matter as our origin, either our natural origin or our spiritual origin.

Because of the bitter warfare that rages between the believers and nonbelievers in God, many people are unsure of exactly what they do believe about the creation of our earth and the man who walks upon it.

At one time, the doctrine that man came into being through an act of the Creator-God was believed almost universally. There were very few avowed atheists. However, today the number of nonbelievers in God (among whom are the atheistic scientists) has increased as a result of our schools' teaching the theory of evolution as fact. Many young people accept these unproven theories of evolution as proven facts. They take man's invalid suppositions into their hearts and minds and discard God as the governor and guide of their lives.

The main purpose of this book is to clarify the truth that the LORD God is the Creator Who made the heavens and the earth and all that is therein and to show that the scientific facts man has discovered to this date DO NOT negate the fact of creation, nor will they ever.

There are four schools of thought involving the origin and history of the earth and its world of inhabitants: creationism and evolutionism (which deal with the origin of the earth and its inhabitants) and catastrophism and uniformitarianism (which deal with their history).

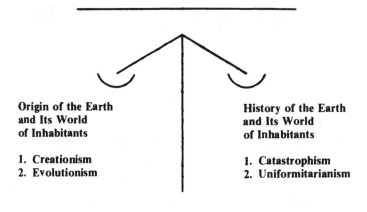

Origin of the Earth and Its World of Inhabitants	History of the Earth and Its World of Inhabitants
1. Creationism	1. Catastrophism
2. Evolutionism	2. Uniformitarianism

I. Creationism

The first basic school of thought concerning the origin of the earth and its inhabitants comes from the Word of God and is accepted by believers as being the infallible truth.

Creationists believe, know, and explain that all existence came from God Himself and was passed down in the form of creation, as is recorded in the Holy Bible.

Creationists believe that God called all things into existence out of nothing; that the universe and the world are the original works, composition, and production of Almighty God; that God is the Cause and Source and Originator of having something "be" out of nothing. Creationists believe that all things exist by the Word of God. They do not believe that things were produced from previously existing matter.

Scientists' tracings start from the end as they search for the beginning. The Bible starts in the beginning with God and continues to the end of creation.

> Before the mountains were brought forth, or ever thou hadst formed the earth and the world, even from everlasting to everlasting, thou art God (Psalm 90:2).

God existed before the creation of time, and He will continue to exist after the cessation of time.

The LORD God is the Creator Who brought to birth the mountains, the great giants of antiquity, which are mentioned by the Psalmist. These ancient giants contribute much to the existence of life upon the earth. They absorb moisture from the clouds, sending it down in the form of springs and brooks. They also draw down electricity from above. But regardless of their importance, God is the eternal, omnipotent Force and Energy Who created them and all other things, and He maintains all things. He is from everlasting to everlasting.

Since all truth is found in the Bible, the Bible is the source that must be used to find true answers to the questions about man's beginning. All existence and creation has proceeded out from the Self-existent God.

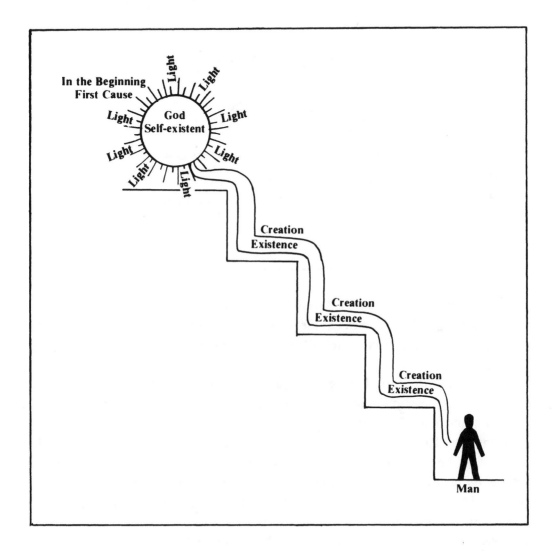

However, before we explore creationism any further, let us note the two classes of existence so that we can draw a balanced and sensible conclusion about the origin of *all* things.

The Bible dispels the darkness that clouds man's mind, which would prevent him from seeing God's orderly and wise plan of all the creation, the creation of both organic and inorganic matter. There is much confusion in the world today about the origin of both living and nonliving matter, about Who brought matter into existence, and about Who maintains the life or existence of all things.

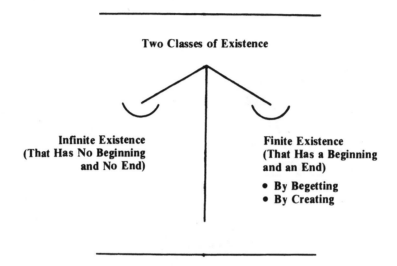

Two Classes of Existence

Infinite Existence
(That Has No Beginning
and No End)

Finite Existence
(That Has a Beginning
and an End)
- **By Begetting**
- **By Creating**

The word *infinite* means a lacking of bounds; extending beyond measure or comprehension; endless; immeasurable; very great; vast; immense; inexhaustible. This is a beautiful description of the infinite God Who is unbegotten and Who always has existed.

The word *finite* means having measurable or definable limits; not infinite. This is a clear, concise description of all created things.

All finite matter, regardless of how large or how small, whether living or nonliving, has had a beginning. Therefore, something or someone outside of the sphere of the finite already had to be in existence in order to initiate finite existence. In the beginning, the infinite divine God existed, Who was and is, with neither beginning nor end. The very word *infinite* signifies One Who is not finite; having no bounds or limits; without limits; unbounded; boundless; not limited or circumscribed. The word is applied to Almighty God, the supreme Being, or to His attributes (such as His goodness and mercy) which are infinite. Infinity is an incalculable number. The infinitude of God's wisdom and knowledge is immeasurable. The Supreme God created all things out of the infinitude of His wisdom and His power.

The mystery of God's will, which has taken myriad ages to unfold, has required cycle after cycle and dispensation after dispensation to be revealed. God's master plan is perfect within Himself, but it has taken Him long ages to unveil and fulfill His mysterious will through the manifold experiences of His creatures. The mystery of God's master plan also will continue unfolding in the myriad ages to come.

Hence, in the beginning of the Bible, God laid the foundation stone of wisdom, understanding, and knowledge concerning the infinite, Self-existent God, Who is the first Cause, the Creator of all matter, both living and nonliving. This is a common belief of all creationists.

The words in Genesis 1:1, "In the beginning God," may appear strange and foreign to a finite mind because of the distance between the human finite mind and the divine infinite mind of God. Infinite existence prior to creation is unfathomable to the finite creature's mind because, as humans, we are blind to the infinity of God's glory, and we are deaf to the infinitude of God's thoughts. Likewise, in the natural realm, the starry heavens are unfathomable to a blind person; and the beautiful sounds of the symphony are incomprehensible to a deaf person. But that does not mean the starry heavens and the sounds of the beautiful symphony do not exist because a man is blind and deaf. Likewise, God's infinity does not cease to exist because man is blind and deaf to it. So God's infinite thoughts are beyond man's finite thoughts.

> For my thoughts are not your thoughts, neither are your ways my ways, saith the LORD. For as the heavens are higher than the earth, so are *my ways higher than your ways, and my thoughts than your thoughts* (Isaiah 55:8,9).

God's infinite thoughts and ways extend far above and beyond man's finite thoughts.

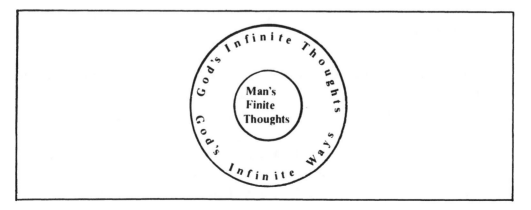

Because God's infinite thoughts and ways are in another dimension, far above the physical world and beyond human comprehension, man might be tempted to reject the eternal existence of God's infinite thoughts and ways. But finite man's rejection of God's eternal existence does not negate His eternal existence.

God's self-existence and His power to create are firmly believed by creationists. To believers, all creation had its beginning with the infinite God.

Creationists believe in an infinite God Who is the Cause of finite creation.

II. Evolutionism

Evolutionism, the second school of thought concerning the origin of the earth and its world of inhabitants, is the theory projected and embraced by most scientists today. The word *evolution* means an unrolling, an opening out, or working out; a process of development, formation, or growth. There are basically three types of evolutionists: 1) theistic, 2) deistic, and 3) atheistic.

A. Theistic Evolutionists

Theistic evolutionists believe that God is Creator and Ruler of the universe, that He is known by revelation, and that He uses the process of evolution to bring His creation onward and upward to perfection.

Theistic evolutionists believe that God not only started the process of life, but that He continues to direct the process of life all through the different stages of evolution to the place it is today. To the theistic evolutionists, present life is a result of God Who is directing this process according to His plan and purpose. They believe in one God Who is Creator and Ruler of the universe and Who is known by revelation through His work in evolution.

B. Deistic Evolutionists

Deistic evolutionists believe that God started the first life and then ignored His original cell of life, allowing naturalistic processes of life to evolve over the ceaseless ages into the present-day creation. No specific purpose is assigned to this development.

Deistic evolutionists believe that God exists and that He created the earth and its world of inhabitants, but that thereafter He assumed no control over the creation or the people. The word *deist* originated from the Latin language, and the word *theist*

32

originated from the Greek language. Conventionally, however, these words are widely different in import.

Deistic philosophy says that reason alone is sufficient to prove the existence of God, with the consequent rejection of revelation and authority. Therefore, although the deists admit the Being of a God, they deny the existence of and the necessity for a divine revelation. They say that the light of nature and reason are sufficient guides in doctrine and practice. They are "free thinkers" and believers in natural religion only. Thus, deistic evolutionists teach that God created original matter and then left matter to its own wisdom and reason to evolve into a perfect, orderly shape and form.

Deistic evolutionists believe in God as the original Creator but disbelieve in God's Son, the Christ, the Word of God.

C. Atheistic Evolutionists

This class of evolutionists believes there is no God involved in the process of life—that all life developed or arose by naturalistic, mechanistic processes without any direct purpose.

Atheistic evolutionists disbelieve the existence of a God. Socrates was put to death for asserting the superiority of divine Wisdom as the Ruler and the Disposer of the universe. Atheism is a scoffing spirit against the existence of God. Atheism protests against the persecution of fanaticism, but it only replaces the system it attempts to destroy with its own system of fanatic persecution. Atheism in our present century includes every philosophic system which rejects the belief in God as a personal Creator.

III. Catastrophism

From the geological and paleontological worlds comes the first scientific school of thought, catastrophism, which concerns the history of the earth and its worlds of inhabitants. Some creationists believe catastrophism to be a fact. This does not disagree with the Bible. On the contrary, it very much substantiates the Scriptural account of the history of the earth and its inhabitants.

The doctrine of catastrophism has its origin from the word *catastrophe*, meaning an upsetting, an overthrowing, a final event, a conclusion, a great misfortune.

Some geologists hold the view that the geological changes of the world and the formation of rocks have been produced by the action of catastrophic or violent physical changes. In France, the distinguished geologists Eliede Beaumont and George Cuvier were great advocates of this theory; and, during their time, the world in general followed their beliefs.

Catastrophism is a geological speculation that changes in the earth were produced by powerful outside forces that were different from those which one presently sees in action in the universe. Many geologists believed that the theory of vast catastrophic changes accounted for the successive breaks that seemed to appear in the earth's development.

They conceived the possibility of worldwide destruction of floras and faunas and the sudden introduction or creation of new forms of life after the forces of nature had sunk into repose. This is certainly congruous with the truth of God's Word.

IV. Uniformitarianism

The second scientific school of thought concerning the history of the earth and its inhabitants, uniformitarianism, was strongly advocated by the geologists Hutton and Lyell, who theorized that there is no need for the hypothesis of alternate periods of repose and convulsion to account for the present appearance of the earth's crust. They believed that visible results of the earth's formation and appearance have been produced by the operation of ordinary causes which are seen today. Their doctrine was that all geological phenomena may be explained as a result of observable processes that operate in a uniform way over long periods of time.

The Academic American Encyclopedia records this information about the theory of uniformitarianism:

> Because geology is primarily observational science, it inherently lacks some of the discipline of the experimental sciences such as chemistry, where simple, repeatable laboratory tests can in many instances settle disputed theories. In Hutton's day, therefore, geology needed a standard of testing theories. Hutton asserted that 'the past history of our globe must be explained by what can be seen to be happening now.' Past geologic events were to be explained by processes that could be tested by observation somewhere in the modern world. This approach had the effect of stimulating investigation into contemporary

geologic processes, and it simplified investigation of Earth's history by eliminating from immediate consideration the more extreme catastrophic explanations. At base, Hutton's principle (which is often called *actualism*) is rooted in the sine qua non of modern science, the belief in the unchanging natural law of an orderly universe.

The subsequent writings of Sir Charles Lyell, particularly the many editions of his *Principles of Geology*, popularized the uniformitarian idea among the English-speaking geologists. Lyell's work, however, extended the meaning of the concept to include the assertion that past geologic processes have operated at a more or less constant rate equivalent to the rates seen today, and that the most important geologic processes are slow. Whereas many important geologic processes, such as erosion or the uplift of folded mountains, are slow, some large results also are not necessarily evidences of slow changes; furthermore, changes in ratio of processes and probably in conditions, such as atmospheric composition, have occurred. Thus, *strict 'Lyellian uniformitarianism (gradualism) is maintained by few geologists today.'* (Emphasis by author.)

However, Lyell's theory was the most influential concept in forming the fourth school of thought—that of evolution. Darwin and Lyell were close friends and correspondents, and although Lyell was slow to accept the theories of Darwin about the development of the species, he eventually believed Darwin's ideas.

In Darwin's *Origin of the Species*, he emphasized that development of life on earth was a slow, gradual process that took aeons of time. This idea he gleaned from Lyell's theory of uniformitarianism.

However, even with the wide acceptance of the theory of evolution, there is still a strong debate over whether evolution always has been a uniform, gradual process, or whether it has been punctuated by rapid bursts of change. This debate continues because scientists cannot answer the riddle of the sudden and apparently catastrophic disappearances of life during different periods of Earth's history.

Summary

As a person who believes that God is the eternal Cause of all things, that He is the Sustainer and Governor of all things, and that His Word is infallible, obviously, I stand opposed to beliefs embraced by atheistic evolutionists. Nevertheless, I believe that all readers, including those who are strong supporters of evolution, will see in the following sections of this book an unbiased presentation of the harmony that exists between God's divine Word and true scientific findings. I believe that they will see a fair and equitable presentation of the fallacies in the theory of evolution. And finally, I believe that those who read this book in its entirety with an open mind will be able to understand clearly why I cannot accept the atheistic theory of evolution as being true.

The four basic schools of thought concerning the origin and history of the earth and its inhabitants have been stated in this section: creationism, evolutionism, catastrophism, and uniformitarianism.

By the time the reader has progressed through the following chapters of this book, he or she should be equipped with sufficient knowledge and understanding of what is taught in God's Word and what has been discovered in the world of science to make a rational decision about these four schools of thought. It is possible that some may want to enroll in a school different from the one they now attend while there is time to get the type of education and attain the moral development that will prepare one for eternity.

Part Two

The Truth That Links the Biblical Account of the History of the Earth and Its Worlds of Inhabitants With Scientific Findings

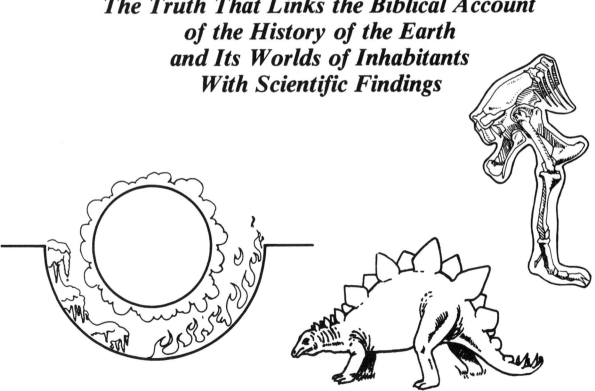

Chapter One

What Happened to the Original Earth and Its World of Inhabitants

THE Bible is an infinite treasure house, filled with the gold of wisdom, the silver of understanding, and the precious stones of knowledge. Any inquiring soul who takes the time to pray and diligently search God's Word can obtain these hidden treasures.

It has been through untold hours of just this kind of searching and praying that the revelation of the creation of the original earth and its three successive restorations has been uncovered. It is this truth that explains why scientific findings, such as the existence of prehistoric men and sudden extinctions of whole species of life on earth, do not negate the Genesis account of creation.

That God has created *more than one* world of inhabitants on this one earth is established clearly in the Bible, although traditional creationists believe that God created only one earth and *one* world of inhabitants. Such a belief leaves too many questions unanswered that have been raised by the scientific world; neither does this belief agree with the revelation of God's Word.

> God, who at sundry times and in divers manners spake in time past unto the fathers by the prophets, Hath in these last days spoken unto us *by his Son*, whom he hath appointed heir of all things, *by whom also he made the* **worlds**; Who being the brightness of his glory, and the express image of his person, and *upholding all things by the word of his power*, when he had by himself purged our sins, sat down on the right hand of the Majesty on high; (Hebrews 1:1-3).

According to His Word, God created *all* the *old worlds*. One after the other, He judged and punished them, leaving each one in a catastrophic, cataclysmic state of chaos, after having cast it into a "pit" because each world sinned and disobeyed Him.

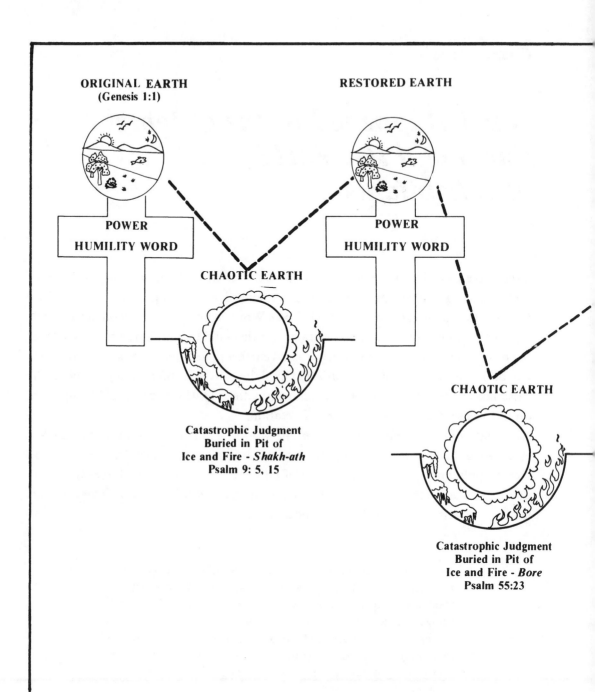

ORIGINAL EARTH
(Genesis 1:1)

RESTORED EARTH

POWER

HUMILITY WORD

POWER

HUMILITY WORD

CHAOTIC EARTH

Catastrophic Judgment
Buried in Pit of
Ice and Fire - *Shakh-ath*
Psalm 9: 5, 15

CHAOTIC EARTH

Catastrophic Judgment
Buried in Pit of
Ice and Fire - *Bore*
Psalm 55:23

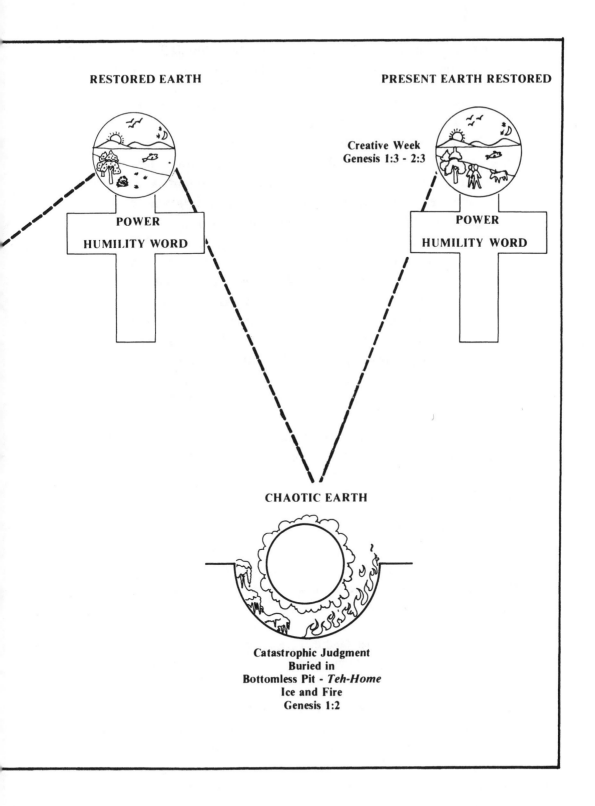

RESTORED EARTH

PRESENT EARTH RESTORED

Creative Week
Genesis 1:3 - 2:3

POWER

HUMILITY WORD

POWER

HUMILITY WORD

CHAOTIC EARTH

Catastrophic Judgment
Buried in
Bottomless Pit - *Teh-Home*
Ice and Fire
Genesis 1:2

41

Let us note what scientists have found that confirms the Biblical account of God's catastrophic judgments of the prehistoric earth and its different worlds of inhabitants.

> Paleontologists have long been aware of abrupt changes in the kinds of plants and animals found on the earth. The fossil record is full of species that lasted for a long time and then disappeared suddenly, to be replaced by entirely new species. The most spectacular as well as the most familiar of these were the dinosaurs, whose sudden disappearance some 65 million years ago signaled the end of what geologists call the Cretaceous period. For almost 200 million years these giant repiles had been the dominant life form on earth, and then in the blink of an eye (geologically speaking) they vanished. Perhaps less well known is the fact that while the dinosaurs were disappearing, fully 70 percent of all living species perished along with them. For some species, such as ocean plankton, the extinction rate exceeded 90 percent. A similar catastrophic extinction occurred at the end of the Permian period, 250 million years ago.*

As Master and Owner of His creation, God has the sovereign right to be its Lawmaker, Lawgiver, Judge, and Punisher, according to the moral standards of the holiness and righteousness of His own laws.

But first, how did God create these worlds?

I. How God Created the Worlds

Through faith we gain the understanding that God framed the worlds by His Word. The worlds did not come into existence through happenstance nor develop by themselves out of pre-existent matter.

> Through faith we understand that *the worlds were framed by the word of God*, so that things which are seen were not made of things which do appear (Hebrews 11:3).

God's Spirit of prophecy enables one to look back to the past, to look into the present, and to look forward into the future. The Spirit of prophecy opens the eye of faith to look in the proper direction, according to the will of God.

*James S. Trefil, *Space Time Infinity* (Smithsonian Institution, Washington, D.C., 1985).

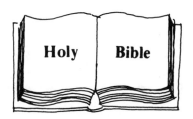

Holy Bible

A Look at the
Past, Present and Future Earths
and Their Worlds of Inhabitants
According to Bible Prophecy

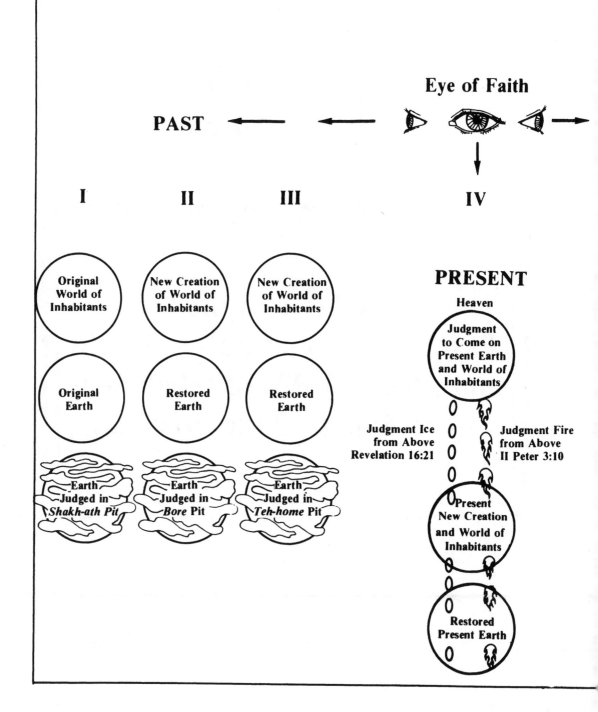

Eye of Faith

PAST

I   II   III   IV

PRESENT

I — Original World of Inhabitants / Original Earth / Earth Judged in *Shakh-ath Pit*

II — New Creation of World of Inhabitants / Restored Earth / Earth Judged in *Bore* Pit

III — New Creation of World of Inhabitants / Restored Earth / Earth Judged in *Teh-home* Pit

IV — Heaven / Judgment to Come on Present Earth and World of Inhabitants

Judgment Ice from Above Revelation 16:21

Judgment Fire from Above II Peter 3:10

Present New Creation and World of Inhabitants

Restored Present Earth

44

FUTURE

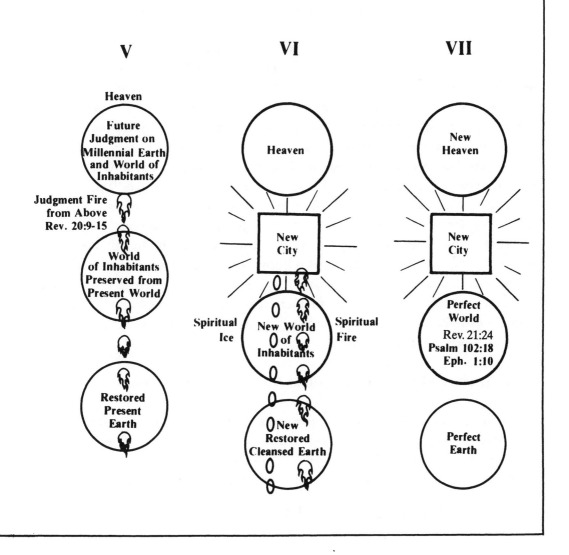

V

Heaven

Future
Judgment on
Millennial Earth
and World of
Inhabitants

Judgment Fire
from Above
Rev. 20:9-15

World
of Inhabitants
Preserved from
Present World

Restored
Present
Earth

VI

Heaven

New
City

Spiritual
Ice

New World
of
Inhabitants

Spiritual
Fire

New
Restored
Cleansed Earth

VII

New
Heaven

New
City

Perfect
World
Rev. 21:24
Psalm 102:18
Eph. 1:10

Perfect
Earth

45

The eye of faith is able to look into God's Word and see a portion of God's master plan for the earth and its worlds of inhabitants that have existed in the prophetic past, that exist in the present, and that will exist in the prophetic future. Therefore looking into God's Word by faith reveals the truth from yesterday, for today, and for tomorrow. One can see in His Word that in the past ages of time God created an original world of inhabitants and two successive worlds. These worlds existed in prehistoric time. Then He created our present world; and in the future He will create a new world of inhabitants to praise His Name.

> This shall be written for the generation to come: and the people
> *which shall be created* shall praise the LORD (Psalm 102:18).

God shall create a people in the future for the purpose of praising His Name!

Man can understand some of the events of creation by looking at the world with the naked eye of logical reasoning, but faith allows him to see and comprehend that the worlds were neither eternal nor self-producing but were framed by another. The eye of faith is able to see in the Bible how God devised and framed His invisible master plan of creation in His mind in eternity past, and how, through the wondrous creative works of His Son, He implemented and framed His master plan visibly. The Holy Scriptures give one wisdom and knowledge, through which many excellent, truthful reasonings about creation also can be framed in one's mind. The eye of faith is able to see God's perfect order, shape, form, and proportions in His creation.

What do we mean by saying that God "framed the worlds" by His wondrous creative works? A frame is that which forms the exterior edging of anything; consequently, it determines the form; it is that which holds the rest together. So God framed the worlds by His exalted Word; then He supported the earth and its world of inhabitants by His humility Word, the Son of God. If God framed *worlds*, then there had to have been an original world.

II. The Creation of the Original Earth and Its Three Restorations

The history of the earth and its inhabitants begins in Genesis, which is the name given to the first book of the Bible because it means origin. Genesis gives the account of the origin of the creation of the heavens and all the host of them, the earth and its worlds of inhabitants, the beginning of life, the creation of all things.

> In the beginning *God created* the heaven and the earth (Genesis 1:1).

The Book of Genesis declares the creation to be the work of the infinite LORD God Almighty. This first verse gives a majestic description of God's original, creative works—the heavens and the earth and the worlds of inhabitants that occupied them. It also introduces us to God Himself and indisputably identifies Him as the Creator.

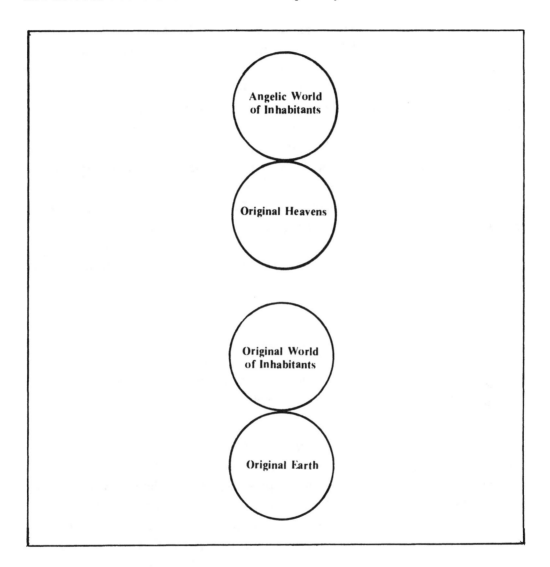

The Name of God is the general designation which refers to the supreme, divine Being Who is the Cause, the fountain and source of all things. In Hebrew the Name of *God* is *Elohim*, which is a uniplural noun signifying both plurality and oneness in the Godhead (Father, Word [Son], Spirit). Almighty God comprehends and unifies all the powerful energy of eternity and infinity. The Scripture states: God created. The Hebrew word for *create* is *baw-raw*. It is used exclusively to describe the divine activity of God Who produced something out of nothing. Man can make and form things from substance that already has been created, but he can never create (*baw-raw*) things from nothing.

The creation spoken of in the beginning verse of the Bible refers to the creation of the original earth. The word *create* (*baw-raw*) means to cut down, select, feed as (formative process), choose, dispatch, do, make fat. The very meaning of the word create reveals the truth that God's formation of the earth was not an instantaneous act. God does not reveal the length of space, time, or ages that He took in forming the original earth. However, the word *created* does show that God selected His master plan in His own mind, and then cut down, as it were, His master plan from His own mind and dispatched it to His Son, Who took the master plan and brought it into visibility by some formative process. God has not revealed the formative process which He used in the creation to bring forth the finished product of His original earth. This much of man's history is unrevealed, and remains God's knowledge alone at this time.

We do know that in the beginning God created the heaven and the earth beautiful and to be inhabited. God's purposive will for the earth, from the beginning, was for it to be inhabited.

> For thus saith the *LORD that created the heavens*; God himself that *formed the earth and made it*; he hath established it, he created it *not in vain*, he *formed it to be inhabited*: I am the LORD; and there is none else (Isaiah 45:18).

The Prophet Isaiah clearly confirmed that God is the sole power and the supreme Creator and that He did not create the original earth in vain or in a waste state. The fact that God created the earth beautiful and to be inhabited reveals that He intentionally created man in the beginning to inhabit the original earth.

The original earth and two of the earth's restorations existed in prehistoric days, and they were inhabited by prehistoric men. With each restoration, God created a new world of inhabitants to occupy each newly restored earth. Our present-day earth was lifted up out of the third pit of destruction, the bottomless pit, and populated with a newly created world of present-day inhabitants. This means that there were three distinct and separate creations of prehistoric man before the present-day creation of man.

This is why scientists are discovering, through studying and testing, that fossil remains are not some form of ape-like creature, but are more closely related to modern man than ever has been thought. A short news column in "U.S. News & World Report," of February 29, 1988, says that a new dating technique, thermoluminescence, if correct, "places modern *Homo sapiens*—the high-domed, big-chinned humans of today—in the Mideast thousands of years before Neanderthals inhabited the region." This relegates the Neanderthals to a lesser role in the evolution of man, the scientists say.

Of course making new discoveries which do not seem to fit with their old ideas raises more and more questions among the scientists. The article further says, "Experts have long debated whether the big-boned Neanderthals were our direct ancestors—a link between archaic *Homo sapiens* and the more recent Cro-Magnon man—or a separate line that ended in extinction and may have shared a common ancestor with modern man."

According to answers we find in the Bible, prehistoric man and modern man (meaning men of today) do not share a common ancestor but a common Creator.

Undeniably, scientists have discovered the existence of prehistoric man. However, scientists' assumption or theory that present-day man has descended or evolved from the prehistoric man, who inhabited the original earth or from the other two classes of created man on the two previous restorations of the earth, is not true. God always created man afresh and anew to inhabit the earth—the original and the restored earths. The existence of similarities between the inhabitants from these different earths is totally and certainly understandable because they are all part of God's wondrous works.

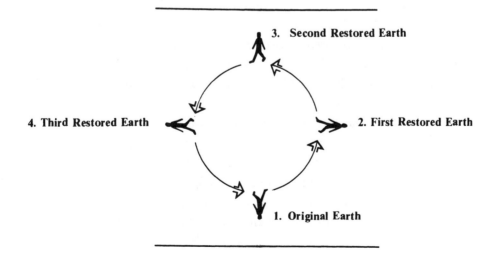

Even in the natural realm, one always is able to detect a similarity in the different works of the same artist or craftsman. It should not come as a surprise, then, when people discover a similarity in the different works of Almighty God.

God, the master Artist and Craftsman, out of His infinite wisdom, fashioned and formed the original earth and its world of inhabitants out of the invisible substance of His Word. He fashioned the earth into a most proper shape and hung it on nothing.

> He stretched out the north over the empty place, and *hangeth the earth upon nothing* (Job 26:7).

To say that God suspended the earth on nothing means there was no visible object of support. God's invisible Word supported it as long as the earth and its inhabitants obeyed His will and worshipped Him. But when prehistoric man sinned, God sent His judgment upon him.

III. God's Laws Which Govern the Destination of the Worlds

There are two basic reasons that God visited judgment upon the original earth and its different worlds of inhabitants, all of which He created: (1) The creation became proud, rebellious, and ungrateful for the wisdom of God's master plan and rejected the humility foundation of Christ the Word. (2) The creation sowed wicked, immoral sins.

Because of these two basic sins, the prehistoric inhabitants and the earth upon which they lived lost the humility foundation that upheld them; consequently, they fell into a pit of judgment, and there they reaped the sins they had sown.

In the beginning, the exalted Christ, the divine Word of God, created the earth and its world of inhabitants. After creating the earth, Christ's living, fiery, exalted breath rose above it to fill its world of inhabitants with continual life so they could become fruitful "trees of righteousness," bearing forth the fruits of holy love, joy, and peace. Only then could the earth's inhabitants fulfill God's purposive will for them.

Original man's first sin was against his humility foundation, the Son of God. The Son of God formed and fashioned man and breathed His fiery breath of life into him. Thus man became a living creature through the life-giving power of the Son.

After the Son of God (the Word of God, Christ the LORD) had received God's blueprint or master plan and commandments and had created all things, giving life to all things, He became the support of all created things.

50

The Word of God, the Christ, having created all things, joyfully humbled Himself to become the humility support of all things by the Word of His power. All things that have their origin in the Father's master plan and all things that remain in the purposive will of the Father's master plan are supported by the Son, the humility Word of God.

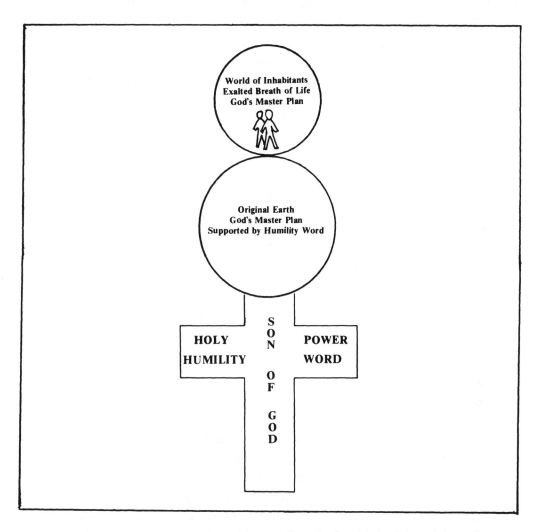

Humility means a lowly and modest quality of mind and spirit which enables one to occupy the lowest place in condition or rank with grateful joy. Humility is the absence of pride. Opposite to the state of humility is the quality or state of being exalted. Exaltation means to rise on high, to be lifted up, or to be elevated, to be raised in dignity, status, power, honour and glory, and to be lifted up with feelings of great, excessive joy.

Spiritual humility is pictured by its natural counterpart, cold air, which always descends to the low place. When cold is sufficiently intense, in the case of water or moisture, ice is the speedy effect. Spiritual exaltation is pictured by its natural counterpart, heat or hot air, which always ascends to the high place. When heat is sufficiently intense, in the case of combustible materials, fire is the speedy effect.

These laws work in the spiritual realm, too. The humility of Christ, or His cold humble breath, always gratefully descends into the low place to support and uphold His Father's master plan and His purposive will. The exalted Christ, or His hot, glorious, resurrected breath, willingly and gratefully ascends to the high place to make the truth of His Father's master plan and divine will known.

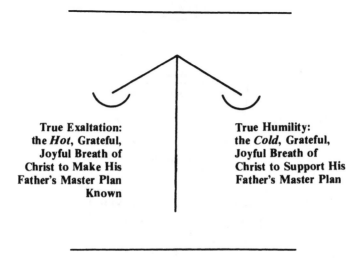

True Exaltation:
the *Hot*, Grateful,
Joyful Breath of
Christ to Make His
Father's Master Plan
Known

True Humility:
the *Cold*, Grateful,
Joyful Breath of
Christ to Support His
Father's Master Plan

God governs both worlds, the natural and the spiritual, by His laws of humility and exaltation. Another example of the law of humility in the natural realm is the root system of a plant, which is the plant's support. The law of exaltation works in the plant kingdom in the natural realm to extol the nature of a plant by the fruit it bears.

With His humility support, the Son of God, the Word, upholds the earth and its world of inhabitants as long as they fulfill the purposive will of His Father's master plan. But when they pridefully cast aside the Father's master plan for them, Christ removes His humility support, and the earth and its inhabitants fall into a *pit*. This spiritual principle holds true for the earth and its world of inhabitants in general, for nations in this present dispensation, for families, and for individuals. The Word, the Son of God, will not lend His humility support when man pridefully casts down the Father's master plan and replaces it with his own proud plan.

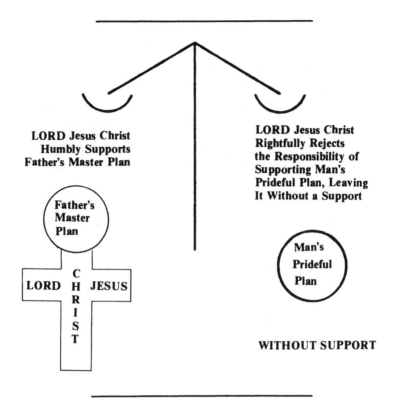

LORD Jesus Christ
Humbly Supports
Father's Master Plan

LORD Jesus Christ
Rightfully Rejects
the Responsibility of
Supporting Man's
Prideful Plan, Leaving
It Without a Support

Father's
Master
Plan

Man's
Prideful
Plan

LORD C H R I S T JESUS

WITHOUT SUPPORT

Corrupt man cannot expect the Word to continue giving His divine, humble support to him from below, when man lifts up his proud, finite plan above God's master plan. Christ will have no part of such unholy union! When man establishes his independence from God and goes about to set up the proud plan of his independence, the Word of God, the Christ, righteously and faithfully removes His humility support. Consequently, without the support of his Creator, the creature falls.

God never has allowed His creation to entertain the vain hope that they can enjoy the divine works of His hands very long and at the same time continually be rebelling against His will, revolting against His dominion, and refusing to perform their duties of serving Him and worshipping Him.

This same spiritual principle is reinforced by Christ in the Book of Matthew.

> And every one that heareth these sayings of mine, and doeth them not, shall be likened unto *a foolish man*, which *built his house upon the sand*: And the rain descended, and the floods came, and the winds blew, and beat upon that house; *and it fell: and great was the fall of it* (Matthew 7:26,27).

The man who built his house upon the sinking sands of the creation instead of building on the Rock, the Word, the Creator, experienced a great fall of his house because he did not have the humility support of the Word of God.

When corrupt man does not have the humility support of the Rock of God's Word, he and his own proud plan sooner or later fall into a pit. What a high and holy privilege we have to accept the Father's master plan and to be upheld with the humility support of the Son of God, the Word of God! This has been and is man's only hope for existence and the maintenance of his existence. This is God's provision for man's salvation.

The second reason the earth and its inhabitants suffered punishment was that they were automatic recipients of the results of God's immutable law of "sowing and reaping."

God's infinite principle of "sowing and reaping" must be understood in order to comprehend the chronological, historical events of the earth because God operates according to spiritual laws as well as natural laws. So when man sinned, he had to reap according to God's laws. Lawlessness does not originate with God. He is orderly and logical, and His acts are governed by His laws. Although, being God, He can supersede them if He so desires.

God is not deceived about the internal and external feelings and actions of either the obedient or disobedient subjects of His creation; therefore, He will not be mocked by His creation. Whatever a man sows, that he also reaps. God rewards according to obedience, and He punishes according to disobedience.

Be not deceived; God is not mocked: for *whatsoever a man soweth, that shall he also reap.* For he that soweth to his flesh shall of the flesh reap corruption; but he that soweth to the Spirit shall of the Spirit reap life everlasting (Galatians 6:7,8).

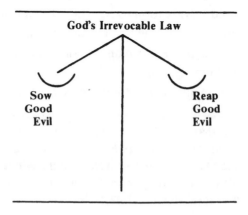

Present seed sowing is an irrevocable, decisive law that determines one's future harvest. Righteousness and unrighteousness always yield their separate harvests. Because man has been deceived by Lucifer, the Devil, he never has understood God's law of sowing and reaping. It is foolish to be deceived about the omniscience and omnipresence of God Who is aware of all sowing. Man is unwise to be deceived about the omnipotence of God Who has all power to reward every seed that has been sown, whether good or evil. Man is not to be deceived about the certainty of the harvest which surely follows all sowing. God will not be mocked by the lawlessness of the disobedient who have broken His established moral laws, nor will He be unmindful of the obedience of the faithful who have kept His moral laws.

Be not deceived, every man is a sower and has been since his beginning. Every man always has had a choice of the kind of seed he has sown, and every sower always has been a reaper.

When one sows sinful seeds, he is punished by reaping the same sinful seeds. If one sows the seeds of corruption, one must expect to reap a harvest of his seeds of corruption. Thus, by having the knowledge of God's irrevocable law of sowing and reaping, if no other information were available, one would know why the original earth, including man, was cast down into a chaotic pit through a catastrophic act of the Judge and Punisher and why the next two restored earths suffered a similar destruction of being cast down into a pit. Also the extent of one's sin begets the sin's proportionate punishment.

When the earth and its world of inhabitants live grateful and holy lives unto the LORD God (their Creator, Owner, and Master), His holy, powerful, humility Word *supports* and *upholds* them. But, when the world of inhabitants upon the earth become rebellious revolters and fill the earth with their corruption, the holy Word of God removes His powerful humility support from them.

These two laws—that humility must be creation's foundation and that sowing determines the reaping—explain why the original earth ended the way it did. Prehistoric man broke God's spiritual laws, so he was punished accordingly. The world sinned against the LORD by becoming ungrateful for their humility foundation and their exalted fiery breath of life. They sowed haughty, proud rebellion against their Creator; they reaped a lowly, degrading pit.

IV. The Places of Judgment for the Sins of the Prehistoric Worlds

The revelation of the kinds of destructions the earth and its worlds of inhabitants have suffered comes through understanding the Scriptural meanings contained in the

Hebrews words for pit —the *shakh-ath* (pit), the *bore* (pit), and the *teh-home* (pit).

The original earth was created by God, and it was occupied by the first world of inhabitants. This was as God had planned; but the original earth and its world of inhabitants sinned, so they were cast into a pit. In Hebrew the word used for the *pit* into which the original earth was cast is *shakh-ath*. The fact that the original earth's inhabitants were brought low into this *shakh-ath* pit permits us to know that they had exalted themselves highly against God. Then, God restored the earth and created a new world of inhabitants to occupy the restored earth.

When God restored the earth, He fashioned it into a new earth, and placed newly created inhabitants on it. After an untold period of time had elapsed, this restored earth and its world of inhabitants sinned against God; consequently, they also were cast down into a pit of judgment, which was a different pit from the one the original earth had experienced. In this instance the Hebrew word for *pit* is *bore*, which differentiates between the first and second judgments of the earth. Once again, after a season, God restored the earth (a second time) and created a whole new world of inhabitants to occupy it.

The earth's pattern of behaviour never changed because the second restored earth and its world of inhabitants sinned against God, too, and He cast the second restored earth and its world of inhabitants into a third pit (in the Hebrew the word is *teh-home*), which was still a different pit from the first and second pits. In due season, God restored the earth and created the present world of inhabitants which now are occupying the third restored earth.

Because each earth and its inhabitants ended in a pit of judgment, it is completely impossible for a series of evolutions to be in effect from the beginning until now! This is the link of knowledge which is missing from the evolutionists' theory. They try to unite God's separate creations into a continuous evolution, but this is not so.

Science has investigated and proven that our earth has been around for a long time, some say over 4.5 billion years. However, since no one was a personal eyewitness to earth's past, and since most scientists are not aware of some Biblical facts concerning the earth's historical experiences, they are limited in their knowledge of the chronological, historical events of the earth.

This truth is substantiated in an article written by Paul Trachtman for the June, 1984, issue of *Smithsonian* magazine. Mr. Trachtman said: "Reconstructing a picture of life's earliest habitat has been a considerable challenge because crucial evidence has been entirely erased. The mystery is what happened on Earth between 4.6 billion years ago, when our planet formed from a vast cloud of gas and dust, and 3.8 billion years ago, the age of the oldest terrestrial rocks. The geological evidence has vanished, leaving what British geologist Stephen Moorbath calls 'an embarrasing little gap of more than 700 million years.'"

In addition to the lack of evidence needed to reconstruct the history of the earth, scientists encounter different opinions about the origins of life on Earth. In the same article Mr. Trachtman had this to say about the origin of life on the earth: "With the wealth of biological precursors [necessary ingredients for life] apparently well established, scientists have turned to the question of how life could have organized itself out of that original organic soup. And here the controversies are as thick as the evidence is thin."

But with the Bible's account of the chronological, historical events of the earth and its world of inhabitants, added to the facts that scientists have discovered, one can enjoy a richer and fuller understanding of the past and present earth and its four different worlds of inhabitants.

People on this present earth have been punished *spiritually* in the same "pits" of judgment that the other worlds experienced *literally*. Therefore, we learn what the type of sin each past earth and its inhabitants were guilty of by the type of sin that was committed by people in the *present* earth who were punished in the same pit, even though in this day the pits of judgments are spiritual places of punishment for sins. The same sin begets the same punishment. God never changes. Since God's law of "sowing and reaping" is irrevocable, we know that God fits the punishment to the crime or sin. So if sinners in this world have been punished by being cast into a particular spiritual pit for committing a particular sin, then we know that God always has punished the same sin in the same way, whether on this present earth or on prehistoric earth.

God's three pits of judgment exist as prisons of punishment for the natural earth and its world of inhabitants after they have filled up their cup of wickedness before God. They also exist in the spiritual world as pits of punishment to make the soul knowledgeable and aware of the wrong it has done when it has taken its own sinful way.

As we study each spiritual pit of judgment, we will learn what sin each previous earth committed and gain some understanding of what punishment is in each of God's pits in the natural realm.

Chapter Two

The Fall of the Original Earth Into the First Pit of Judgment, the "Shakh-ath" Pit

GOD created the original earth clean and holy, and He created a world of clean, holy inhabitants to live upon it so they could fulfill His purposive will. God did not create the earth or its world of inhabitants for them to use their existence for wickedness and corruption.

Therefore, when the original world of inhabitants corrupted themselves and the original earth beyond measure, the Word removed His upholding humility support, and the earth tottered, shook, and fell from its suspended positon into a pit of ice and fire, the *shakh-ath* pit of judgment, thus destroying its inhabitants.

> Thou has rebuked the heathen, thou hast destroyed the wicked,
> *thou hast put out their name for ever and ever.* . . . The heathen
> are sunk down into the pit [*shakh-ath*] that they made: in the
> net which they hid is their own foot taken (Psalm 9:5,15).

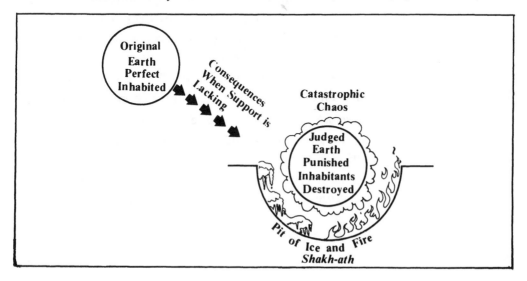

Scientists have discovered some of the ice ages of the earth. However, God is the only One Who knows how many aeons the earth lay in the *shakh-ath* pit of ice and fire. No one from the present creation was an eyewitness to this catastrophe, so the amount of facts that present man can learn about it is limited.

Each time the earth and its world of inhabitants have sinned and filled up their cup of wickedness, they have fallen into a deeper pit.

The Hebrew word for *pit* in the ninth Psalm is *shakh-ath*, meaning a trap, destruction, corruption, to decay, to cast off, lose, mar, perish, spill, spoiler, to spoil pleasant words, sinking into the ground, vitiate a convenant, ditch, groove, break in pieces, destroy. The word *shakh-ath* comes from a Hebrew root word *shoo-akh*, meaning to sink, to bow down, to incline, humble, to sink down into death, to lie depressed, to be dejected, to get low, to let oneself sink down, to become despondent, utterly waste, to destroy, to become corrupt morally, to be spoiled, marred, laid waste, to devastate lands or cities, to vitiate a covenant, to violate feelings of pity, to act without mercy, to ruin oneself, to ruin or mar a tree, or to be of disorderly conduct.

What God *has done* should be a warning to all. He has rebuked; He has destroyed; and He has blotted out forever the names of the inhabitants of the world from the original earth. God's retribution always has overtaken wicked aggressors, whether they be worlds, nations, cities, or individuals.

By destroying the first lawless world and blotting out its name forever, God rebuked or gave threatening warnings to all the nations who have followed His first creation.

The downfall of any lawless world or any lawless nation is a warning to *all* who refuse to honour and obey God's moral law. God, in His righteousness and justice, always has been faithful to punish sinful worlds, sinful nations, sinful cities, and sinful people who have refused to repent and render obedience to His Holy Word.

God has given some details in the Bible about the first pit of judgment that the earth and its prehistoric world of inhabitants experienced. What is recorded in God's Word is sufficient to inform man of its existence and enlighten him as to its purpose.

The punishment in the *shakh-ath* pit reveals the depth of the sinful pride that was sown by the world of inhabitants from the original earth because they reaped the depth of punishment and destruction in the *shakh-ath* pit.

The world of inhabitants on the original earth became sinful, merciless, corrupt, and destructive people. Therefore, God punished them with a proper proportion of destruction.

The very Hebrew word *shakh-ath* reveals how the inhabitants upon the original earth corrupted themselves morally, and how they ungratefully vitiated God's covenant of humility support, and how, through their pride, they violated all feelings of pity, which caused them to act without mercy toward God and toward one another. Therefore, God ruined and marred the trees, spoiled, marred, and laid waste the land, and cast the inhabitants into the pit because of their disorderly conduct.

I. Sin Against the Wisdom and Humility of the Name of the LORD Is Punished in the *Shakh-ath* Pit

Knowledge of God's law of justly measuring one's reaping in proportion to one's sowing makes a person clearly understand the kind of spiritual pit of immorality into which the original inhabitants had sunk because God justly measured out the *shakh-ath* pit to them. God was provoked to destroy the original earth and the *wicked* inhabitants who were upon it because of the pit of immorality into which they had descended.

The sin of the world of inhabitants on the original earth was against the *wisdom* of the LORD's Name and the humility of His Name. Initially, they despised and rejected God's eternal order of building which starts with a humility support or foundation. This is God's divine order for all building; without following God's order, there can be no support or maintenance of a superstructure of honourable exaltation.

> The fear of the LORD is the instruction of wisdom; and *before honour is humility* (Proverbs 15:33).

Humility wisdom or the humble Son of God, the Christ, Who is the humility foundation of every true spiritual building, instructs one in the fear or reverence and respect of the LORD. The fear of the LORD is the beginning of wisdom. The fear of the LORD is the instruction and correction of wisdom, which is one's guide to receiving a mature spiritual foundation. Humility wisdom is the preparative for the superstructure of honour and exaltation.

> Before destruction the heart of man is haughty, and *before honour is humility* (Proverbs 18:12).

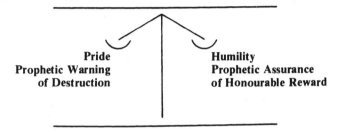

Pride
Prophetic Warning
of Destruction

Humility
Prophetic Assurance
of Honourable Reward

Proud man is always the most haughty before his downfall. After man fills his cup of pride to the brim, God overturns his cup.

> *By humility and the fear of the LORD* are riches, and honour, and
> life (Proverbs 22:4).

Humility is reverence for God's majesty and authority and a willingness to submit to His master plan and His divine will. Humility is a prophetic sign of assurance of God's future reward of riches, honour, and life.

The Christ, the Son of God, was the instructive example to the original world of inhabitants because He was willing to submit to being the humble upholding foundation of the earth, according to His Father's master plan and divine will.

The world of inhabitants on the original earth had a choice to accept their humility foundation and live. But they rejected their humility foundation and chose their haughty pride instead. Hence, they were cast down to ruin and destruction in the *shakh-ath* pit.

Not one earthly name can be found of the original inhabitants from the original earth because God blotted out their names forever. The original earth and its wicked inhabitants sank into the pit (*shakh-ath*) that they had made for themselves with their own wicked doings. God punished these lawless people on the original earth by a catastrophic destruction which took them to a pit of ice and fire.

God always has brought diverse, catastrophic judgments of ice and fire upon the earth when the different worlds of inhabitants have rebelled against Him in the past aeons. Scientists have found evidence of mass extinctions of life during times of temperature changes.

An article by Steven M. Stanley in the June, 1984, issue of the *Scientific American* magazine deals with the subject of mass extinctions. Mr. Stanley said, "At various times, however, there have been sharp peaks in the number of vanishing species. Such mass extinctions have affected terrestrial as well as marine organisms, but the fossil record documenting their occurrence is more abundant in the marine realm. During geologically brief intervals of several million years some of these events have eliminated most of the species in the ocean and as many as half of the families. Devastation of this magnitude could have been inflicted only by radical changes in the environment, on a regional or even global scale, . . ."

Mr. Stanley offers evidence in his article that climatic cooling has been a primary culprit behind past marine crises. "First [he says], in some cases there is independent indication, such as the presence of glacial gravels, that cooling occurred at the same time as a mass extinction." He adds these statements later in his article: "A large number of species did vanish from the oceans during these glacial periods, but the geographic pattern of the extinctions suggests they were caused by cooling rather than by shrinkage of the shallow sea floor. The connection is only now becoming clear, because for a long time paleontologists overlooked the Ice Age mass extinctions. . . . The study of microscopic fossils, such as those of planktonic foraminiferoas (floating organisms like amoebas but with skeletons), has now produced more accurate age assignments showing that the extinctions were actually bunched in the Ice Age. In many fossil faunas only four million years old more than half of the species are extinct."

While scientists have discovered that our earth has been subjected to intense cold (ice) and heat (fire) from time to time, they also admit that establishing dates from geological information is neither easy nor accurate. Dr. James Trefil said in his book, *Space Time Infinity*, that "There is no question that establishing the dates of the geological formations in which fossils are found is often a difficult task, and dates for a given formation can often differ by 10 percent (or much more). But 10 percent of 250 million years, the length of time covered by the data base used, is 25 million years—a period as long as the time between successive extinctions. It is difficult to establish the regularity of a sequence of events when the time at which each event occurs could vary by such an appreciable amount."

So although man has discovered mass extinctions from global changes in the environment, he does not know their sequence nor, unless he searches the Scriptures, does he know their cause.

Man also has discovered that part of the earth's bowels is filled with fire, but he has not yet discovered the other part of the earth's bowels that is filled with ice. The earth and its worlds of inhabitants have been purged in times past by ice and fire from below, but in the future, according to God's Word, they will be purged with ice and fire from above. It is interesting to note a question Dr. James Trefil poses in the closing pages of his book. He asks this question about the future of the universe: "Will it end in emptiness? Or, indeed, will it end in fire or in ice?"

God blotted out the names of the people from the original earth forever and ever. Scientists never have discovered fossils from the world of inhabitants during this aeon of time because God buried them in the pit forever and ever. The downfall of menacing lawlessness on the original earth is not only an historical warning but also a future prophetic warning to the earth and to its world of inhabitants that God has not and will not tolerate unrestrained immorality.

II. The LORD's *Shakh-ath* Pit Is Punishment for the Guilty: Nations, Cities, Individuals

The historical measure of judgment upon the original earth and its world of inhabitants is a preview of God's faithfulness as a just Judge and a righteous Punisher Who destroys all insurrection against His master plan, His purposive will, and His moral law. God's just retribution always overtakes wicked aggressors.

Man always has reaped according to the seeds he has sown, whether they be good or wicked. God's divine judgment of wicked man is a striking sign of the existence of God. Because God always has created man with a free moral choice, He respects man's power of choice; therefore, He always allows the wicked to prepare for their own downfall, after they have chosen to disobey their Creator.

The angel or destroyer from the *shakh-ath* pit is also called *Shakh-ath*. The Word of God reveals that God created this angel of destruction.

> Behold, I have created the smith that bloweth the coals in the fire,
> and that bringeth forth an instrument for his work; and *I have
> created the waster* [*shakh-ath*] *to destroy* (Isaiah 54:16).

God created this angel of destruction (*Shakh-ath*) for the proud. The prideful heart never is grateful for the gifts of freedom and blessings from the LORD's perfect will. A prideful heart always feels that God has withheld the best from it. Therefore, it ungratefully seeks what it thinks to be the greater freedom and greater blessings from its own will. It imagines that what it has found for itself outside of God's will is the best.

God's Word gives examples of ones on this present earth who sinned against the humility and wisdom of the LORD's Name and never repented. In their rejection of the humility foundation of God's Word, they chose to sow destruction; consequently, they reaped the destruction of the spiritual *shakh-ath* pit. By studying these examples, one's mind can be enlightened in a greater way about the wicked pride that destroyed the first world of inhabitants.

A. The Nation of Judah Reaped *Shakh-ath* Destruction in the Present Day—an Example of the Sin Sown and the Judgment Reaped by the Original Earth and Its World of Inhabitants

When Judah and Jerusalem's pride caused them to cast down God's Word and God's master plan, substituting their own prideful plan to worship idols, God sent the

Prophet Jeremiah to make a demonstration of the spiritual destruction (*shakh-ath*) that would come upon them when they lost God's supporting Word.

> Then I went to Euphrates, and digged, and took the girdle from the place where I had hid it: and, behold, the girdle was marred, it was profitable for nothing. Then the word of the LORD came unto me, saying, Thus saith the LORD, After this manner will I *mar* [*shakh-ath*] *the pride of Judah*, and the great pride of Jerusalem (Jeremiah 13:7-9).

The prophet took a linen girdle, after having worn it a short time, and hid it in a cavity on the banks of the Euphrates. After a long season, the prophet retrieved the girdle, only to find it completely rotten and useless. This was a demonstrative parable about Judah, who had been as close to God as a girdle is to one's body. But, Judah had proven herself unworthy of this honour, so God intended to *mar* (*shakh-ath*) her pride, which appeared to God as a rotten girdle.

The pride of Judah's morally corrupt and offensive idolatry was like a decayed and decomposed girdle that should have been destroyed and discarded. God demonstrated that He could mar (*shakh-ath*) Judah's pride as easily as a rotten girdle breaks and disintegrates. The natural law of entropy that caused the girdle to rot was made by the same Creator Who used His law of entropy in the spiritual realm to mar or destroy Judah's pride.

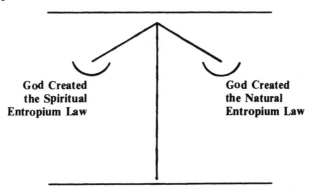

God is the Governor of the dissipation of energy, the loss of usefulness, in both the natural and the spiritual realms.

B. The City of Jerusalem Reaped *Shakh-ath* Destruction

Jeremiah's prophecy to Judah also included the city of Jerusalem.

Then I went to Euphrates, and digged, and took the girdle from the place where I had hid it: and, behold, the girdle was marred, it was profitable for nothing. Then the word of the LORD came unto me, saying, Thus saith the LORD, After this manner will I *mar* [*shakh-ath*] *the pride of Judah, and the great pride of Jerusalem* (Jeremiah 13:7-9).

God cast out the former inhabitants of Jerusalem who were called the Jebusites. Before King David conquered Jerusalem, the city was called Jebus.

And David and all Israel went to *Jerusalem, which is Jebus*; where the Jebusites were, the inhabitants of the land (I Chronicles 11:4).

The city of Jerusalem was special because it was where the LORD God had chosen to place His holy Name.

And Rehoboam the son of Solomon reigned in Judah. Rehoboam was forty and one years old when he began to reign, and he reigned seventeen years in *Jerusalem, the city which the LORD did choose* out of all the tribes of Israel, *to put his name there.* . . . (I Kings 14:21).

God cast out the former inhabitants of Jebus or Jerusalem because they had totally degenerated themselves. He cleansed and sanctified the city of Jerusalem and the children of Israel, and then He placed the Ark of the Covenant, which contained the *Torah* (Law) and His holy Name, in the city of Jerusalem.

But *the ark of God* had David brought up from Kirjath-jearim to the place which David had prepared for it: *for he had pitched a tent for it at Jerusalem* (II Chronicles 1:4).

God cleansed and sanctified Jerusalem, and He cleansed and sanctified the Israelites, making them clean and holy inhabitants that were fit to live in His holy city. Then the nation could fulfill God's purposive will by living holy lives and by lifting up the holy Name of the LORD God in worship, praise, and thanksgiving.

God did not cleanse and sanctify the city of Jerusalem and its inhabitants so they could use their existence for wickedness and corruption.

Therefore, when the inhabitants of Jerusalem had corrupted themselves and the city of Jerusalem beyond measure, the Word removed His humility support, and they fell into God's spiritual *shakh-ath* pit of judgment.

And say unto the people of the land, Thus saith the Lord GOD of the inhabitants of Jerusalem, and of the land of Israel; They shall eat their bread with carefulness, and drink their water with astonishment, *that her land may be desolate from all that is therein, because of the violence of all them that dwell therein.* And the cities that are inhabited shall be laid waste, and the land shall be desolate; and ye shall know that I am the LORD (Ezekiel 12:19,20).

God is not a respecter of persons. He always has punished evil and wicked doers who have sinned against His holy, righteous Name.

When Israel and Jerusalem sinned against the wisdom from and in the LORD's holy Name, by bowing down to idols or false gods and by inclining their hearts to strange gods, the LORD God caused them to reap what they had sown. After Israel and Jerusalem had sown the seeds of the depths of idolatry, they reaped the fruition of those seeds in the form of the depths of God's *shakh-ath* judgments.

When Jerusalem and Israel took the fame and renown they had acquired because of the glorious presence of God's holy temple, His holy covenant, and His holy Name and joined them to idols, using their fame and renown to lead others in the way of idolatry, God cast them down into the spiritual *shakh-ath* pit. God *marred* (*shakh-ath*) Israel's fame and renown, so they appeared among the nations as a weak, rotten, and marred girdle.

When Jerusalem served the LORD God in faithfulness and sincerity, she was exalted among the nations. Kings and queens came from afar off to see the splendours and glory of the temple wherein dwelt the holy covenant and the holy Name of the LORD God. But when Jerusalem and Israel sank down into spiritual death through idolatrous worship of false gods, the LORD God punished Jerusalem and Israel with His judgment of the spiritual *shakh-ath* pit.

God sent the Chaldeans to spoil, to war, to lay waste, and to devastate Jerusalem and the land. The Jewish people and the holy vessels of the holy temple were carried captive into Babylon.

What God did to Jerusalem and its inhabitants should be a warning to all. God's righteous retribution always has overtaken wicked aggressors and punished lawless, sinful people and lawless, sinful cities.

Jerusalem and its inhabitants had been the most privileged city and the most blessed people upon the face of the earth because the LORD God had chosen to place His holy Name, His holy covenant, and His holy temple there.

However, since the LORD God is not a respecter of persons, and inasmuch as He is holy, just, and righteous, He punished Jerusalem and its inhabitants with the *shakh-ath* judgments from the spiritual *shakh-ath* pit.

C. Uzziah Reaped *Shakh-ath* Destruction

King Uzziah is another classical example of one whose prideful heart sowed corruption; consequently, he reaped corruption through his *shakh-ath* punishment.

In the beginning of his reign, King Uzziah walked in the ways of piety and holiness and trustfully leaned upon the Word, the Wisdom of God, for his support.

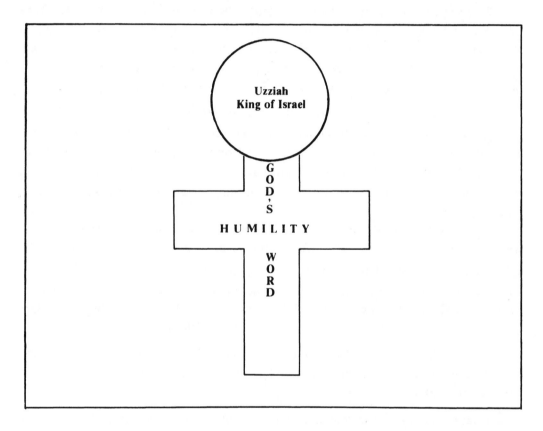

As a result of King Uzziah's trust in God and his obedience to God, he was blessed in a manifold way with victory over his enemies, with great fame, and with the love of his loyal subjects. But when he became proudly puffed up by the blessings of his success, he presumed to burn incense upon God's altar in the Holy Place as the priests did.

However, the complete ministry of burning incense had been committed to the priests by God. When Uzziah intruded into the Holy Place, he viciously resisted the attempted restraint of the eighty priests who were in the Holy Place of the temple. Then God smote Uzziah with leprosy as punishment for his deliberate defiance.

> But when he was strong, *his heart was lifted up to his destruction*
> [*shakh-ath*]: for he transgressed against the LORD his God, and
> went into the temple of the LORD to burn incense upon the altar
> of incense (II Chronicles 26:16).

When Uzziah's heart was lifted up by pride, he lost the awareness that his freedom of existence depended solely upon the upholding support of God's humility Word. Therefore, when Uzziah cast away his awareness and his gratefulness for the humility support of God's Word, the Son of God removed His support, and Uzziah fell into the spiritual pit of destruction (*shakh-ath*).

When some people sin outside of God's temple, they are too ashamed to face God in His house, so they stay away from God's temple. But Uzziah went inside God's temple and deliberately sinned before God's face by casting down God's Word and God's master plan and by trying to establish his own prideful plan. As a result of his haughty arrogance, he lost his freedom of existence as a person and as a king. Until his death, Uzziah was quarantined in a separate house, never to return to his own house, to the house of God, or to his throne. He was punished spiritually by *shakh-ath* destruction.

D. Lucifer Reaped *Shakh-ath* Destruction

Lucifer, at one time, was a beautiful and anointed cherub in heaven. Because of his beauty, he lifted up his heart in vanity and pride. Then, after the conception of his own prideful plan, he cast down the master plan that God had for him. He *corrupted* (*shakh-ath*) or *destroyed* humility wisdom as the upholder of his free existence in heaven; consequently, he was cast out of heaven.

> Thine heart was lifted up because of thy beauty, *thou hast*
> *corrupted* [*shakh-ath*] *thy wisdom by reason of thy brightness*: I
> will cast thee to the ground, I will lay thee before kings, that they
> may behold thee (Ezekiel 28:17).

Lucifer sinned by sowing the seed of rebellion against God's will and by casting down God's master plan for him in heaven. As a result, he reaped the punishment of being cast down out of heaven. Jesus Christ declared that He had witnessed this punishment of Lucifer.

> And he said unto them, I beheld *Satan as lightning fall from heaven* (Luke 10:18).

Lucifer originally was upheld in the perfect will of God in heaven by the humility Word of God, the Wisdom of God, the Son of God.

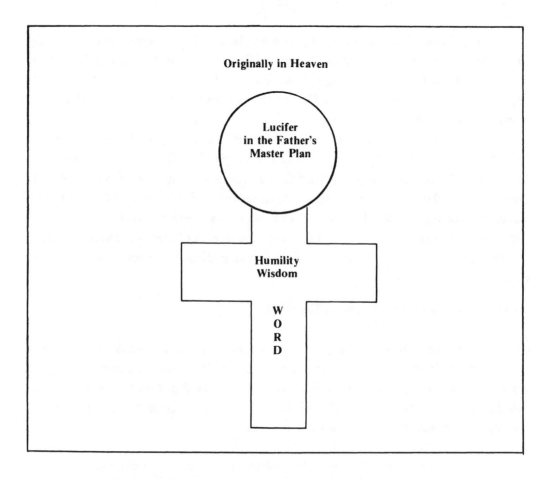

Lucifer's pride and rebellion against God's master plan for his life cost him the humility support of the Word of God. His freedom of existence in heaven did not continue because Wisdom removed Himself as Lucifer's support, and he was left without a foundation. Because of his own prideful plan, he and his plan were cast down out of heaven.

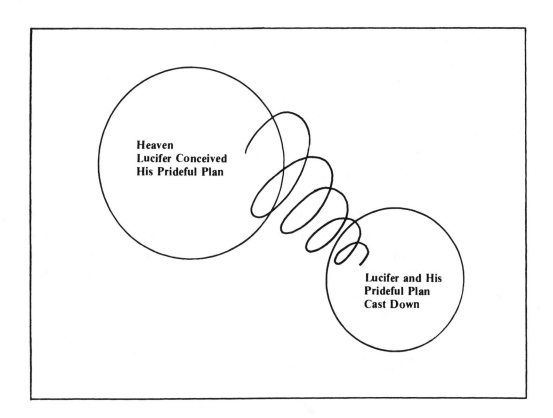

The Wisdom of God, the Son of God, has one purpose in His holy life, and that is to support His Father's master plan. Therefore, when any creature or creation rejects the Father's master plan, the Son of God withdraws His support from that creature or creation, and it falls into the pit.

III. The LORD Delivers from the *Shakh-ath* Pit

The LORD God takes no pleasure in punishing His creation. God's pleasure consists in turning His creation from wrong to right, from error to truth, and from unrighteousness to righteousness. God delights in delivering His people from the *shakh-ath* pit when they repent and return unto Him as their Creator, Owner, and Master.

One does not have to stay in a spiritual pit forever. Errors are punished in order to correct wrong behaviour, so if a person errs, and if he willingly accepts his punishment, repents, and learns his lesson, God will deliver him. The Bible also gives some examples of times God has delivered people on this present earth from the spiritual *shakh-ath* pit.

A. Israel Delivered from *Shakh-ath* Destruction in Egypt

The infant nation of Israel spent over four hundred years in Egypt. During much of this time, she was in slavery and bondage to the Egyptians. Then God sent His messengers, Moses and Aaron, to Pharaoh, the Egyptian king, commanding him to let His people go free.

God's master plan for Israel must be understood, however, in order to comprehend the *shakh-ath* pit judgment that fell on Pharaoh and the Egyptians in their day.

God's wise master plan for the nation of Israel called for a house of freedom to be built for Israel. God desired that the humility foundation of Israel's house of national freedom be laid in Egypt through the blood of the lamb. God purposed that the exalted, honourable superstructure of Israel's house of national freedom be built in the wilderness, and He willed that the crown of Israel's house of national freedom be built in Canaan's land.

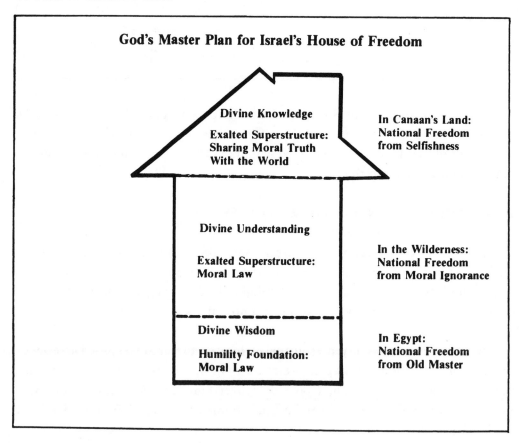

God's Master Plan for Israel's House of Freedom

Divine Knowledge

Exalted Superstructure:
Sharing Moral Truth
With the World

In Canaan's Land:
National Freedom
from Selfishness

Divine Understanding

Exalted Superstructure:
Moral Law

In the Wilderness:
National Freedom
from Moral Ignorance

Divine Wisdom

Humility Foundation:
Moral Law

In Egypt:
National Freedom
from Old Master

The wise design of God's master plan for Israel called for a humility foundation of freedom from Egyptian bondage and slavery to be laid through the blood of the lamb. God liberated Israel from her old master, both naturally and spiritually, and He became the new Owner and Master of the tiny new nation, laying a new foundation of freedom in it by the wisdom of His redemption.

God's divine understanding of His master plan for Israel constrained Him to build the exalted superstructure of her house of freedom in the wilderness through His gift of light of truth to her in His law. Israel's comprehension of God's moral law, the *Torah*, freed her from moral ignorance and darkness.

Through His divine knowledge of His master plan for Israel, God built a crown of freedom on her house of freedom in Canaan's land. Israel's selfless sharing of God's law, the *Torah*, with the whole world freed her from spiritual selfishness. Thus, the nation of Israel, having followed God's purposive will, was crowned with total freedom from selfishness by obediently sharing her treasures of truth with the whole world. The building of Israel's national house of freedom extended from Egypt to Canaan's land.

Pharaoh's sin was great because he tried to prevent Israel from laying the humility foundation of her house of national freedom by holding her as a bondslave in Egypt. If Pharaoh could have prevented the foundation of Israel's house of national freedom from being laid, then Israel also would have been prevented from erecting the superstructure of her house of national freedom in the wilderness. Furthermore, it would have prevented her house of national freedom from being adorned with its crown of dominion and honour in Canaan's land. After Israel's long bondage and slavery in Egypt, God judged her cruel taskmasters. God gave Israel the protective covering of the lamb's blood on her doors while He sent His final judgment upon Egypt, which consisted of the plague of *shakh-ath* destruction upon Egypt's firstborn.

> For the LORD will pass through to smite the Egyptians; and
> he seeth the blood upon the lintel, and on the two side posts,
> the LORD will pass over the door, and will not suffer the
> *destroyer* [*shakh-ath*] to come in unto your houses to smite
> you (Exodus 12:23).

The destroyer (*Shakh-ath*, the angel from this particular pit), ministered the final judgment upon the Egyptians. The *Shakh-ath* Angel slew the firstborn of the Egyptians with his icy fingers of death. The Egyptians had sown the seeds of death in the families of Israel (Exodus 1:16); they had used their icy fingers of death and destruction to destroy the firstborn sons of Israel; consequently, they reaped the icy fingers of death and destruction of their firstborn sons which was carried out by the destroyer, *Shakh-ath*, who came out of the *shakh-ath* pit.

When God saw the shed blood of the lamb over Israel's doors, He passed over the door, protecting the dwellers inside by forbidding the *Shakh-ath* destroyer to come in. God delivered Israel from the destroying angel, *Shakh-ath*, in Moses' day because Israel accepted God's master plan of redemption and protection through the shed blood of the lamb.

This is true today. God delivers, from this level of wicked pride and powers of darkness, all who accept His master plan of redemption and protection through the blood of His true Lamb, Jesus Christ.

B. Jonah Delivered from *Shakh-ath* Destruction

Jonah was a unique example of one who experienced reaping the *shakh-ath* pit because, in contrast to those who remained in the pit, Jonah was delivered from it.

> I went down to the bottoms of the mountains; the earth with her bars was about me for ever: yet hast *thou brought up my life from corruption* [*shakh-ath*], O LORD my God (Jonah 2:6).

When Jonah disobeyed God, God allowed Jonah to see His punishment of the wicked by taking Jonah's soul out of the whale's belly, and taking it not only to hell, but also to the spiritual *shakh-ath* pit of corruption. When Jonah repented of his rebellion, God brought his soul up out of the spiritual pit of corruption (*shakh-ath*), and Jonah went on to obey God's purposive will.

There is such a great amount of information about this pit (*shakh-ath*) and its angel (*Shakh-ath*) in the Word of God that it is impossible to give every detail in this book. However, the information given establishes the fact that this pit does exist in both the natural realm and in the spiritual realm.

C. Job Delivered from *Shakh-ath* Destruction

Job is also a witness from the present creation that this same force from the *shakh-ath* pit still works spiritually today in man's earth. Elihu, who was a type of Christ, gave Job instructions for delivering his soul from this class of pit or destruction.

> Lo, all these things worketh God oftentimes with man, *To bring*
> *back his soul from the pit* [*shakh-ath*], to be enlightened with the
> light of the living (Job 33:29,30).

Elihu summed up the great and gracious designs of God's providence toward the children of men, which is to bring them back from the spiritual *shakh-ath* pit of destruction or from the pit of misery and wretchedness to a state of health, happiness, and prosperity. God's will is for the inhabitants of earth to live in a happy and prosperous state under His Sovereign dominion. However, man's rebellion against God's ownership and mastership frequently plunges him into the spiritual *shakh-ath* pit of misery and wretchedness because he rejects God's master plan for his life, replacing it with his prideful plan which is doomed to destruction. But the LORD is forever faithful to redeem repentant man from the darkness of this wretched pit and illuminate his soul and spirit with the new, fresh light and life of His glorious presence.

D. David Delivered from *Shakh-ath* Destruction

David, the Psalmist, assured all repentant souls, who bless the holy Name of the LORD, of the LORD's forgiveness and of His redemption from the spiritual pit (*shakh-ath*).

> Who forgiveth all thine iniquities; who healeth all thy diseases;
> *Who redeemeth thy life from destruction* [*shakh-ath*]; who crown-
> eth thee with lovingkindness and tender mercies; (Psalm 103:3,4).

David testified that when man is guilty of iniquities or crookedness, God is ready to forgive, if man repents and turns to Him. Each deviation from God's straight, moral path of righteousness casts man into the spiritual *shakh-ath* pit of misery and unhappiness from which he needs to be redeemed and forgiven. A person's feelings of deep misery and wretchedness are witnesses that his emotions have fallen into the pit because he has strayed from the LORD, either in thought or in deed. God's gracious mercy uses man's spiritual "pit" experiences to chastise him, to discipline him, to instruct him, and to help him progress in his spiritual journey. God makes all things work together for the good of one's spiritual education and for one's moral development. Any deviation from God's straight and narrow way of truth renders the soul sick and in need of healing. God is able to dissolve man's knots of sickness and disease which prevent his spirit, soul, and body from progressing and developing according to the divine purpose of His holy will.

God constantly redeems man's life from the spiritual pit of destruction, the pit of misery and wretchedness, as man continually turns back to God.

When Israel's pride angered the LORD, He permitted Satan to stand up against King David and coerce him to number the children of Israel in a way that was contrary to God's will and His Word. When David numbered the people, he deliberately omitted having them pay the atonement money that God had commanded to be paid on the occasion of this kind of census (Exodus 30:12). David's sinful ambition and vainglorious desire to number his military strength caused him to lose his spiritual freedom that rested upon God's Word and the humility, upholding support of God's protection against death. Therefore, God sent the destroying angel (*Shakh-ath*) to chastise and punish King David and Israel.

> And when *the angel stretched out his hand upon Jerusalem to destroy* [shakh-ath] it, the LORD repented him of the evil, and said to the angel that destroyed the people, It is enough: stay now thine hand. And the angel of the LORD was by the threshingplace of Araunah the Jebusite (II Samuel 24:16).

When man departs from the Word of God, the humility support of his freedom of existence, he can expect destruction and death as the speedy consequence.

However on this occasion, after three days of punishment, God mercifully stayed the angel (*Shakh-ath*) from further destruction. God changed His mind about the evil that He had thought to do to Jerusalem; therefore, He stayed the destruction.

When the Scriptures say God *repents*, it simply means that He changes His mind. It does not mean that He sinned and had to repent. The Word says that He repented of the evil He had previously thought to do to Jerusalem.

The word *evil* in Hebrew is *rah*, meaning misery, woe, and affliction. God has no desire to punish His creation beyond effecting the necessary repentance and correction that He desires from them.

All who sow rejection against the humility support of God's Word can expect to reap the punishment of the *shakh-ath* pit. So, while there are those who have been delivered from the spiritual *shakh-ath* pit because they have repented, there are others who have reaped the destruction of this pit because they never have repented.

IV. Obedience to God's Law of Circularity Delivers from the *Shakh-ath* Pit

During the first aeon of the earth and its world of inhabitants, God, as their Ruler and Guide, gave His master plan to govern them, and He gave them Wisdom, the Son of God, to be their foundation. They had the privilege to choose, willingly and gratefully, the rulership of the Father and the support of the Son of God, the Word. They could have retained their freedom of existence, serving and worshipping the LORD God in His perfect will.

However, they chose to beget wicked rebellion in their free moral will and refused to humble themselves in order to be ruled over by God's master plan and to be supported beneath by the humility truth. As a result, they lost their freedom of existence.

God gave, by gift, an exalted position on His newly created earth to its world of inhabitants. He gave them a humility foundation, by gift, to support both them and His newly created earth. Therefore, they had no excuse for not striding forward in their spiritual education and in their moral development.

God's ultimate goal for the original earth and its inhabitants was the same as it is for present-day man and that is that he accept the right foundation and grow spiritually by practicing the spiritual law of circularity. For every natural law in existence, there is a spiritual law that is its counterpart. Later in this book the relation of God's natural law of circularity to His spiritual law of circularity will be shown. At this point it is necessary to explain the spiritual law because it relates to God's law of humility and exaltation and because it was the abuse of this law that led the original earth and its world of inhabitants into the *shakh-ath* pit.

The wheel of God's spiritual law of circularity begins with humility and turns upward to exaltation, returns to humility, only to begin the cycle over again.

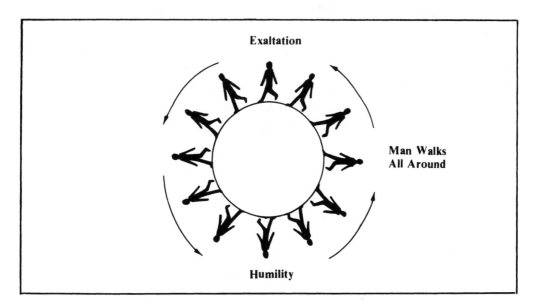

Exaltation

Man Walks
All Around

Humility

77

All true spiritual progress is experienced and accomplished by riding the wheel of God's spiritual law of circularity. When we accept and experience a new increase in God's wisdom of humility, He sets His spiritual wheel of circularity in motion so we can ascend to new heights of exalted understanding and knowledge of His truth. Then we descend and begin the cycle of new growth all over again. This wheel of God's law of circularity is ever turning.

God's spiritual law of circularity is like His natural law of circularity which is seen in the cycle of water that replenishes the earth. The sun draws up the vaporous water from the sea below into the clouds above, which are God's floating reservoirs. Then the wind carries the clouds with their waters over the earth, and by God's wise design, they release their precious liquid in the form of rain upon the earth. Thus the rain gives the earth drink and fills the streams and rivers whose waters rush back to the sea, only to begin their cycle all over again.

If the wheel of circularity were stopped, either in the humility low place of the sea or in the exalted high place of the clouds, the earth soon would become a waste and a howling desert. All freedom of existence on the earth soon would be extinguished. Yet, man in his diseased perception of reality imagines he can continue making spiritual progress on one hand, while stopping God's spiritual law of circularity on the other hand. God plainly declares in many places in His Word that we either humble ourselves voluntarily, or we will be abased involuntarily. By gift, God has given His spiritual law of circularity, which consists of humility and exaltation, because He expects man to practice humbling himself so he can be exalted in due time with greater understanding and knowledge; thus, he will grow in his spiritual education and in his moral development.

The original earth and its world of inhabitants had a humility foundation for their support *by gift*, and they also had God's exalted master plan for their government *by gift*. However, they did not have humility and exaltation *by growth*. Gifts are given as a result of God's choice, but spiritual growth is a result of one's personal choice to accept God's blueprint for spiritual building.

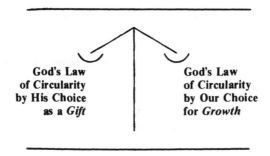

God's Law   God's Law
of Circularity   of Circularity
by His Choice   by Our Choice
as a *Gift*   for *Growth*

God's blueprint for spiritual building requires humility before exaltation. Exaltation by growth in knowledge and honour cannot be experienced before the humility root of wisdom is experienced in the foundation.

The sole purpose and desire of Christ, the humility Root, is to support His Father's master plan. Therefore, the bigger a believer grows in the humility Root, the Wisdom of Christ, the greater his desire will be to support God's master plan for his life, and the more the believer will grow in the exaltation of God's knowledge. Thus, man fulfills the command to grow in grace and knowledge (II Peter 3:18).

Also, the law of circularity clearly is seen in the relationship between God the Father and His only begotten Son, the Christ, the Wisdom Word.

The Son's only motive in descending in humility is for the sole purpose of supporting His Father's master plan.

> And he went a little farther, and fell on his face, and prayed,
> saying, O my Father, if it be possible, let this cup pass from me:
> nevertheless *not as I will*, but *as thou wilt* (Matthew 26:39).

When it appeared that Jesus was dying in the Garden before reaching His goal and objective in this life, which was to die on the Cross for man's redemption, He prayed for the cup of death *to pass from Him in the Garden*. He did not wish to die in the Garden if it were the Father's will for Him to continue on to the Cross. Yet, Christ Jesus was in complete submission to His Father's will and was ready to support any change in the Father's master plan for Him. However, the Father heard the Son's prayer and redeemed Him from death in the Garden and strengthened Him so He could go on to the Cross (Hebrews 5:7). Jesus Christ supported the Father's master plan in the humble place below, and He made it known from the exalted place above. After the Son died on the Cross, was buried and rose again, He ascended on high to lift up His Father's Name and to make His master plan known.

The Son of God descended by His Father's will to reveal Himself as the humility redeeming support of the whole world. Through the Son's condescension, man learns of God's humility and of His love for His whole creation.

Jesus continually witnessed about the wheel of circularity, the humility and exaltation, that exists between Him and His Father.

> All things are delivered unto me of my Father: and *no man*
> *knoweth the Son, but the Father; neither knoweth any man the*
> *Father, save the Son*, and he to whomsoever the Son will reveal
> him (Matthew 11:27).

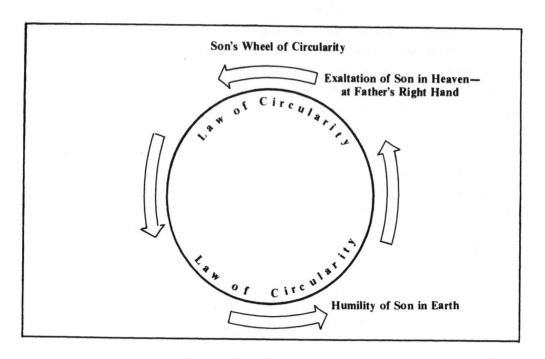

The intimacy between the Father and the Son is so great that no one can know the Son except the Father draw him to the Son. Likewise, no one can know the Father except the Son reveal the Father to him.

> No man can come to me, except the *Father which hath sent me*
> *draw him*: and I will raise him up at the last day (John 6:44).

The Father draws to His Son by the gentle influencing power of His Holy Spirit. The Father does not force anyone to His Son. The Father draws to His Son by working a change in one's will so one's heart willingly can accept the gentle influences of His Holy Spirit. The Father draws to His Son by sharing with the human will a small portion of His love for His Son. A touch of the Father's love works a willing desire in one's will and heart to come to His Son. When the heart and will are drawn by the Father to the Son, the Son begins to lead a person to the Father by instructing and teaching him how to surrender to the Father's divine will and how to support His master plan. There is neither salvation nor spiritual growth without this wheel of circularity of the Father and the Son.

During the first aeon of the earth, the world of mankind sinned by their ungrateful rejection of the humility foundation of Christ, the Word, and by their ungrateful rejection of the Father's master plan.

The first pit (*shakh-ath*) existed for the purpose of punishing the first level of rebellious, ungrateful *wicked* ones who preferred to stand on their own foundation of pride and who preferred to be ruled over by the illness, the miserableness, and the wretchedness of their own prideful plan instead of being supported by the humility Word and being ruled over by the sovereign dominion of God's master plan. Mankind in general always has preferred his own sick foundation and his own unsuccessful, prideful plan instead of the healthy foundation of God's Word and His prosperous master plan. So, this original earth and its world of inhabitants were cast down into the *shakh-ath* pit for the proud exaltation of their own plan, with its consequent rejection of God's humility Word, and for their immoral sins which they had sown.

Chapter Three

The First Restoration of the Earth and Its Fall into the Second Pit of Judgment, the "Bore" Pit

THE revelation of man's sin and God's judgment and punishment that have come upon the earth and its world of inhabitants is seen clearly as one searches the Scriptures.

Because of His immutability, Christ the Creator lifted the original earth from its state of ruin and decay. He set it again in its place in the universe, restoring it to its fruitful condition and exalted position, rebuilding it, and making it a fit place on which a new world of created inhabitants could live.

God reclaimed the earth from its state of degeneracy, according to His master plan and in conformity to His divine purpose which had and has been interrupted for a season.

The immutable Christ worked in harmony with the master plan of His Father to bring the earth back to its former state of purity and cleanness, restoring it from its fall into the *shakh-ath* pit. The earth was made free from moral corruption. It once again became a clean earth.

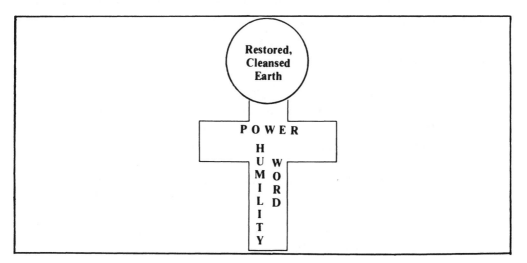

As the immutable supporter and upholder of the righteousness and purity of the Father's master plan, Christ, as the holy upholding Word, again became the upholder and supporter of the earth, joining Himself to it.

Three main reasons substantiate this conclusion. The first reason is based on pure logic; the earth could not have fallen into a second pit if it had not indeed been raised up from the first pit. As we shall see, it did fall into a second pit, the *bore* pit.

The second reason is based on a clear understanding of the Sovereignty of God's divine will for the earth; God originally prepared the earth beautiful and to be inhabited. This is His intended purpose for the earth, which Lucifer has tried to thwart by polluting the earth with his sin and death. But Christ will be victorious in His plan for the earth and its world of inhabitants.

> For thus saith the LORD that created the heavens; God himself
> that formed the earth and made it; he hath established it, *he*
> *created it not in vain, he formed it to be inhabited*: I am the
> LORD; and there is none else (Isaiah 45:18).

The reasonableness of God's procedures prevents Him from working for nothing. He does not begin working and then cease His working because some greater force than Himself has defeated the omniscience of His master plan and conquered His omnipotent power. This is impossible since God is the Supreme Being. No other is greater! The same God Who created the earth in the beginning and framed the world of inhabitants upon it will continue working with the earth and its world of inhabitants until He has established His goal and objective for them forever.

The third reason is based on the infallibility of God's divine Word. We find this second pit, the *bore* pit, and the particular people who are cast into it, recorded in God's Word. Ezekiel the prophet wrote about the people of *old times* who were cast down to the second pit, the *bore* pit.

> For thus saith the Lord GOD; When I shall make thee a desolate
> city, like the cities that are not inhabited; when I shall bring up the
> deep upon thee, and great waters shall cover thee; When *I shall*
> *bring thee down with them that descend into the pit* [bore], *with*
> *the people of old time,* and shall set thee in the low parts of the
> earth, in places desolate of old, with them that go down to the pit,
> that thou be not inhabited; and I shall set glory in the land of the
> living; I will make thee a terror, and thou shalt be no more: though
> thou be sought for, yet shalt thou never be found again, saith the
> Lord GOD (Ezekiel 26:19-21).

Ezekiel, through the gift of prophecy, looked both into the future and into the past and saw God bringing the inhabitants of the city of Tyre down to the second pit (*bore*) into which He had cast the first *restored* earth and its newly created world of inhabitants in old times.

God's Word states clearly that God intended to bring the inhabitants of the city of Tyre down where the people of old time (eternity-past) abode. These people from eternity-past were cast down into the *bore* pit.

Ezekiel the prophet warned the inhabitants in the city of Tyre that for this same wickedness they, too, were going to be humbled, mortified, reduced to ruin, and lowered into the *bore* pit with the people of old time (*o-lawm* or eternity-past). Although God had cast the earth into the *bore* pit, He promised the earth that it again would be set in the land of the living as a clean land, and that it would receive a new world of created inhabitants to lift up and glorify the Name of the LORD. The Son of God always is ready and willing to give His support to a clean earth and to a clean world of inhabitants for the purpose of lifting up His Father's master plan and His Father's holy Name.

Although the Bible does not disclose a vast amount of revelation about the dispensation of the *first restoration* of the earth, the fact remains that the earth and its world of inhabitants fell into a second pit, proving that the earth had to have been raised up and restored after having been judged in the first pit, the *shakh-ath* pit.

While not much *specific* information is given in the Scriptures about how the first restoration of the earth was accomplished, Jesus Christ, the divine Word and Creator, is the same yesterday, today, and forever; therefore, we can know through the details that are given in the Book of Genesis about the restoration and creation of our *present* earth and its world of inhabitants that God, being unchangeable, used the same ways to restore the earth from the two different pits into which it was cast in *former* days, and that He created a new world of inhabitants following the same plan each time.

> Jesus Christ *the same* yesterday, and to day, and for ever
> (Hebrews 13:8).

The immutability of Jesus Christ permits us to understand that He is always the same. The immutable, unchangeable Workings of the infinite Christ are the same yesterday, today, and forever. Christ always has worked in the same manner, using the same methods, and He always will work in the same manner, using the same methods. So, after a person perceives how God works today, he will understand how God worked yesterday and how He will work tomorrow. Jesus Christ is the same in His person, His Works, and His teaching. Christ, as the Creator, maintains His infinite sameness, yet without monotony. Christ does not have to change to become perfect because He is the perfect, infinite Word of God.

The immutableness of Christ's mercy and the changelessness of His grace help poor mortal creatures change their imperfections for His perfection, if they so desire. Man can make progress in his spiritual education and in his moral development only through change, by putting off the old man or flesh, and by putting on the new man in Christ Jesus. There is a keen awareness of great sublime satisfaction when a person presses past the changeableness of his corrupt human nature and goes on to acquire the immutable nature of Christ, the divine Word of God.

So, we can know from Christ's immutability that He has a reasonable master plan, and He has rational, moral consistency and practical intelligence to implement His master plan. God's immutability certifies the ultimate finishing of His master plan.

Because God is a Being with a free moral will, He always has created the *worlds* of mankind with a free moral will which gives them the power to make choices. Man has been given the prerogative in this earthly life to choose righteousness with its ensuing good and to refuse wickedness with its ensuing evil, or to choose wickedness with its ensuing evil and to refuse righteousness with its ensuing good.

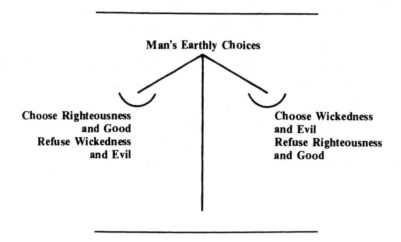

Man's Earthly Choices

Choose Righteousness and Good Refuse Wickedness and Evil

Choose Wickedness and Evil Refuse Righteousness and Good

God, during the dispensation of time, has given mankind the power of choice either to accept the rulership of His master plan and the redemptive, supportive work of His Son, or to reject the redemptive support of the Son and the rulership of the Father. However, in eternity-future, man will be forced to accept the rulership of God's master plan and to bow his knees in submission to the support of Jesus Christ (Philippians 2:9-11). In the beginning of each aeon of creation, earthly man, exercising his free moral will, always has chosen wickedness and evil in preference to righteousness and good.

In the beginning of this present world, when Adam male and female were clean and perfect, they chose the wickedness of passive and active disobedience, with its ensuing evils of suffering and death, in preference to the righteousness of passive and active obedience with its ensuing goodness of freedom of existence. The wickedness of sinful disobedience to God has existed from the beginning of the original earth and its world of inhabitants, up to and including this present earth and its present world of inhabitants.

While the basic sin of the original earth and its inhabitants was against the *wisdom* that is from and in the Name of the LORD, the second world sinned against the *understanding* that is from and in His Name.

I. Sin Against the Understanding That Is from and in the LORD's Name Is Punished in the *Bore* Pit

The Hebrew word for the *pit* into which the second world of inhabitants and the restored earth were cast is *bore*, meaning a pit, hole, cistern, prison, dungeon, fountain, well; it comes from the Hebrew word *boor*, meaning to examine and to declare.

The restored earth and its created world of inhabitants sowed sins against the understanding that is from and in the LORD's Name, so they reaped the punishment of being cast into the "*bore* pit," which God has reserved for their type of sin.

The *bore* pit is in the underworld, and it is inhabited by the dead of old. The word for *old* in Hebrew is *o-lawm*, meaning eternity-past, ancient time, beginning of the world. The people of old time (eternity-past) are the people from the first restored earth who, for their wickedness and sin against the understanding that is from and in the LORD's Name, were cast into the second pit (*bore*).

God created and reserved this second pit to be used for the punishment of a deeper level of wickedness than that practiced by the original earth and its world of inhabitants. God has both a spiritual pit and a natural pit called *bore* in the Hebrew. He has punished the guilty sinner man, cities, nations, and the whole world alike by casting them into His natural *bore* pit.

God also has punished and does punish His own people who believe on His Name, and yet who have been and are guilty of sinning against the understanding that is from and in the LORD's Name, by casting them into spiritual *bore* pits for chastising and correction. God's purpose in casting His people into a spiritual *bore* pit is that, through grief and sorrow of mind and spirit, their sin and the fear of God's wrath might be called to remembrance so they can repent.

Many of God's saints and servants have been chastised in the *bore* pit through the sorrows of heart and troubles of mind they have experienced.

> *I am counted with them that go down into the pit*: I am as a man
> that hath no strength: Free among the dead, like the slain that lie
> in the grave, whom thou rememberest no more: and they are cut
> off from thy hand. *Thou hast laid me in the lowest pit* [*bore*], in
> darkness, in the deeps (Psalm 88:4-6).

When God lays His children in the low spiritual pit (*bore*) of darkness, gloom, and despair from whence there is no human help, it is for their refinement and illumination, not for their annihilation and destruction. From this low pit, God illuminates a person's understanding so he can cease leaning upon the arm of flesh and give reverence and honour to the holy delivering Name of the LORD.

By examining the present creation's sin and judgment in the *spiritual bore* pit, insight is given into the sinful and wicked disobedience of the second world of created inhabitants who fell into the second pit, the *natural bore* pit.

When the earth and its world of inhabitants do not gratefully accept and lovingly honour God's gift of His powerful Word that supports them as a humility foundation, and when they do not willingly accept and lovingly honour the gift of the understanding that is from and in the LORD's Name, which helps them submit rightfully to God's rulership and to His master plan, God ultimately is forced to cut them off.

When the second created world of mankind refused to use the understanding that is from and in the LORD's Name which would have helped them to practice God's spiritual law of circularity of the humility of the Son and the exaltation of the Father, they continually sank further and further into the depths of sin and wickedness. Finally God was forced to cast them down in judgment to the *bore* pit.

What was the understanding against which this creation sinned? Understanding means to have the use of intellectual faculties; to be able to comprehend or apprehend the meaning, import, motive, or intention of anything; to be an intelligent and conscious being.

Understanding causes one to believe, to learn, to be informed, and to know. The capability of being intelligible, comprehensive, and perceptive of ideas and thoughts expressed by others comes to one through understanding. Understanding gives one clear insight and intelligence, both in natural matters and in spiritual matters. The power to form sound judgments in regard to any course of action comes from understanding.

The LORD's Name is the source of *all* understanding. He is the One Who gives wisdom and understanding to His creation.

> Only *the LORD give thee wisdom and understanding*, and give
> thee charge concerning Israel, that thou mayest keep the law of the
> LORD thy God (I Chronicles 22:12).

The LORD is the only One Who gives man the understanding to lift up His holy Name and to perform His divine will.

> But there is a spirit in man: and the inspiration of the *Almighty*
> *giveth them understanding* (Job 32:8).

The LORD's Name gives the extraordinary influence that illuminates the understanding which in turn raises and purifies the moral senses of man so that he can use his understanding in obedience to God's purposive will.

The LORD's Name is great and full of infinite understanding.

> Great is our Lord, and of great power: *his understanding is infinite*
> (Psalm 147:5).

The understanding that is from and in the LORD's Name is numberless, incalculable, and past searching out.

The insight or understanding that is from and in the LORD's Name is not a commodity that a finite creature can count. The greatness of the insight or understanding that is from and in the LORD's Name prevents people and things from being insignificant to God. The LORD's understanding preserves the separate identity of all things and weighs the inner value of all people and all things.

> Hast thou not known? hast thou not heard, that the everlasting
> God, the LORD, the Creator of the ends of the earth, fainteth not,
> neither is weary? *there is no searching of his understanding* (Isaiah
> 40:28).

When the LORD does not respond or intervene in response to man's pleading cries, it is not for lack of power. His understanding is beyond man's searching out.

Understanding is a deep wellspring of life. A well in the natural realm supplies life-giving refreshment to all who draw and drink of its waters. Likewise, the understanding that is from and in the LORD's Name is a deep well of infinite understanding that supplies its life-giving waters of refreshment to all who draw and drink.

> *Understanding is a wellspring of life* unto him that hath it: but
> the instruction of fools is folly (Proverbs 16:22).

The waters of the LORD's understanding give abundant satisfaction to one's own heart and to the hearts of others with whom they are shared.

The understanding that is from and in the LORD's Name can be acquired by applying one's heart to search for it and by lifting up one's voice to ask for it.

> So that thou incline thine ear unto wisdom, and *apply thine heart*
> *to understanding*; Yea, if thou criest after knowledge, and *liftest*
> *up thy voice for understanding*; (Proverbs 2:2,3).

For man to make only his ears attentive unto the LORD is not sufficient to gain understanding; he must also incline his heart as a witness to his eagerness. He also must lift up his voice, which is an indication of his intense desire for the LORD's understanding.

The LORD's purposive will in giving man understanding from His Name is to enable man to dig, examine, and declare the truth of the LORD's Name and His Word.

> *Whoso is wise*, and will observe these things, even they *shall*
> *understand* the lovingkindness of the LORD (Psalm 107:43).

The heart that is filled with understanding from the LORD's Name will dig into, examine, and declare the lovingkindness and mercy of the LORD which are revealed through His rule and reign in one's own affairs and in the affairs of mankind.

> For *God is the King* of all the earth: *sing ye praises with*
> *understanding* (Psalm 47:7).

The LORD gives understanding from His Name so that a person can take his newly-won understanding and raise his voice in joyous song because of his fresh, blissful awareness of the LORD and because of his new union with the LORD's Name.

God gives understanding to the human heart so it can fear or reverence the glorious and fearful Name of the LORD.

> If thou wilt not observe to do all the words of this law that are
> written in this book, *that thou mayest fear this glorious and
> fearful name, THE LORD THY GOD*; (Deuteronomy 28:58).

Understanding from the LORD's Name empowers one to give the reverential obedience due His holy Name and causes one to fear His fearful Name.

If we do not apply our hearts and lift up our voice for the LORD's understanding that comes from out of the pit of His deep "wellspring," we may expect to receive the plagues and punishments from His *bore* pit.

When the soul of man fears the fearful Name of the LORD, the Sun of Righteousness rises upon that soul.

> But unto *you that fear my name shall the Sun of righteousness
> arise* with healing in his wings; and ye shall go forth, and grow up
> as calves of the stall (Malachi 4:2).

The Sun of Righteousness rises upon the reverent soul, spreading out the rays of His healing wings, radiating His powerful healing light to broken hearts and to confused minds, illuminating the gloom and darkness of souls in sorrow and affliction.

The LORD God gave understanding, which comes out of His deep wellspring of understanding, to the newly created world of inhabitants on the newly restored earth so they would know how to fear His fearful Name. Because they sinned against the LORD's understanding from the deep, they were cast into the depths of the *bore* pit.

God gave the restored earth with its world of created inhabitants understanding that is from and in His Name so they could discern and comprehend how to measure out a true measure or true proportion of praise, worship, and reverence to the LORD's holy Name. However, instead of using their understanding for exalting the LORD's holy Name, which was God's intended purpose, they yielded when "Wickedness" tempted them. Consequently they filled their measure of understanding with all manner of false measurements with which to justify themselves for putting down the Name of the LORD and lifting up their own name.

Christ Jesus warned His people against the false measure of wickedness.

> Judge not, that ye be not judged. For with what judgment ye
> judge, ye shall be judged; and *with what measure ye mete, it shall
> be measured to you again* (Matthew 7:1,2).

Christ Jesus has warned us against using our understanding for a wicked or false measurement of others. In our understanding we have different "baskets," as it were, for measurements. We have one "basket" that we use for judging others, and we have another "basket" that we use for judging ourselves.

If we are judging others' faults and failings, we use the largest size "basket" that we can find in our understanding so we can have plenty of room for our vicious judging, our censorious criticism, our malignant faultfindings, and our corrupt critiques. When we falsely judge others, we delightfully and pleasurably fill the large "basket" in our understanding with wicked, uncharitable, and unmerciful judgments, as though God had appointed us to be the supreme, sovereign judge. We cannot become a better person until we allow the LORD to enlighten our understanding so we can mete out true judgment.

However, if we are judging our own faults and failings, we take the smallest "basket" that we can find in our understanding so we will not have much room to fill up because we assume our faults and failures are so very few. We also make excuses for not adding the rest of our faults and failures to our small "basket." Then because there is so much room left in our small "basket," we throw in a lot of false compliments to ourselves.

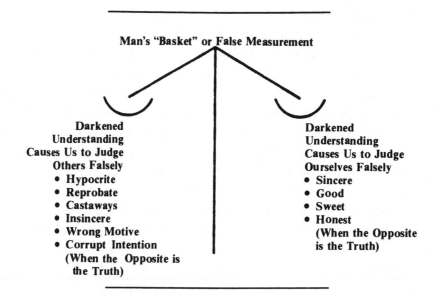

Man's "Basket" or False Measurement

Darkened
Understanding
Causes Us to Judge
Others Falsely
- Hypocrite
- Reprobate
- Castaways
- Insincere
- Wrong Motive
- Corrupt Intention
  (When the Opposite is
  the Truth)

Darkened
Understanding
Causes Us to Judge
Ourselves Falsely
- Sincere
- Good
- Sweet
- Honest
  (When the Opposite
  is the Truth)

This class of darkened understanding caused the second world of inhabitants to sin against the Name of the LORD which resulted in their reaping God's judgment in the *bore* pit.

II. God's Judgments Are Measured According to the Measure of Man's Sins

God always measures out His judgments according to the measure of man's sins. This spiritual principle is seen in connection with Israel's possession of Canaan's land.

> Speak not thou in thine heart, after that the LORD thy God hath cast them out from before thee, saying, For my righteousness the LORD hath brought me in to possess this land: but *for the wickedness of these nations* the LORD doth drive them out from before thee (Deuteronomy 9:4).

Moses made the truth plain to Israel about the reason for her inheritance of Canaan's land. Moses clarified that it was *not* because of Israel's righteousness as compared with the wickedness of the inhabitants of Canaan's land that she was counted worthy to possess the land.

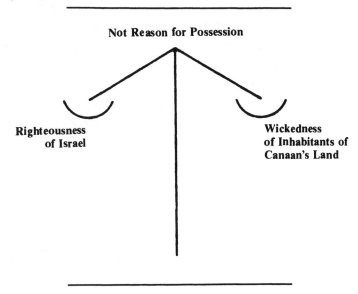

Not Reason for Possession

Righteousness of Israel

Wickedness of Inhabitants of Canaan's Land

It is true that the inhabitants of Canaan's land had lost their land because of their wickedness. But Israel did not inherit their land because her righteousness made her more worthy to have the land than the Canaanites. Israel inherited Canaan's land because of God's divine promises to Abraham, Isaac, and Jacob and because God measured out His judgments according to the measure of the sins and wicked disobedience of Canaan's original inhabitants.

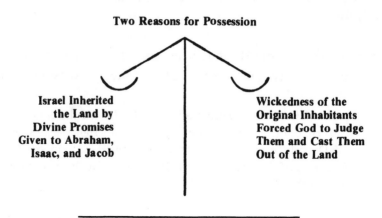

Two Reasons for Possession

Israel Inherited
the Land by
Divine Promises
Given to Abraham,
Isaac, and Jacob

Wickedness of the
Original Inhabitants
Forced God to Judge
Them and Cast Them
Out of the Land

These are the two reasons Israel inherited the land. God taught Israel that her own righteousness had nothing to do with her inheritance of the land. His actions toward the original inhabitants of Canaan's land also teach everyone a lesson—that His holy nature never will tolerate full measure of wickedness in any land; He will mete out a just and true measure of judgment for sin. The immutable, holy nature of God never has tolerated a full measure of wickedness, either in the whole earth or in any particular part of the earth, without judging accordingly. Biblical history and secular history confirm God's faithfulness and moral justice in judging and punishing those who have filled up their measure of wickedness. God already delivered His righteous verdict that the wicked shall fall by his own wickedness.

> The righteousness of the perfect shall direct his way: *but the wicked shall fall by his own wickedness* (Proverbs 11:5).

Righteousness leads a willing soul in the perfect will of God which is the only route to eternal prosperity and everlasting happiness. But wickedness leads a rebellious soul to fill up his cup of wickedness, which ultimately will cause God to cast him down in judgment.

III. Man Uses His *Bore* Pits to Punish the Innocent

The *bore* pits that man has used for punishment of the innocent is opposite to the *bore* pit that the LORD has used to punish the *guilty*. The Bible gives examples of both *bore* pits—man's and the LORD's.

94

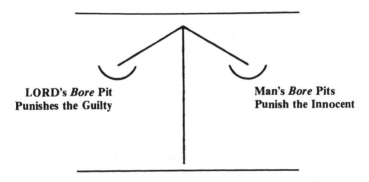

LORD's *Bore* Pit
Punishes the Guilty

Man's *Bore* Pits
Punish the Innocent

A. Innocent Joseph Punished in Man's *Bore* Pits

Joseph, the son of Jacob, is the first example of an innocent one who suffered wicked, undeserved punishment in man's *bore* pits.

> And they took him, and *cast him into a pit* [*bore*]: and the pit was
> empty, there was no water in it (Genesis 37:24).

In obedience to his father's command, Joseph went to visit his brothers who were feeding his father's flock. Although Joseph was aware of his brothers' malicious envy and hate toward him, he willingly obeyed his father and went to them in love, kindness, and respect. However, Joseph's brothers conspired to return evil for good by conceiving a destructive design to cast Joseph into a *bore* pit.

The cruel crew stripped Joseph of his coat of many colours and cast him into the *bore* pit. When envy and malice reign, justice and pity and love are banished. When injustice reigns, humanity is obliterated.

Joseph wept and pled his innocence. And out of the anguish of his soul, he besought his brothers for mercy.

> And they said one to another, We are verily guilty concerning our
> brother, in that *we saw the anguish of his soul, when he besought
> us*, and we would not hear; therefore is this distress come upon us.
> And Reuben answered them, saying, Spake I not unto you,
> saying, Do not sin against the child; and ye would not hear?
> therefore, behold, also his blood is required (Genesis 42:21,22).

Reuben, the firstborn, could not prevail upon his brothers nor restrain them from casting Joseph into the horrible *bore* pit. Their vicious hate made them willing to bury Joseph alive, leaving their brother to die by degrees in the *bore* pit.

The callousness of their hearts allowed them to sit down and eat bread nearby while Joseph was grieving and groaning in the *bore* pit.

Because of man's lack of understanding, God's providence sometimes seems to be diametrically opposed to His purpose. However, in Joseph's case, as in all other cases, God is the head over all circumstances. So, in spite of contrary appearances, the brothers' injustice and condemnation of innocent Joseph ultimately brought Joseph to the throne of government in Egypt. God was faithful to accomplish His purpose in innocent Joseph's life, so the evil that was intended against Joseph became a blessing to him and all his people.

The brothers eventually took Joseph out of the *bore* pit and sold him to a band of Ishmaelites who carried him to Egypt. Then Joseph was sold to Potiphar, captain of Pharaoh's guard. Because Joseph was a loyal and faithful servant in the house of Potiphar, God blessed Joseph. And because God's blessing was on Joseph, Potiphar's house also was blessed.

Eventually, Potiphar's wife cast her eyes upon Joseph and begged him to commit adultery with her. When Joseph steadfastly resisted and willfully rejected the alluring approches of Potiphar's wife, she falsely accused him of trying to seduce her, so her husband, Potiphar, had him thrown into a dungeon (*bore* pit) in Egypt. Once again, Joseph was an innocent victim of the hate and injustice of man.

> For indeed I was stolen away out of the land of the Hebrews: and
> here also have I done nothing that they should *put me into the*
> *dungeon* [*bore*] (Genesis 40:15).

Man's wicked punishment of the innocent cannot prevent God from using their *bore* pits as steppingstones for the implementation of His master plan. Joseph soon gained favour with the keeper of the prison, and because of the position the keeper assigned Joseph, he met Pharaoh's butler, who eventually recommended Joseph to Pharaoh.

> Then *Pharaoh sent and called Joseph, and they brought him*
> *hastily out of the dungeon* [*bore pit*]: and he shaved himself, and
> changed his raiment, and came in unto Pharaoh (Genesis 41:14).

Pharaoh fetched Joseph, the innocent one, out of the dungeon or *bore* pit, and exalted him to a place of rulership in Egypt. While Joseph was serving Pharaoh, God gave him understanding of Pharaoh's dreams concerning the seven years of plenty and the seven years of famine. God used Joseph to store up grain in the time of plenty so he could preserve life in the time of famine.

Man's wicked punishment of the innocent in his *bore* pits cannot thwart God's purposive will in the earth.

B. Innocent Jeremiah Punished in Man's *Bore* Pits

Jeremiah, the great and good prophet of the LORD, was another innocent one who suffered the wicked punishment of man.

> Wherefore the princes were wroth with Jeremiah, and smote him, and put him in prison in the house of Jonathan the scribe: for they had made that the prison. When *Jeremiah was entered into the dungeon* [*bore* pit], and into the cabins, and Jeremiah had remained there many days; (Jeremiah 37:15,16).

Because Jeremiah, by the Spirit of God, had counseled Judah to surrender and be submissive to the Babylonians (whom God had sent to rule over Judah and Israel), the princes were angry with him and falsely accused Jeremiah of being a deserter. Therefore, they cast innocent Jeremiah into a dungeon (*bore* pit) for many days. Because of the truth, Jeremiah was cast into a *bore* pit, wrongfully suffering man's unjust judgment.

King Zedekiah sent for Jeremiah and took him out of the *bore* pit. Then he secretly asked the LORD's prophet, Jeremiah, to tell him what the mind of the LORD was for him. Jeremiah declared the prophetic truth that King Zedekiah eventually would be taken captive to Babylon. Because of Jeremiah's continued declaration of the truth, they cast him into another *bore* pit.

> Then *took they Jeremiah, and cast him into the dungeon* [*bore* pit] of Malchiah the son of Hammelech, that was in the court of the prison: and they let down Jeremiah with cords. And in the dungeon [*bore* pit] there was no water, but mire: so Jeremiah sunk in the mire (Jeremiah 38:6).

Man's wicked punishment of innocent Jeremiah could not thwart God's prophetic predictions from comming to pass. So in the meantime, God raised up Ebedmelech, an Ethiopian (an alien) who respected Jeremiah, to rescue him from man's *bore* pit.

Jeremiah testified of his suffering in the *bore* pit. In his innocence, Jeremiah suffered persecution at the hands of his own fellow countrymen. Stones were cast upon him, and the waters flowed over his head. All possibility of the enjoyment of life seemingly was cut off.

> Mine enemies chased me sore, like a bird, without cause. *They have cut off my life in the dungeon* [*bore* pit] and cast a stone upon me. Waters flowed over mine head; then I said, I am cut off. I called upon thy name, O LORD, out of the low dungeon [*bore* pit]. Thou hast heard my voice: hide not thine ear at my breathing, at my cry. Thou drewest near in the day that I called upon thee: thou saidst, Fear not. O Lord, thou hast pleaded the causes of my soul; thou hast redeemed my life. O LORD, thou hast seen my wrong: judge thou my cause (Lamentations 3:52-59).

Out of the low dungeon (*bore*), Jeremiah cried unto the LORD Who heard his prayers and delivered him from man's *bore* pit.

God delivered His innocent ones, both Joseph and Jeremiah, from man's wicked punishment in the *bore* pit.

IV. The LORD's *Bore* Pit Is Punishment for the Guilty: Nations, Cities, Individuals

God's desire for man is that he grow in the wisdom of the humility foundation of the Son of God, which supports and lifts up the Father's purposive will and master plan. The LORD also desires that man grow in understanding so he can fulfill God's exalted purposive will, which is to lift up the LORD's holy Name in praise and thanksgiving.

The restored earth and its created world of mankind fell into the second pit or *bore* pit, after they had filled up their measure of wickedness by passive and active disobedience.

The whole motive and purpose of the Son of God, the Word, in creating the creation and in humbling Himself to uphold it and to lift it up on high is for the creation of mankind to assume its duty and responsibility in its understanding by lifting up the Father's unbegotten tetragrammaton Name of *LORD* in praise and thanksgiving.

When sinful man, in his understanding, fills up his cup of wickedness to the full by casting down the holy Name of the LORD and by lifting up his own corrupt name, the Son of God, the holy Word, removes His righteous support from unrighteous man and his evil deeds. Thus, unrighteous men, whether they be worlds, nations, cities, or individuals, fall into the *bore* pit.

98

A. Inhabitants of Assyria Reaped the *Bore* Pit

Through the prophetic "eye" of faith, Ezekiel the prophet looked to the future and saw God bringing the inhabitants of the nation of Assyria down into the *bore* pit, just as he had looked into the past and saw how God had brought the world of mankind, who had lived on the first restored earth, down into the *bore* pit.

> To the end that none of all the trees by the waters exalt themselves for their height, neither shoot up their top among the thick boughs, neither their trees stand up in their height, all that drink water: for they are all delivered unto death, *to the nether parts of the earth, in the midst of the children of men, with them that go down to the pit* [*bore*] (Ezekiel 31:14).

> I made the nations to shake at the sound of his fall, when I cast him down to hell with *them that descend into the pit* [*bore*]: and all the trees of Eden, the choice and best of Lebanon, all that drink water, shall be comforted in the nether parts of the earth (Ezekiel 31:16).

Assyria used his God-given understanding to worship his many gods and goddesses of stone and clay, the works of his own hands. The great god of Assyria was Asshur, who was depicted as the figure of a man, armed with a bow, issuing from the center of a winged sphere.

Because of Assyria's gross idolatry and refusal to humble himself and repent before the true God of heaven, he, as a nation, was cast down by God's just judgment and righteous punishment into the "*bore* pit."

The wickedness of the prideful people of old time (eternity-past), the wickedness of the haughty inhabitants of Tyre, and the wickedness of the arrogant inhabitants of Assyria are historical warnings to all. Lands and all peoples who are tempted to follow the wicked example left by the people from eternity-past will find that abusing and misusing their God-given understanding to put down the Name of the LORD, the supreme, Self-existent Sovereign and divine Creator, while exalting the works of their own hands by making idols out of them, will lead to punishment in the *bore* pit. The lesson that all should learn from the history of rebellious man is that God faithfully judges and punishes prideful wickedness: in the beginning, past time; in present time; and in all future time.

All the nations of old time (eternity-past) were comforted in the nether parts of the earth when they saw Assyria joining their company because they saw and beheld that God is not partial in His judgment and punishment of idolatrous worship.

B. Inhabitants of Egypt Reaped the *Bore* Pit

Ezekiel the prophet looked through the prophetic "eye" of faith, both toward the future and toward the past, and saw God bringing Egypt down into the *bore* pit, joining them through His judgment and punishment to the people of old time or eternity-past.

> Son of man, wait for the *multitude of Egypt,* and *cast them down,* even her, and the daughters of the famous nations, *unto the nether parts of the earth, with them that go down into the pit* [*bore*] (Ezekiel 32:18).

The Egyptians knew there was a supreme, Sovereign, Self-existent LORD and Creator, but they refused to use their understanding to lift up the holy Name of the LORD God in praise and thanksgiving. Instead, by the works of their own hands, they created many gods from the things of creation.

They filled their minds and understandings with ideas that were mixed with the basest forms of polytheism and idolatry. Every city had its own particular divinities and its sacred fetishes. Each city had its various orders of gods and a revolving order for specially honouring each god, called the "society of the gods."

Vast temples were built to honour, worship, and lift up the names of the Egyptians' gods instead of to honour, worship, and lift up the Name of the true LORD God.

Ezekiel saw God judging Egypt and bringing her inhabitants down to the *bore* pit because of her abuse and misuse of her understanding as demonstrated by her polytheistic, idolatrous worship.

C. Inhabitants of Elam Reaped the *Bore* Pit

Ezekiel also looked through his prophetic "eye" of faith to the future and to the past and saw God bringing Elam down into the *bore* pit, joining them by His judgment and punishment to the people of old time (eternity-past).

> *There is Elam* and all her multitude round about her grave, all of them slain, fallen by the sword, which are *gone down uncircumcised into the nether parts of the earth*, which caused their terror in the land of the living; yet have they borne their shame *with them that go down to the pit*. They have set her a bed

in the midst of the slain with all her multitude: her graves are
round about him: all of them uncircumcised, slain by the sword:
though their terror was caused in the land of the living, yet have
they borne their shame *with them that go down to the pit* [bore]:
he is put in the midst of them that be slain (Ezekiel 32:24,25).

The country of Elam was peopled by the descendants of Shem. It was called after
Shem's son Elam (Genesis 10:22), and it lay south of Assyria and west of Persia.

A remarkable statement concerning Elam has been deciphered from Assyrian
cylinders in the British Museum which confirms the truth of the Scriptures. Assur-
bonipal records the destruction of the wicked king of Elam and the evil people of
Elam.

The inhabitants of Elam also sinned by abusing and misusing their
understanding. As descendants of Shem, they had learned about the supreme,
Sovereign, Self-existent LORD, the Creator. But they, too, refused to use their
understanding to lift up the holy Name of the LORD God in worship, praise, and
adoration. They chose to lift up the names of their own gods; and by their sinful and
wicked oppression, they put down the LORD's Name. They filled their minds and
understanding with the basest forms of idolatry.

Ezekiel, by prophetic vision, saw God judging Elam and bringing her inhabitants
down to the *bore* pit because she abused and misused her understanding by engaging
in idolatrous worship.

D. Inhabitants of Edom Reaped the *Bore* Pit

As Ezekiel looked into the prophetic future, he also saw Edom brought down to
the *bore* pit by God's judgment and punishment, which joined them to the people of
old time (eternity-past).

There is *Edom*, her kings, and all her princes, which with their
might are laid by them that were slain by the sword: *they shall lie
with the uncircumcised, and with them that go down to the pit*
[bore] (Ezekiel 32:29).

Edom also is called Idumaea and Mount Seir. Edom extended from the Dead Sea
southward to the Gulf of Arabah and from the valley of the Arabah eastward to the
desert of Arabia.

The nation of Edom was one of the most powerful and formidable nations of her
age. However, they, too, abused and misused their understanding of the supreme,

Sovereign, Self-existent LORD, the Creator, by filling their thoughts with base and vile forms of idolatry and hatred toward their brethren which were manifested in crimes of robbery and bloodshed.

E. Inhabitants of Zidon Reaped the *Bore* Pit

Ezekiel, the faithful prophet of God, looked into the future and saw God also bringing the Zidonians down to the *bore* pit by His judgment and punishment, joining them to the people of *old time* (eternity-past) who had preceded them to the *bore* pit.

> There be the princes of the north, all of them, and *all the Zidonians*, which are gone down with the slain; with their terror they are ashamed of their might; and *they lie uncircumcised with them* that be slain by the sword, and bear their shame with them *that go down to the pit* [*bore*] (Ezekiel 32:30).

Zidon was one of the most ancient cities of this present world. It was named after Zidon, the great-grandson of Noah. The name Zidon also denoted the Phoenicians in general.

The Zidonians or Phoenicians were not unknowledgeable of the supreme, Sovereign, Self-existent LORD, the Creator. They were descendants of the righteous and just Noah and lived adjoining Israel. They helped to build the temple in Jerusalem (I Chronicles 22:4). In spite of all the truth they knew from the past, they used their idolatrous abominations to corrupt Israel.

> For *Solomon went after Ashtoreth* the goddess of the Zidonians, and after Milcom the abomination of the Ammonites (I Kings 11:5).

> Because that they have forsaken me, and *have worshipped Ashtoreth the goddess of the Zidonians, Chemosh the god of the Moabites, and Milcom the god of the children of Ammon*, and have not walked in my ways, to do that which is right in mine eyes, and to keep my statutes and my judgments, as did David his father (I Kings 11:33).

> And the high places that were before Jerusalem, which were on the right hand of the mount of corruption, which *Solomon the king of Israel had builded for Ashtoreth the abomination of the*

Zidonians, and for Chemosh the abomination of the Moabites, and for Milcom the abomination of the children of Ammon, did the king defile (II Kings 23:13).

When Solomon was old, his foreign wives were able to influence him, to weaken his powers of resistance, and to fill his understanding with thoughts of abominable, idolatrous worship. Therefore, Solomon did not remain whole-heartedly loyal and loving toward the Name of the LORD. He condoned the abominable, idolatrous practices of his wives, who were brought to Israel from Zidon. He had idolatrous images and shrines provided for them.

Ashtoreth is the Hebrew name for Astarte, the most important goddess of the Zidonians; their chief male deity was Baal. Astarte symbolized the moon while Baal symbolized the sun.

What unmitigated shame, and what unparalleled brazenness that man should take his God-given understanding and use it to honour, worship, and idolize the creation instead of reverencing and worshipping the supreme, Sovereign, Self-existent LORD and Creator.

God never has failed to exercise His just judgment and righteous punishment on worlds, nations, cities, and individuals who have corrupted their God-given understanding by pridefully misusing and abusing it in worshipping idols.

F. Lucifer Reaped the *Bore* Pit

When Lucifer, the anointed cherub of heaven, filled his understanding with sinful pride, revolting and rebelling against the Name of the LORD, God also brought him down to the *bore* pit, where Lucifer reaped God's just judgment and righteous punishment.

Yet *thou shalt be brought down to hell*, to the sides of the pit [*bore*] (Isaiah 14:15).

Lucifer, the light-bearer, the morning star of heaven, corrupted his understanding and abused and misused it by leading some of the angels of heaven in rebellion and revolt against the Name of the LORD. Instead of lifting up the Name of the LORD in worship and praise, and instead of teaching others to do likewise, he used his corrupted understanding to snatch the souls of angels who had followed him because he seemed to be victorious in his revolt against God. Now he himself is cast down to the *bore* pit.

When Lucifer conceived his prideful desire to ascend and exalt his throne above all the stars or angels of God, he corrupted his understanding, and God cast him down to the *bore* pit.

God never has allowed any individual, city, nation, or world to corrupt his or its understanding without faithfully administering His judgment and punishment.

V. The LORD Delivers from the *Bore* Pit

Many who reaped the just punishment from the *bore* pit because of their deeds of idolatry went to their eternal end without repenting. Others took their God-given punishment, repented, and God forgave and delivered them from the *bore* pit.

A. Nebuchadnezzar Delivered from the *Bore* Pit

Nebuchadnezzar, the Babylonian king, is a classical example of one who corrupted his understanding. After the God of heaven had given him a throne and a kingdom, Nebuchadnezzar's heart and understanding became filled with pride.

God had forewarned him of what was destined for him unless he humbled himself by repenting and giving glory to the God of heaven with *his understanding*. God granted the king a period of grace in which to repent of his pride and arrogancy, but the king failed to utilize his God-given opportunity. So, one day, while the king was walking in the royal palace of Babylon, he, in his unbounded arrogance, announced that he had built the royal palace by the might of his own power and for the glory of his own majesty.

His distinguished arrogance was the cause of God's immediate judgment and punishment. God took away the king's understanding so that he behaved like an ox. He roamed, roved, and wandered in the fields unclothed; his body was wet with dew, and he ate grass like an ox. His hair grew like eagles' feathers, and his nails grew like birds' claws. The king lived in this despicable state of humiliation for seven years before he lifted up his eyes unto heaven and recognized the LORD as the supreme, Sovereign God and Creator.

> And *at the end of the days I* Nebuchadnezzar *lifted up mine eyes* unto heaven, *and mine understanding returned unto me*, and I blessed the most High, and I praised and honoured him that liveth for ever, whose dominion is an everlasting dominion, and his kingdom is from generation to generation: (Daniel 4:34).

The arrogant, prideful words that Nebuchadnezzar spoke against the glory and majesty of the Most High God have been recorded in many cuneiform inscriptions and have been deciphered by modern scholars.

God's purposive will in giving man understanding was so man would lift up the holy Name of the LORD in praise, giving God the glory, honour, and majesty due His holy Name. When man sins by corrupting his understanding, he is judged and punished.

Nebuchadnezzar finally repented of his proud thoughts and desires that had made him take unto himself the glory and praise that rightfully belonged to God. After he repented, he used his understanding according to God's purposive will, giving glory and honour to the LORD, the Most High God. Thus, Nebuchadnezzar escaped the judgment and punishment of the *bore* pit.

God's merciful dealings and patience with Nebuchadnezzar teaches that God does not send any world, nation, city, or individual to the *bore* pit without first granting ample time and grace for them to repent. The immutable nature of the LORD assures us that He always has worked, and is working, and will work the same way with His creation, both in merciful long-suffering and in just judgment and righteous punishment.

B. King David Delivered from the *Bore* Pit

King David is a classical example of a great warrior who fought against the wickedness of false measurement. Being guilty of false measurement causes one to descend to the *bore* pit in the spiritual realm. Sometimes David was victorious and escaped being cast down to the spiritual *bore* pit.

> Unto thee will I cry, O LORD my rock; be not silent to me: *lest*, if
> thou be silent to me, *I become like them that go down into the pit*
> [*bore*] (Psalm 28:1).

This Psalm is a short song of praise to the LORD for His power and strength that are found as a result of an intimate spiritual relationship with the LORD and His Holy Word. David depended upon the LORD's Word to support every moment of his life. David keenly was aware that if God were silent or inactive in His support of him that he would fall into the spiritual *bore* pit.

In this verse, David was calling upon the LORD and acknowledging Him as the sole foundation of his existence, spiritually and naturally. David confessed that if God, Who was his support, were separated from him, he would go down to the spiritual *bore* pit and experience a suffering similar to the people's from old time in eternity-past who are imprisoned in the *bore* pit.

On some occasions David failed to continue his victorious walk with the LORD and was cast into the spiritual *bore* pit.

> I waited patiently for the LORD; and he inclined unto me, and heard my cry, He brought me up also out of an *horrible pit* [*bore*], out of the miry clay, and set my feet upon a rock, and established my goings (Psalm 40:1,2).

At this point in his life, David momentarily had lost his close relationship with God's humility foundation, the Word, and he had failed to use his understanding to measure out proper reverence, praise, and worship to the LORD's holy Name. As a result, he fell into the spiritual *bore* pit.

David's soul was filled with spiritual desolation, barrenness, vagueness, and absence of happy thoughts when he fell into the spiritual *bore* pit. David was fettered with such great spiritual difficulties that he could not extricate himself from them. His soul was in such a state of destructive bondage that he felt as though he were confined in a loathsome dungeon. But when David cried to God in repentance, God, in His great graciousness, brought David's soul up and out of the spiritual *bore* pit, out of the dirt and mire of false measurement and reasoning. God set David's feet upon Christ, the solid Rock foundation, the humility support of all creation.

God established David's "goings" after He had restored his humility foundation. He also put a song in David's heart after He had restored David's humility foundation and had given him new illumination in his understanding.

God always gives security and song after one is retrieved from the spiritual *bore* pit into which he has been cast as a result of his wicked false measurement.

Because of his lack of understanding, David had committed adultery with Bathsheba, and God had cast him into the spiritual *bore* pit.

The wise man in Proverbs revealed the truth that man is without understanding when he commits adultery.

> But *whoso committeth adultery* with a woman *lacketh understanding*: he that doeth it destroyeth his own soul (Proverbs 6:32).

When man commits adultery with a woman, he lacks the understanding that for momentary gratification he gives up his life and his relationship with God, destroys his own soul, and incurs God's wrathful judgment in the *bore* pit. An adulterer is one who rejects the wisdom and understanding of the LORD's Name.

David's former experience in the *bore* pit constrained him to cry unto the LORD for help so he would not have to return there again.

> Hear me speedily, O LORD: my spirit faileth: hide not thy face
> from me, *lest I be like unto them that go down into the pit* [*bore*]
> (Psalm 143:7).

David knew by experience that if God hid His face in wrath from him that he would go down to the *bore* pit. In his wretchedness, David pled for the LORD not to withdraw His face from him.

When man's understanding is illuminated, he is able to discern God's favours and frowns. Therefore, he is able to repent speedily when his words or deeds have brought an angry frown to God's face.

C. Hezekiah Delivered from the *Bore* Pit

Isaiah was a famous prophet. He was the evangelist among the prophets in the Old Testament. The Messianic prophecies reach their highest perfection in the ministry of Isaiah. His prophetic ministry began under the reign of King Uzziah and continued during the succeeding reigns of Jotham, Ahaz, and Hezekiah.

Isaiah the prophet gave some more truth concerning the *bore* pit when he revealed King Hezekiah's experience with the LORD during Sennacherib's invasion of Israel. Hezekiah, an eminently righteous man, was the successor of the apostate Ahaz. He restored the Mosaic law to a place of honour, abolished idolatry, and repaired the temple of the LORD. He celebrated the Passover with festivities that had not been equaled for magnificence and solemnity since the days of Solomon and David (II Chronicles 29:3).

Hezekiah's godly zeal is seen clearly in the high esteem he held for Isaiah; he frequently consulted with the prophet.

Hezekiah fell sick with a serious illness three days before God miraculously destroyed Sennacherib's armies, while Sennacherib himself fled to Nineveh. After God healed Hezekiah and delivered him from the Assyrian hosts, he went up to the house of the LORD to offer up his prayer, praise, and thanksgiving for physical victory and for political victory.

Hezekiah promised God to go softly all his years in the bitterness of his soul. In other words, he promised always to retain a lasting impression of the affliction in his soul, and, thereby, he always would be grateful and thankful for God's delivering him from the *bore* pit. God in His great love forgave Hezekiah, put his sins behind His back, and healed him physically.

> Behold, for peace I had great bitterness: but *thou hast* in love to my soul *delivered it from the pit of corruption*: for thou hast cast all my sins behind thy back. For the grave cannot praise thee, death can not celebrate thee: they that go down into the pit [*bore*] cannot hope for thy truth (Isaiah 38:17,18).

Hezekiah revealed that the grave cannot praise the LORD, death cannot celebrate the LORD, and the *bore* pit cannot hope for the truth.

Those who go down eternally to the *bore* pit are no longer on the earth in a state of probation and choice where they willingly can lay hold of the truth and understanding of God's holy Name.

Hezekiah was so thankful that he could come to the temple of the LORD and use his understanding to praise and magnify the Name of the LORD.

Isaiah the prophet also instructed us about the way God is going to judge and punish the high ones, the proud ones, in days to come, just as He judged and punished the second world of created inhabitants on the restored earth—by gathering them together in the *bore* pit.

> And it shall come to pass in that day, that *the LORD shall punish the host of the high ones that are on high*, and the kings of the earth upon the earth. And *they shall be gathered together*, as prisoners are gathered *in the pit* [*bore*], and shall be shut up in the prison, and after many days shall they be visited (Isaiah 24:21,22).

God in His faithfulness will punish all the host of high ones who are so corrupted and puffed up in their understanding as to think that in all the height of their grandeur they are beyond the reach of the Most High God.

VI. The End of the Sin Against the Understanding That Is from and in the LORD's Name

The immutable, changeless God always has punished the haughty pride in man's understanding, and He always will until every creature in heaven, in earth, and under the earth is brought to bow before the LORD and His Christ! Then all people will use their understanding to glorify and magnify the Name of the LORD.

Zechariah the prophet revealed that in eternity-future the LORD God, once and for all, will destroy "Mother Wickedness," who has been the leader in false measurement.

> Then the angel that talked with me went forth, and said unto me, Lift up now thine eyes, and see what is this that goeth forth. And I said, What is it? And he said, This is an ephah that goeth forth. He said moreover, This is their resemblance through all the earth. And, behold, there was lifted up a talent of lead: and this is *a woman that sitteth in the midst of the ephah*. And he said, *This is wickedness*, And he cast it into the midst of the ephah; and he cast the weight of lead upon the mouth thereof. Then lifted I up mine eyes, and looked, and behold, there came out two women, and the wind was in their wings; for they had wings like the wings of a stork; and they lifted up the ephah between the earth and the heaven. Then said I to the angel that talked with me, Whither do these bear the ephah? And he said unto me, To build it an house in the land of Shinar: and it shall be established, and *set there upon her own base* (Zechariah 5:5-11).

The Prophet Zechariah saw a woman called "Wickedness" shut up in an ephah (an ancient Hebrew dry measure equal to about 37 quarts). The permanent home of Wickedness is to be Shinar, a poetical name for the confusion found in the *bore* pit. The female called "Wickedness," who taught the creation on the restored earth to sin by false measurement, will be placed in the very "ephah" or false measurement that she taught others to use. She will be sealed inside the false ephah with a weight of lead cast upon the top of it. "Wickedness" will then be carried to the pit of confusion and will be set upon her own base, a place specially prepared for her. She will be fastened to her base, never to corrupt the earth and its world of inhabitants again by tempting them to use false measurements, either in the spiritual or in the natural realms.

False measurement has been one of the most destructive forces from the beginning of time until this present time. Sinful man always has struggled with the problem of false measurement in his mental world, his social world, his religious world, and his financial world.

God has forbidden the use of false measurements in any form. Every sincere soul sometimes struggles against the temptation to use the false ephah in their understanding for injurious measurements of others and of themselves instead of trusting God to help them wisely use their understanding to measure out proper praise, worship, and reverence toward Him and to measure out proper merciful respect to others.

Mother Wickedness, until she is sealed in the false ephah once and for all, always will tempt us to make a "sinner" out of the other person and to make a "saint" out of ourselves. May our gracious and good LORD help us to become wise so we will repent of using our understanding foolishly and wickedly.

The first restored earth with its created world of mankind literally was cast down into the *bore* pit as a result of disobedience and wickedness. It is not known how many aeons the earth lay in this particular pit before God lifted it up again. However, when the history of the earth is traced as it is recorded in the Bible, one can certainly understand why the scientists have found that our earth is billions of years old.

The earth never again will be cast down to the natural *bore* pit as a result of the works of "Mother Wickedness." And one day mankind never again will fall into the spiritual *bore* pit of despondency and disparagement as a result of having "Mother Wickedness" influence them to disobey God.

Chapter Four

The Second Restoration of the Earth and Its Fall Into the Third Pit of Judgment, the "Teh-home" Pit

GOD did not leave the earth buried permanently in the *bore* pit. After a certain lapse of time, God again lifted up the earth and restored it the second time since its original creation. To live upon it, He created a whole new world of inhabitants.

The first reason for knowing that the earth was raised out of the *bore* pit and restored a second time is the fact that it later fell into a *third pit*, which fact is recorded in God's Word. God never permanently leaves His creation in rack and ruin.

The second reason for knowing that the earth was raised up from the *bore* pit is the surety of the changeless nature of the LORD's faithfulness to His creation. God does not and will not cease working with His creation until His master plan and purposive will are accomplished in them and for them.

> Having made known unto us the mystery of his will, according to his good pleasure which he hath purposed in himself: That in the dispensation of the fulness of times *he might gather together in one all things in Christ*, both which are in heaven, and which are on earth; even in him: (Ephesians 1:9,10).

God always has had "set seasons" to accomplish His holy mysterious will. He has seasons for those who have and who voluntarily will receive His salvation; and He has appointed seasons to refine the righteous. God also has appointed aeons to punish and purge rebellers and revolters so that He might bring them in subjection to Christ.

> *Thou hast put all things in subjection under his feet*. For in that he put all in subjection under him, *he left nothing that is not put under him*. But now we see not yet all things put under him (Hebrews 2:8).

Theoretically, God has put all things under the feet of Christ Jesus. However, we do not see now all things experientially under His feet because God has an appointed time, age, or season for this to occur.

To every thing there is a *season, and a time to every purpose* under the heaven: (Ecclesiastes 3:1).

The Hebrew word for *time*, here, is *ayth*, signifying a circle around a point, a circle of time, a circle of seasons; hence time is a circle around a point.

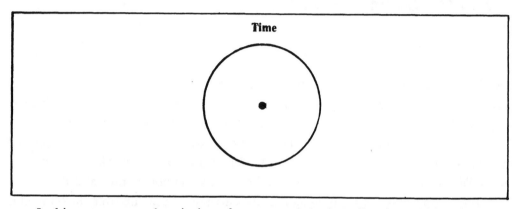

Is this not a proper description of our natural clocks? Likewise, within His master plan, God has many different sizes of "clocks" which tick off the appointed moments, the set seasons, the fixed years, and the established aeons of His master plan.

God has a law of circularity in the natural realm, and He has a law of circularity in the spiritual realm. After God's faithful clock of the aeons marks off sufficient time, the aeon or age of unity and harmony will arrive in which God will bring all things under subjection to His only begotten Son, Christ Jesus, the Messiah.

The third reason we know the earth was raised up from the *bore* pit and restored is the immutability of God's purposive will for the earth to be beautiful and to be inhabited.

For thus saith the LORD that created the heavens; God himself that formed the earth and made it; he hath established it, *he created it not in vain, he formed it to be inhabited*: I am the LORD; and there is none else (Isaiah 45:18).

God created the earth beautiful so that man could dwell upon it in peace and harmony, not in agitation, insecurity, and disharmony.

God does not hide Himself in gloom and darkness, but reveals Himself in love, light, justice, and righteousness.

God did not create the earth to be ugly and chaotic. He formed it into a most proper shape and size by His infinite divine wisdom. God established the earth in its proper place according to His purposive will. He did not create the earth in vain. He designed it and fitted it for the use of His world of creation, which included man's using it as an habitation. The supreme, Sovereign, self-existent LORD, the Creator, in His infinite, almighty power, did all these things.

God never allows one world of rebellious inhabitants to negate His master plan and purposive will. God's master plan ultimately will be set forth in all its perfection and beauty because He is an omniscient and omnipotent self-existent Being.

After the first restored earth had been raised up from the *bore* pit and restored a second time to a place of exaltation, a newly created world of inhabitants was placed upon it. Then Christ, the humility Word of God, once more assumed the responsibility of supporting and upholding this clean earth with its new world of clean inhabitants.

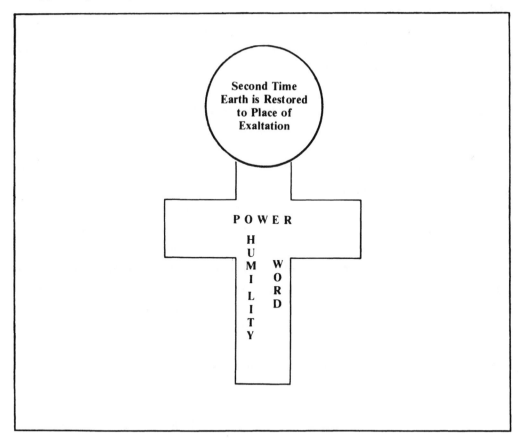

God did not have to *recreate* the earth each time it fell into a pit of judgment. He simply lifted it up, *restored* it to its original freshness and cleanness, and created a new world of inhabitants to live upon it. Once this was accomplished, the Word of God, the Christ, returned as the humility support and foundation of the new world.

One of God's appointed "times" was the time given to the second restored earth and its new world of created inhabitants in which they could choose to serve the LORD and worship Him. But they followed the first two worlds in choosing against their Creator.

In due season, the second restored earth fell into a pit of judgment, the bottomless pit, called the *teh-home* (pit) in Hebrew.

The original world of inhabitants sinned against the wisdom that is from and in the LORD's Name and was cast into the *shakh-ath* pit by God's just judgment and righteous punishment.

The second world of created inhabitants sinned against the understanding that is from and in the LORD's Name and was cast into the *bore* pit by God's just judgment and righteous punishment.

Then the third world of created inhabitants sinned against the knowledge that is from and in the LORD's Name and was cast into the *teh-home* pit by God's just judgment and righteous punishment.

I. Sin Against the Knowledge That Is from and in the LORD's Name Is Punished in the *Teh-home* Pit

True knowledge of the LORD's Name consists of the rule and order of His Name. The LORD, in His graciousness and kindness, revealed the knowledge, rule and order, of His Name to the third created world of inhabitants upon the second restored earth. He gave them clear perception of the rule and order of His holy Name.

The knowledge or rule of the LORD's immutable, changeless Name consists of the infinite, eternal, fixed principles of the holiness of it. Knowledge or rule from His holy Name always leads and moves in the straight paths of righteousness. With justice and righteousness, the knowledge or rule of the LORD's holy Name governs and guides His creation. The knowledge or rule of the LORD's holy Name always influences and restrains His creation with perfect love. The absolute authority of the LORD's justice and righteousness always prevails through the knowledge or rule of His holy Name.

The knowledge or order of His holy Name always designs, fixes, and arranges all things according to His master plan and according to the holiness and righteousness of

His Name. The knowledge or order of His holy Name is an eternal state of peace and serenity.

What a great privilege man has had and does have to be familiar and intimate with the knowledge, rule and order, of the immutable, changeless, eternal, holy Name of the LORD, the Most High God.

All knowledge is an extension of the knowledge, rule and order, of the LORD's high and holy Name. The origin of all knowledge, all rule and order, is the eternal treasure house of the LORD's righteous and holy Name. Lucifer's knowledge originated from God; however, Lucifer has corrupted his knowledge and now projects it to the human race in a corrupt form.

How unfortunate and shameful that many drink at distant streams of knowledge, rule and order, which have their origin in the fountainhead of the LORD's holy righteous Name; yet, they either do not come to the fountainhead, or they deny the existence of the fountainhead.

God's purposive will in every stream of knowledge is to lead the thirsty pilgrim to the fountainhead of the LORD's holy, serene, satisfying Name. The knowledge, rule and order, of the LORD's holy Name is the *end* of all learning.

The eternal pleasure of the knowledge, rule and order, of the LORD's holy Name far surpasses all other temporal, deceitful pleasures.

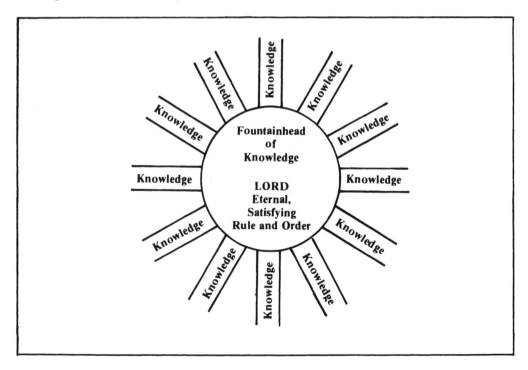

Balaam had a vision of the knowledge, rule and order, of the holy Name of the Most High God, but he never attained being joined personally with it in the fountainhead.

Job is an example of one who displayed a lack of knowledge of the LORD's Name. But unlike Balaam, who had a vision of the knowledge of the LORD's Name, yet who never was joined to it, Job only lacked knowledge at first. But after the LORD had chastened him, and after he had received the LORD's knowledge, Job repented. Job's lack of knowledge of the LORD's Name was evident in his complaining against God's method and manner of dealing with him. Job's fault was that he did not yet have the knowledge, rule and order, of the LORD's holy Name in the fountainhead.

> Job had spoken *without knowledge*, and his words were without wisdom (Job 34:35).

> Therefore doth Job open his mouth in vain; he multiplieth words *without knowledge* (Job 35:16).

> Then the LORD answered Job out of the whirlwind, and said, Who is this that darkeneth counsel by *words without knowledge* (Job 38:1,2).

However, Job finally humbled himself and confessed his sins of ignorance against the knowledge, rule and order, of the LORD's holy Name. Because Job repented, God lifted him up out of his affliction and blessed him with a double portion of blessing from the fountainhead.

King David, on the other hand, is an example of one who had an intimate experience in the knowledge, rule and order, of the holy Name of the LORD.

> Thou hast beset me behind and before, and laid thine hand upon me. Such *knowledge is too wonderful for me*; it is high, I cannot attain unto it (Psalm 139:5,6).

In His righteous, holy knowledge, the LORD had hemmed David in like a besieged city so that he could not escape. God had grasped David with His hand so he could not get away and had drawn him near to the fountainhead of knowledge, rule and order, of His holy Name. David declared that such knowledge was too wonderful, too high, and too unattainable for him.

How can one gain the high, wonderful knowledge of the LORD's Name? God reveals in the Book of Proverbs that the knowledge of His Name is obtained in the same manner as the understanding of His Name—by applying one's heart to search for it.

> Bow down thine ear, and hear the words of the wise, and *apply*
> *thine heart unto my knowledge* (Proverbs 22:17).

When one applies his heart to the knowledge, rule and order, of the LORD's holy Name, the consequence is pleasant, peaceful, and satisfying.

The firstfruits of an experience with the knowledge, rule and order, of the LORD's holy Name are manifested in the form of the fear or respect and reverence for the LORD.

> *The fear of the LORD is the beginning of knowledge*: but fools
> despise wisdom and instruction (Proverbs 1:7).

Since the LORD God is the Creator of the universes, it is impossible for man to know and accept his place in the design and purpose of God's master plan without humbly applying his heart to the knowledge, rule and order, of the LORD's holy Name. What peaceful rest and what joyful pleasantness fill the heart of one who fears, respects, and reverences the knowledge, rule and order, of the LORD's holy Name.

The lips of those who are able to utter the knowledge, rule and order, of the LORD's holy Name are a precious jewel.

> There is gold, and a multitude of rubies: but *the lips of knowledge*
> *are a precious jewel* (Proverbs 20:15).

Many people may have gold and rubies in their treasure chests, but their hearts may be empty and poverty-stricken as far as having the riches of the knowledge, rule and order, of the LORD's holy Name.

Although God's Word has much more to say about the knowledge, rule and order, of the immutable, changeless Name of the LORD, these few truths are sufficient witnesses to the eternal holiness of His Name.

When the third world of inhabitants upon the restored earth sinned against the knowledge, rule and order, of the LORD's holy Name, God cast them down to the *teh-home* pit by His just judgment and righteous punishment.

The English word *deep* that is used in Genesis 1:2 is *teh-home* in Hebrew, which is the same Hebrew word that is used in the Hebrew New Testament to describe the *bottomless pit.*

By examining the Hebrew word *teh-home*, the deep, the bottomless pit, one can understand better why God was angry with the third world of creation. Since God is immutable and unchangeable, one can ascertain, by noticing the punishment that this particular creation reaped, what kind of sinful seeds they had sown.

The Hebrew word *teh-home* is derived from the root word *hoom*, meaning to set in commotion, to disturb, drive, destroy utterly, break, consume, crush, discomfit, trouble, vex, to make a noise, to rattle, to impel, urge forward, to be in a stir, a preliminary state of glowing, ebullition, effervescence, surging, billowing, turmoil.

The earth, as it appears in Genesis 1:2, lay in confusion, in a seething, boiling, bottomless pit. Gross darkness covered this seething, noisy turmoil of the deep, the *teh-home* or bottomless pit. The light from the solar system was not great enough to penetrate the darkness that covered the earth in the deep, nor to awaken the slumbering seeds in the fallen earth while it lay in the *teh-home* or bottomless pit.

The *teh-home* pit is not bottomless to God, but it appears to be bottomless to the earth and to the creatures cast inside of it since they cannot find the top, the bottom, or the sides of it. The *teh-home* is the pit that lies *under* the underworld. It is the deepest of the pits.

In addition to Moses' account in the Book of Genesis, Jeremiah the prophet also gave a graphic description of this particular fall of the earth into the *teh-home* pit.

> I beheld the earth, and, lo, *it was without form* [*to-hoo*]*, and void* [*bo-hoo*]; and the heavens, and they had no light. I beheld the mountains, and, lo, they trembled, and all the hills moved lightly. I beheld, and, lo, *there was no man*, and all *the birds of the heavens were fled*. I beheld, and, lo, the fruitful place was a wilderness, and all the cities thereof were broken down at the presence of the LORD, and by his fierce anger. For thus hath the LORD said, The whole land shall be desolate; yet will I not make a full end (Jeremiah 4:23-27).

The Prophet Jeremiah looked through his prophetic "eye" into eternity past, beholding what had happened to the second restored earth as a result of its fall into the *teh-home* pit as described in Genesis. He saw the second restored earth become waste and void and fall into the *deep*, the *teh-home*, bottomless *pit*, because of its sin against the knowledge, rule and order, of God's Name.

When the earth fell into the *teh-home* pit, the bottomless pit, it was covered with darkness and appeared empty, void, and without form. Despite the earth's massive weight, it moved to and fro as though it were a small, light ball when God's just judgment and righteous punishment fell upon it. The created world of inhabitants upon the earth also was devastated and destroyed. All the cities, the fruitful fields, and all the living creation were devastated and destroyed because of the fierce anger of the LORD.

The earth became *without form* (in the Hebrew, the term is *to-hoo*) and *void* or empty (or in the Hebrew, *bo-hoo*). When the earth sank into the bottomless pit, it became without form, meaning it lost its newly created form of grass, plants, herbs, and trees. It lost its newly created form of mountains and hills since they were shaken and moved out of their former places. The earth became void and empty of its world of inhabitants when it sank into the bottomless pit.

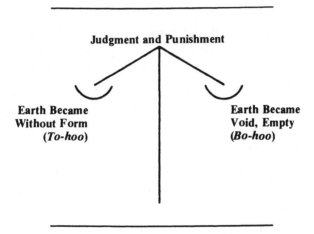

The earth became without form (*to-hoo*). The Hebrew word *to-hoo* means to lie waste, a desolation of surface, desert, worthless thing, vain thing, confusion, empty place, nothing, thing of nought, and wilderness. *To-hoo* comes from an old Biblical Hebrew root word *taw-aw*, meaning to be laid waste or desolate, to be strewn or prostrated, to lie desolate. In Rabbinic Hebrew, the root word *taw-aw* has the meaning of the kind of astonishment that one has when trying to recognize something which is still unknown. *Taw-aw* means a state of regretting, being sorry for something; it also means an unclear, muddled impression of something, or a chaotic condition.

Thus when the earth lost its form, it became an astonished desert and wilderness, as it were. It was sorrowful and regretful of its condition, which was totally chaotic. The Prophet Jeremiah confirmed the condition of the earth as it lay in the bottomless pit when he said it was *without form* (*to-hoo*).

The Prophet Isaiah proclaimed clearly that God *did not create* the earth in the *to-hoo* condition, without form.

> For thus saith the LORD that created the heavens; *God himself that formed the earth and made it*; he hath established it, *he created it not in vain, he formed it to be inhabited*: I am the LORD; and there is none else (Isaiah 45:18).

God created the earth not in vain (*to-hoo*), not without form. In the beginning, God created the earth *with form* and with a world of life and inhabitants upon it.

Not only did the earth become without form, it also became void (*bo-hoo*), empty, waste. The Hebrew word for *void* is *bo-hoo*, meaning to be empty, to be laid waste. The word *bo-hoo* or void in old Biblical Hebrew means an expression of pain, a chaotic condition of something as being intolerable, full of contradiction and struggle. God, in His perfection, created the earth *with form*, beautiful, and to be inhabited. However, when the earth fell out of the perfect will of God into the permissive will of God, it suffered the intolerable pain of contradiction and struggle.

When the earth lay in the bottomless pit as a confused, entangled mess, it felt the pain of the contradiction it had brought about by being disobedient to the purpose God had for it in His perfect will, and it experienced a painful and continual struggle to free itself from the permissive will of God.

Jeremiah also confirmed the void (*bo-hoo*) condition of the earth. The words *without form* (*to-hoo*) and *void* (*bo-hoo*) describe the condition of the earth when it fell into the *teh-home* pit from God's perfect will and His perfect purpose for it. The word *deep* (*teh-home*) describes the place or pit of judgment into which God cast the second restored earth and held it as a prisoner.

II. The LORD Uses the Natural and the Spiritual *Teh-home* Pit as Punishment for the Guilty on This Present Earth: the World, Nations, Cities, and Individuals

Some people become very angry at the thought that a supreme God exists Who judges and punishes. However, a few people would like to live in a society without any existing forms of judgment or laws for punishing guilty offenders. No parent would like to assume the responsibility of parenthood and not have jurisdiction to make rules and regulations, or not have any authority to establish order, or not have any power to enforce rule and order upon their children. If, out of their love, finite creatures have a right to establish law and order for the benefit of their offspring, God our eternal Creator has, out of His love, a right to establish law and order for His creation's benefit.

120

God has all righteous right to make laws and to give laws for His creation to abide by, and He has all moral right to judge and punish all those who are disobedient to His law and order.

A. The Guilty Inhabitants of the World Reaped the Natural Judgmental Waters from the *Teh-home* Pit in Noah's Day

God opened the fountains of the *teh-home* pit when He judged the earth and its world of inhabitants with an overflowing flood in Noah's day.

> In the six hundredth year of Noah's life, in the second month, the seventeenth day of the month, the same day were *all the fountains of the great deep* [*teh-home*] *broken up*, and the windows of heaven were opened (Genesis 7:11).

> And God remembered Noah, and every living thing, and all the cattle that was with him in the ark: and God made a wind to pass over the earth, and the waters asswaged; *The fountains also of the deep* and the windows of heaven *were stopped*, and the rain from heaven was restrained; (Genesis 8:1,2).

God opened up the fountains of the deep (*teh-home*) from below and swept the earth with a mammoth and monstrous tidal wave that covered the earth. He simultaneously opened up the windows of heaven with a torrential downpour of rain from above in order to judge the earth and its world of inhabitants.

God's judgment and punishment upon the earth and its world of inhabitants in Noah's day came from the waters below (the *teh-home*) and from the waters above. After God had cleansed and sanctified the earth from those who had sinned against the knowledge, rule and order, of His holy Name, He shut the windows of heaven and sealed the fountains of the *teh-home*.

B. Inhabitants of Assyria Reaped the *Teh-home* Pit

When the great nation of Assyria fell under God's judgment, He caused the deep (*teh-home*) to mourn because God had used the blessing from the *teh-home* to help exalt Assyria.

The waters made him great, *the deep set him up on high with her rivers running round about his plants*, and sent out her little rivers unto all the trees of the field (Ezekiel 31:4).

The *teh-home* depths had supported the rivers, lakes, fountains, and wells of the country of Assyria, turning her land into a fruitful and flourishing place. The Assyrian kingdom grew and flourished as a result of the *teh-home* waters that were raised up from under its frozen face or the circle of the Name of the LORD, the knowledge of true rule and order. But later Assyria abused the knowledge of the Name of the LORD and misused the deep water from beneath in order to lift himself on high and to lead his people away from the LORD into abominable idolatry. Therefore, Assyria was punished with the spiritual waters of judgment from the *teh-home*.

Thus saith the Lord GOD; In the day when he went down to the grave I caused a mourning: *I covered the deep* [*teh-home*] *for him, and I restrained the floods thereof, and the great waters were stayed*: and I caused Lebanon to mourn for him, and all the trees of the field fainted for him (Ezekiel 31:15).

When God commanded the deep, the natural *teh-home*, to withdraw its support, then the field, fruits, and trees in the land of Assyria languished and mourned.

The people who had preceded Assyria to the *teh-home* pit mourned for him because they saw how Assyria, too, had abused the knowledge, rule and order, of the LORD's holy Name. Assyria had removed himself from under God's supreme Sovereignty and had created his own gods, taking the blessings of the LORD's Name and pouring them out on false gods in idolatrous worship. Therefore, Assyria went to the spiritual *teh-home* pit of judgment.

God's just judgment and righteous punishment of Assyria should be an instructive example to all that He judges righteously and faithfully punishes the full measure of wickedness.

C. Inhabitants of Egypt Reaped the *Teh-home* Pit

God punished Egypt with the *teh-home* pit, both naturally and spiritually.

The depths have covered them: they sank into the bottom as a stone (Exodus 15:5).

Pharaoh and the Egyptians had sown hardness against the knowledge, rule and order, of the LORD's holy Name, so they reaped hardness. Their bodies sank to the bottom of the Red Sea while their souls sank into the spiritual depths of God's *teh-home* pit, a witness to their hardness.

God controlled the *teh-home* that supported the Red Sea, and He controlled the Red Sea in order to make a way of escape for His people and in order to judge the Egyptians for their sin against the knowledge, rule and order, of the LORD's holy Name.

> And with the blast of thy nostrils the waters were gathered together, the floods stood upright as an heap, *and the depths were congealed in the heart of the sea* (Exodus 15:8).

The blast from the LORD's nostrils gathered the waters of the Red Sea together, and they towered upwards into icy frozen walls, while the mouth of the *teh-home* was solidified in ice in the heart of the sea. Thus Israel safely crossed the sea.

The rule and order of the LORD's mighty, holy Name has complete, unfettered control of all matter and all laws of nature. God uses all matter to redeem, to save, to judge, and to punish according to His purposive will. Therefore the fact that God heaped up the tiny, small drops of water into strong icy walls, creating a way of salvation and a path of freedom for His people was a simple thing for Him to do.

> They go up by the mountains; they go down by the valleys unto the place which thou hast founded for them. *Thou hast set a bound that they may not pass over*; that they turn not again to cover the earth. *He sendeth the springs into the valleys*, which run among the hills. They give drink to every beast of the field: the wild asses quench their thirst (Psalm 104:8-11).

The LORD saved His people for the sake of the knowledge, rule and order, of His holy Name so that His Name might be known in the earth.

The LORD, in His Sovereign, complete, unfettered control, conducted His people through the Red Sea, as a shepherd would lead his flocks through the fields.

At the LORD's Sovereign command, the same tiny, small drops of water that had been solidified into a wall were separated, and as they returned to water, they completely covered the adversaries of God's people. The LORD, in His complete, unfettered control, gathered the tiny drops of water together to save His people; then He separated the drops in order to destroy the enemies who were guilty of sin against the knowledge of His Name.

God is the Owner and Master of all His creation, and He will not cease working with His creation in this world and in the world to come until they all learn to bow to the rule and order of His holy Name.

D. The City of Tyre Reaped the Natural *Teh-home* Pit

God warned the city of Tyre, through the Prophet Ezekiel, that He was going to bring the judgmental waters of the great deep (*teh-home*) upon her.

> For thus saith the Lord GOD; When I shall make thee a desolate
> city, like the cities that are not inhabited; *when I shall bring up the*
> *deep* [*teh-home*] *upon thee,* and great waters shall cover thee;
> (Ezekiel 26:19).

God warned the city of Tyre that He would raise up the waters of the *teh-home* upon her so she would be covered abundantly by the flood waters, which would wash away her layers of earth, leaving her a dry, barren, hard, and uninhabitable rock.

When God, by His knowledge, commands the judgmental waters of the deep (*teh-home*) to be loosed, no creature can stay them.

E. Jonah Reaped the *Teh-home* Pit

Jonah is also a classical example of one who sinned against the knowledge, rule and order, of the holy Name of the LORD. The rule and order of the LORD's holy Name includes His love for all mankind, both Jew and Gentile.

The LORD commanded Jonah, the Jewish prophet, to rise and go to the Gentile city of Nineveh in the country of Assyria and preach a message of repentance unto them. The LORD *knew* that if the Assyrians were warned, they would repent; therefore, He could forgive them. Jonah *knew* this also, but he begrudged the LORD's love, care, and forgiveness toward the Gentiles. Regardless of how Jonah felt, all the LORD's creatures are worthy of pardon and forgiveness if they repent. Jonah, however, went in a diametrically different direction from the one the LORD had commanded. Hence, his body ended up in the whale's belly (Matthew 12:40), and his soul ended up in the spiritual *teh-home* pit under the just judgment and righteous punishment of the LORD because Jonah had deliberately sinned against the knowledge, rule and order, of the LORD's holy Name.

> And said, I cried by reason of mine affliction unto the LORD, and
> he heard me; out of the belly of hell cried I, and thou heardest my

voice. *For thou hadst cast me into the deep*, in the midst of the seas; and the floods compassed me about: all thy billows and thy waves passed over me. Then I said, I am cast out of thy sight; yet I will look again toward thy holy temple. The waters compassed me about, even to the soul: *the depth* [*teh-home*] *closed me round about*, the weeds were wrapped about my head (Jonah 2:2-5).

The sea weeds wrapped around Jonah's body in the great fish, while the spiritual judgmental waters of the *teh-home* encompassed his soul. Jonah repented over his rebellion and disobedience to the LORD and was forgiven. So the LORD raised Jonah's body out of the great fish and his soul out of the *teh-home*.

After Jonah had experienced fresh repentance while he was in the *teh-home* pit, he went to Nineveh and preached a powerful message of repentance. Consequently, the whole city of Nineveh repented and turned to the LORD. However, Jonah continued begrudging the LORD's love, mercy, and forgiveness toward the Gentile city of Nineveh.

Jonah is an instructive example of what *not* to do. Although he ultimately obeyed the LORD and preached the message of repentance as the LORD had commanded him, he continued to rebel against the knowledge, rule and order, of the LORD's holy Name by begrudging the love and forgiveness that the LORD shared with the Gentiles.

F. David Reaped the Spiritual *Teh-home* Pit

King David also experienced the suffering, woes, and afflictions from God's spiritual *teh-home* pit. However, David's unswerving faith in God made him to know that, through God's almighty power, he would be quickened and delivered from the *teh-home* pit of destruction.

> Thou, which hast shewed me great and sore troubles, shalt quicken me again, and *shalt bring me up again from the depths of the earth* (Psalm 71:20).

God's billows and waves of judgmental waters that dashed and crashed upon David's soul washed away superfluous desires that had led him astray from the knowledge, rule and order, of the LORD's holy Name. David's steadfast resistance in the midst of the billows and waves had left the rock of his soul polished and smooth and his heart tender, sweet, and mellow. Therefore, David became a sweet singer in Israel unto the knowledge, rule and order, of the holy Name of the LORD.

G. The Antichrist Will Arise from the Spiritual *Teh-home* Pit

God has revealed much about the bottomless pit (*teh-home*) through the Apostle John in the Book of Revelation. John looked through the "eye of faith" into the prophetic future and saw the Antichrist arising out of the spiritual *teh-home* pit as a resurrected being.

> *The beast* that thou sawest was, and is not; and *shall ascend out of the bottomless pit* [*teh-home*], and go into perdition: and they that dwell on the earth shall wonder, whose names were not written in the book of life from the foundation of the world, when they behold the beast that was, and is not, and yet is (Revelation 17:8).

> And when they shall have finished their testimony, *the beast that ascendeth out of the bottomless pit* [*teh-home*] shall make war against them, and shall overcome them, and kill them (Revelation 11:7).

The whole world will accept the "Wonder Man," the Antichrist, who will soon make his appearance on the world scene when he rises out of the bottomless pit, the spiritual *teh-home*.

The throne of the Antichrist will be a throne of blasphemy, idolatry, and persecution. Because the inhabitants of the world will accept this tyrannical, cruel Beast from the *teh-home* pit, unanimously and zealously devoting themselves to this usurper and imposter, the righteous LORD will judge and punish the world of inhabitants by loosing upon them special creatures out of the *teh-home* pit.

> And the fifth angel sounded, and I saw a star fall from heaven unto the earth: and to him was given the key of the bottomless pit. *And he opened the bottomless pit* [*teh-home*]; and there arose a smoke out of the pit, as the smoke of a great furnace; and the sun and the air were darkened by reason of the smoke of the pit. And there came out of the smoke locusts upon the earth: and unto them was given power, as the scorpions of the earth have power. And it was commmanded them that they should not hurt the grass of the earth, neither any green thing, neither any tree; but only those men which have not the seal of God in their foreheads (Revelation 9:1-4).

A "star angel" from heaven will be sent with a key to open the spiritual *teh-home* pit, loosing the hordes of peculiar locusts that will devour and destroy men who will not have the seal of God in their foreheads. Because the world will *sow* its wicked choice for a governor and guide from the *teh-home* pit (the Antichrist, the Beast), the world will *reap* God's righteous punishment and just judgment through the beastly locusts from the *teh-home* pit.

H. Lucifer Will Reap the *Teh-home* Pit

At the end of the tribulation period, fallen Lucifer, who is known by the names Satan, Devil, Serpent, and Dragon, will be chained in the spiritual *teh-home* pit for a thousand years.

> And I saw an angel come down from heaven, having the key of the bottomless pit and a great chain in his hand. And he laid hold on the dragon, that old serpent, which is the Devil, and Satan, and bound him a thousand years, *And cast him into the bottomless pit* [*teh-home*], and shut him up, and set a seal upon him, that he should deceive the nations no more, till the thousand years should be fulfilled: and after that he must be loosed a little season (Revelation 20:1-3).

Lucifer's Dragon strength, Serpent subtlety, Devil's roar, and Satanic opposition will not be sufficient to rescue him from the mighty angel's great chain. Fallen Lucifer, who has sown the depths of darkness and destruction in the hearts of men, will reap God's just judgment and righteous punishment for a thousand years in the *teh-home* pit. He will be shut up in the *teh-home* with a seal set upon him. When the infinite God shuts by His omnipotent power and seals with His Sovereign Authority, no finite creature can break the seal and rescue himself.

God also revealed to the Apostle John that the Dragon and Serpent nature of fallen Lucifer will remain locked in the spiritual *teh-home* pit after Lucifer has been released in his Satan and Devil natures at the end of the thousand years.

> And when the thousand years are expired, *Satan shall be loosed out of his prison*, And shall go out to deceive the nations which are in the four quarters of the earth, Gog and Magog, to gather them together to battle: the number of whom is as the sand of the sea. And they went up on the breadth of the earth, and compassed the camp of the saints about, and the beloved city: and fire came down from God out of heaven, and devoured them. And the devil that deceived them was cast into the lake of fire and brimstone, where

the beast and the false prophet are, and shall be tormented day and night for ever and ever (Revelation 20:7-10).

When God removes the restraints on fallen Lucifer, he soon will begin his work as Satan, standing against the people of God. As the Devil, Lucifer will deceive the people of God.

Satan "stands against" to stir up disturbance and war. The Devil deceives to make people believe that he has a good cause in which they should engage, when in reality his cause is a wicked one.

Lucifer (Satan and Devil) will *sow* his fires of wrath, anger, and warfare in the minds of people. As a consequence, he will *reap* God's righteous fire from *above* and His just fire from *below* in the lake of fire.

The *teh-home* pit is the largest and greatest of the pits. It is the place of judgment and punishment for those who sin against the knowledge, rule and order, of the LORD's holy Name.

III. The LORD's Natural *Teh-home* Blesses the Following: the World, Nations, and Individuals

From the beginning of the original creation, the fountains of the deep (*teh-home*) have existed to bless the earth by providing the necessary moisture to make the land productive.

God's Word tells of the origin of the depths.

> When there were no depths, I was brought forth: when there were no fountains abounding with water. Before the mountains were settled, before the hills was I brought forth: While as yet he had not made the earth, nor the fields, nor the highest part of the dust of the world. When he prepared the heavens, I was there: *when he set a compass upon the face of the depth*: When he established the clouds above: *when he strengthened the fountains of the deep* [*teh-home*]: (Proverbs 8:24-28).

These Scriptures tell that before the depths (*teh-home*) were brought forth, God brought forth His Wisdom, His Word, His Son. The Son, Wisdom, the Word, was with God when He established the heavens, and when He set His compass, the circle of the knowledge of His Name, upon the face of the deep (*teh-home*). Wisdom, the Word, was there with God before any creation took place. God set His governing force to strengthen the fountains of the deep (*teh-home*) by firmly fixing Wisdom, the Son, as the support of the great *teh-home*. God placed the *teh-home* beneath the earth and securely established it in its place *under* the underworld.

A. The Earth and Its World of Inhabitants Receive Blessings from the LORD's *Teh-home*

The blessings of the natural deep (teh-home) is God's subterranean reservoir of waters from which He moistens the earth and maintains its water level, causing the land to remain fertile and fruitful.

God also blesses the earth by using the waters of the deep as great flood waters to cleanse and sanctify the earth from its filth and corruption, as He did in Noah's day.

When God desires to water the earth by a special cloudburst, He sends a whirlwind or a water spout, and the waterspout calls to the *teh-home*, and the *teh-home* (deep) calls to the particular portion of *teh-home* waters that are reserved by God for His special purpose. This special portion of the *teh-home* waters are lifted up into the whirlwind cloud and are carried to a particular place and then released upon the earth according to God's purposive will. God miraculously has provided the waters of the deep, the *teh-home*, to moisten the earth and to keep its water level at the proper height, maintaining the land's productivity.

Scientists tell us that one of the most amazing facts about the earth's hydrosphere is that practically all of the earth's water was produced very early in its history. The molecules of water washing up on the beaches of the world today are the same molecules that formed the oceans over four billion years ago.*

B. Israel Received Blessing from the LORD's Natural *Teh-home*

God led Israel through a desert wilderness in which there was no water; yet, He miraculously gave Israel water from *above*, out of the Rock which followed them. After God had brought Israel into Canaan's land, He gave them the blessings of water from *below*, from the *teh-home*, the deep.

> For the LORD thy God bringeth thee into a good land, a land of
> brooks of water, of *fountains and depths* [*teh-home*] *that spring*
> *out of valleys and hills*; (Deuteronomy 8:7).

*Trefil, James S., *Space Time Infinity* (Smithsonian Institution, Washington, D.C., 1985).

The blessings of the *teh-home* produced great masses of water in the form of springs, wells, fountains, rivers, and lakes which made the fields rich and productive in fruits and grains.

C. Joseph Received Blessings from the LORD's Natural *Teh-home*

Jacob prophesied to his son Joseph about the blessings that the LORD had reserved in the deep (*teh-home*) for him.

> But his bow abode in strength, and the arms of his hands were made strong by the hands of the mighty God of Jacob; (from thence is the shepherd, the stone of Israel:) Even by the God of thy father, who shall help thee; and by the Almighty, who shall bless thee with blessings of heaven above, *blessings of the deep* [*teh-home*] *that lieth under*, blessings of the breasts, and of the womb: (Genesis 49:24,25).

Joseph's brothers envied him, hated him, and sold him for a slave. But, because of Joseph's God-given knowledge of the rule and order of the LORD's Name, Joseph did not seek revenge on his brothers. Joseph's bow abode in strength upon his shoulder. He never took it down to shoot malicious and noxious arrows of retaliation at his brothers. He drank of the waters of truth from on high, which established that the righteous, holy LORD was his Owner, Master, Governor, and Guide. He knew that whatever his brothers had done would only help him obtain the LORD's purposive will and master plan for his life. Thus, his father prophesied that Joseph would be rewarded with the blessings of the deep (*teh-home*) in his territory in Canaan's land.

Moses also prophesied about the blessings from the deep (*teh-home*) that would encircle Joseph's territory in Canaan's land.

> And of Joseph he said, *Blessed of the LORD be his land*, for the precious things of heaven, for the dew, and *for the deep that coucheth beneath*, (Deuteronomy 33:13).

Joseph had sown faithfulness to the waters of God's moral *Torah* from above, by drinking of its life-giving water and by guarding and obeying it, so he reaped a rich reward of natural waters of the *teh-home* that generated special rivers, lakes, fountains, and wells in his territory, making his fields productive and fruitful.

D. David Received Blessing from the LORD's *Teh-home*

David not only had the knowledge, rule and order, of the LORD's holy Name concerning the natural *teh-home*, but he had the knowledge, rule and order, of the LORD's holy Name in the spiritual *teh-home*. God's spiritual waves and billows of afflictions, testings, and trials from His spiritual *teh-home* had dashed and crashed upon the rock of David's soul; however, David's knowledge of God's law and order assured him that God's all-seeing eye was governing and guiding with steadfast faithfulness. He knew that the rolling waves of suffering would carry away only the undesirable refuse that God had appointed to their power.

How precious and powerful is the knowledge, rule and order, of the mighty Name of the LORD. David was mightily blessed by the knowledge he had of God's law and order.

IV. The Knowledge, Rule and Order, of the LORD's Holy Name Controls the *Teh-home* Both Naturally and Spiritually

The Sovereign LORD has complete, unfettered control of all matter, all creation.

> *Whatsoever the LORD pleased, that did he* in heaven, and in earth, in the seas, and all deep places (Psalm 135:6).

The celestial matter and forces are not free agents. They obey the knowledge, rule and order, of the LORD's holy Name according to His purposive will.

Neither are the terrestrial matter and forces, including the *teh-home*, free agents. They, too, are under omnipotent control of the LORD God.

The *deep* (*teh-home*) lifts up his hands, his mighty waves, in reverence and surrender to his Owner and Master, the LORD God, and His purposive will. The *teh-home* is described thus by the Prophet Habakkuk:

> The mountains saw thee, and they trembled: the overflowing of the water passed by: the *deep* [*teh-home*] *uttered his voice, and lifted up his hands on high* (Habakkuk 3:10).

When the mountains saw their Creator, they trembled and were seized with pangs of travail that brought forth a new shape and form, as a woman in childbirth brings forth a new shape and form.

The circle of knowledge, rule and order, of the LORD's holy Name upon the face of the deep causes the *teh-home* waters to obey, with joy and gladness, the voice of their Owner, Master, and Creator.

God's desire is to instruct and teach each person how to be encircled with the knowledge, rule and order, of His holy Name, so that all may lift up holy hands in obedient surrender to Him as the supreme Governor and Guide. What joy and gladness is experienced in the human heart when the deepest waters of the human will lift up their hands, as it were, in obedient surrender to the LORD's master plan and purposive will.

In order to control the waters that would deluge the lands with a great flood, God freezes the face of the deep (*teh-home*).

> The waters are hid as with a stone, and the *face of the deep* [*teh-home*] *is frozen* (Job 38:30).

God sent His cold breath and solidified every drop of water on the face of the deep (*teh-home*), hardening his face like stone. God's creation is ruled and regulated according to the order of His divine will.

The waters of the sea are controlled by God, and He controls the waters of the *teh-home*. God's visible "law of nature" is nothing but an extension of the rule and order of the knowledge of His holy Name, which proceeds in accordance with His holy will.

> He gathereth the waters of the sea together as an heap: *he layeth up the depth* [*teh-home*] *in storehouses* (Psalm 33:7).

The almighty Sovereignty of God gathered the waters of the Red Sea together as an heap, as icy walls, and His almighty Sovereignty separated the waters of the *teh-home* into storehouses. The supreme Sovereignty of God gathers the waters or separates the waters according to His purposive will.

If God were not to place the deep waters in storehouses or vaults, they would inundate the dry land. All nature is governed by the knowledge, rule and order, of God's holy Name. The mighty waves and tides of the seas roar and thunder furiously upon the shores of the dry land, but they have to return and subside because their boundaries are fixed by the supreme, Sovereign God.

God has great storehouses or reservoirs in which He stores the sweet water pools and keeps the salt water pent up. How almighty is our God!

The omnipotent, almighty God not only controls the billowy deep of the natural *teh-home*, He also controls the spiritual *teh-home*.

> *Deep* [*teh-home*] calleth unto deep at the noise of thy waterspouts:
> all thy waves and thy billows are gone over me (Psalm 42:7).

David said the natural deep (*teh-home*) appears like an uncontrollable, overpowering mass of water. But, through the knowledge, rule and order, of the holy Name of the LORD, David knew that the *teh-home*, which feeds the oceans and seas, moves according to God's directive will with clock-like regularity, not uncontrollably. The infinite divine law of rule and order of God governs and guides the mighty mass of waves easier than man can govern and guide small quantities of water through channels and lakes.

David said in the Psalm that the deep calls to the deep; in other words, the wave that rises calls for another one to follow. The rushing, powerful waves dash and crash upon the rocks in a vain effort to break them, but the waves are defeated and broken by the powerful resistance of the rock. The waves are broken by the very objects they mean to destroy. So, through the rocks' resistance to the impact of the waves, they are left smooth and polished.

The knowledge, rule and order, of the LORD's holy Name controlled the *teh-home* from the beginning of its creation.

The discourse that the LORD had with Job sheds more light on the *teh-home* and its obedience to God's controlling force.

When the LORD desired to humble Job concerning his sinful complaining against the knowledge, the rule and order, of His holy Name, He asked him if he ever had walked in the recesses of the deep (*teh-home*). Had Job walked in the *teh-home*, he would have seen, upon the face of the *teh-home*, the circle of knowledge, rule and order, of the LORD's holy Name. What a contrast between the face of the deep (*teh-home*), with its knowledge of the LORD's holy Name, and Job's sinful complaining face, which did not have the knowledge, rule and order, of the LORD's holy Name on it.

> Hast thou entered into the springs of the sea? or *hast thou walked*
> *in the search of the depth* [*teh-home*]? (Job 38:16).

Job never had walked in the illimitable waters of the abyss, the deep (*teh-home*), which is governed by the rule and order of the LORD's holy Name and from which God replenishes the waters of the seas and the waters of the earth. Job was very unwise in his ignorance to complain against the knowledge, rule and order, of the LORD's holy Name since he did not possess the knowledge of the rule and order of the LORD's

Name. Therefore, he knew very little about God's master plan, for himself or for the other creation.

God's judgments are like the vast, deep (*teh-home*) waters; there is no escape from them when God looses them. Man cannot control God's judgments that descend from above nor His judgments that rise up from below.

> Thy righteousness is like the great mountains; *thy judgments are a great deep* [*teh-home*]: O LORD, thou preservest man and beast (Psalm 36:6).

This verse teaches that without the rule and order of the LORD's Name there would be neither spiritual existence nor natural existence. The earth consists of mountains, plains, and valleys which are surrounded by oceans and seas which, in turn, are supported by the *teh-home*. It is only through their reciprocal actions and interdependence that the existence of life is maintained on the earth. The *teh-home* supports the ocean and seas which give birth to the clouds in the sky, which in turn moisten the earth with their liquid life, without which the earth would shrivel to a burning desert, and all life would be extinguished.

Likewise, in the spiritual, without the mutual interaction of the righteousness and judgments of the LORD's Name, man's spiritual education and moral development would cease to flourish. Without God's cleansing judgmental waters from His spiritual *teh-home*, the mental and moral faculties of man would degenerate beyond recovery. God's judgmental waters of suffering penetrate the ground of the heart and the soil of the mind, plowing up the fallow ground so the heart and mind can receive new seeds of righteous truth. Thus, man's mind and heart can become a productive and fruitful garden.

God controls His righteousness which is immovable and conspicuous like the great mountains. He controls His judgments which are as deep as the great *teh-home*. Man does not control the knowledge, the rule and order, of God's holy Name; therefore, he cannot walk in either God's natural *teh-home* or His spiritual *teh-home*. Man cannot measure God's great depths with his own plumb line just because he may desire or pretend to do so.

God has a great storehouse of the knowledge of His Name, both in the natural and spiritual *teh-home*.

> By his knowledge the depths [*teh-home*] are broken up, and the clouds drop down the dew (Proverbs 3:20).

By the knowledge, the rule and order, of His holy Name, God governs the *teh-home* pit, and by the knowledge, the rule and order, of His holy Name, the depths are opened up. By wisdom, God founded the earth, and by understanding He established the heavens (Proverbs 3:19). But, by the knowledge, the rule and order, of His holy Name, He governs and guides the depths (*teh-home*). The knowledge of the LORD's Name is the controlling force of the physical universes that raises up the great waters of the depths and brings down the small drops of dew according to His purposive will.

There are more Scriptures that reveal additional information about the *teh-home* pit; however, the ones just covered are sufficient to give some insight into the kind of pit in which God buried the second restored earth. Three times God judged the earth and its world of inhabitants with ice and fire in the pits below. However, God's future judgments, reserved for the earth and its world of inhabitants, call for ice and fire from above (Revelation 8:7,8,10; 16:8; 20:9; 11:19; 15:2).

Because the earth and its worlds of inhabitants sinned against the LORD's holy Name each time, they always ended in a pit of judgment. However, ultimately, God's master plan for the creation will reach fruition.

God created the earth and its world of inhabitants with a free moral will and with the power of knowledge so they willingly could learn to praise His holy Name and the wisdom, the understanding, and the knowledge of the rule and order of it. The LORD is a supreme, Sovereign School Master; therefore, if any person refuses to go to God's school of surrender and subjection in the dispensation of *free will*, the LORD will force him to go to His school of surrender and subjection in the world to come, under the dispensation of *restrained will*.

As the supreme, Sovereign God, the LORD justly commands and rightly expects His creation to praise Him.

> *Praise the LORD* from the earth, ye dragons, and *all deeps*:
> (Psalm 148:7).

All creation, including *all* in the *teh-home*, ultimately must come to the knowledge, rule and order, of the LORD's holy Name. Someday they, too, will bow their knees and give all glory and all honour unto the LORD God and His Son, their Creator (Philippians 2:10,11).

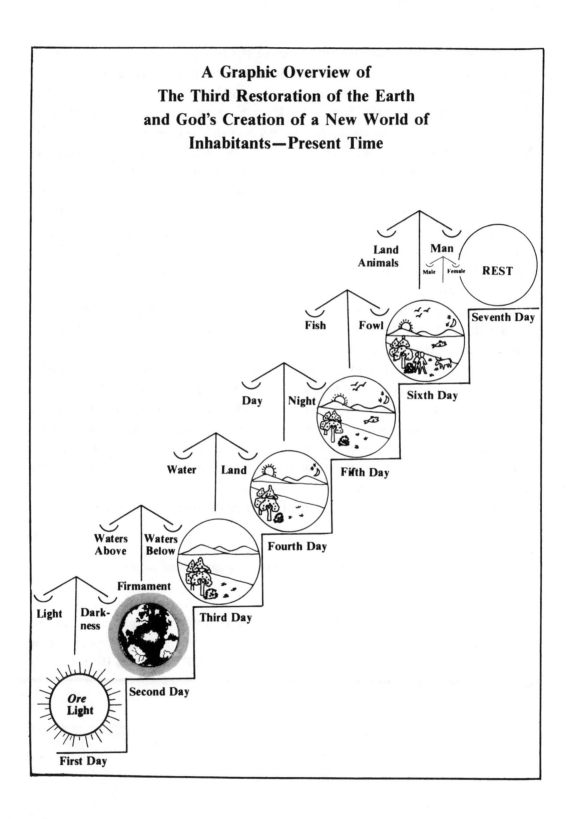

A Graphic Overview of
The Third Restoration of the Earth
and God's Creation of a New World of
Inhabitants—Present Time

Chapter Five

The Third Restoration of the Earth and God's Creation of a New World of Inhabitants—Present Time

IT IS SO comforting to know that in the midst of the darkness, destruction and gloom of the earth's fall into the *teh-home* pit that the immutable God promised not to make a full end of the earth by leaving it eternally in a chaotic state under His judgment and punishment. In other words, He promised to restore the earth again.

It is necessary to deviate from our progression in the history of our present earth at this point in order to establish some truths about its "creation," or what in fact is its restoration with newly created inhabitants.

God is immutable and changeless; He is the same yesterday, today, and forever. Therefore, when God explains His principles of *future* workings, we can understand His principles of *past* workings because they are the same.

Let us examine God's master plan for our present earth and notice, for instance, what the state of the galaxy, which contains the earth, will be at the end of this present dispensation. This will help us understand how the earth reached its present state.

Science has proven that the moon is of great antiquity like the earth. Study of the moon also has disclosed the many craters on it, which proves that large pieces of space debris have joined to it along the pathway of its great historical experience. This growth by accretion is part of the process that formed our solar system, our sun, moon, all the planets and their satellites, asteroids, and meteorites.

God's Word also declares that the light of the sun and the moon again will be increased tremendously, comparable to the increased size of the earth after it has gone through its next judgment.

> Moreover the light of the moon shall be as the light of the sun, and *the light of the sun shall be sevenfold*, as the light of seven days, in the day that the LORD bindeth up the breach of his people, and healeth the stroke of their wound (Isaiah 30:26).

There will be a miraculous increase in the radiance of the heavenly luminaries or light bearers when God increases the size of the earth after the tribulation period. The moon in that day will shine as our sun of today, and the sun will become seven times brighter.

Because of their increased size and form, God speaks of the earth and the heavens as being new. Scientists know that about four and one-half billion years ago the day on Earth was shorter than it is now. Dr. Trefil mentioned in his book that the luminosity of the sun probably has increased by up to 20 percent during the past 4.5 billion years. This lets us know that there have been increases in the size of the sun and the earth in the past which have lengthened our days. Actually each time the earth has fallen into a pit of judgment it has become larger after God has restored it. The prophecy in the Book of Revelation tells us that our present earth will be larger after it has been restored from its fourth judgment, which will be a judgment of ice and fire from above.

> And I beheld when he had opened the sixth seal, and, lo, there was a great earthquake; and the sun became black as sackcloth of hair, and the moon became as blood; And *the stars of heaven fell unto the earth*, even as a fig tree casteth her untimely figs, when she is shaken of a mighty wind. *And the heaven departed* as a scroll when it is rolled together; and every mountain and island were moved out of their places (Revelation 6:12-14).

At the end of the tribulation period that is soon coming to try the whole earth, the LORD will return again to the earth. Just prior to His return, the sixth seal of judgment will be loosed, and as a result of this judgment, many stars of the present galaxy will fall on the earth. Some will fall into the sun, so it will appear as black as sackcloth for a season.

Many years previous to the Apostle John's prophecy in the sixth chapter of the Book of Revelation, the Prophet Isaiah foretold the same scene.

> And all the host of heaven shall be dissolved, and the heavens shall be rolled together as a scroll: *and all their host shall fall down, as the leaf falleth off from the vine*, and as a falling fig from the fig tree (Isaiah 34:4).

Isaiah prophesied how the heavenly luminaries, the stars, shall fall as the leaves of autumn. The heavens shall roll together as a scroll of parchment.

This does not mean that the LORD will annihilate what He already has created. But He will reshape and reform the earth and the heavens so they will be new creations. For this reason, then, the LORD revealed, through both His prophet and His apostle, the truth about this new creation that *will be* brought to pass.

> For, behold, *I create new heavens and a new earth*: and the former shall not be remembered, nor come into mind. But be ye glad and rejoice for ever in that which I create: for, behold, I create Jerusalem a rejoicing, and her people a joy (Isaiah 65:17,18).

> *And I saw a new heaven and a new earth*: for the first heaven and the first earth were passed away; and there was no more sea. . . . And he that sat upon the throne said, Behold, I make all things new. And he said unto me, Write: for these words are true and faithful (Revelation 21:1,5).

The LORD's glorious and marvelous new creation of the new heaven and the new earth will cause our present earth, solar system, and galaxy to undergo a complete transformation. The former shapes and conditions of the heavens and the earth, prevailing before the advent of the LORD's new creations, neither will be remembered by the LORD, nor come into His mind.

"New creations" of the LORD does not mean that He has annihilated what He has previously created. If He previously has created something, and if He creates something new out of the old, it means He has sanctified, rearranged, and reshaped the old into something new.

This is also true of God's spiritual principles in His spiritual world.

> *Create in me a clean heart, O God; and renew* a right spirit within me (Psalm 51:10).

> Therefore if any man be in Christ, *he is a new creature*: old things are passed away; behold, all things are become new (II Corinthians 5:17).

> For in Christ Jesus neither circumcision availeth any thing, nor uncircumcision, but *a new creature* (Galatians 6:15).

David besought God to take his heart and sanctify it, purge it, cleanse it, and reshape it into a *new creation*, which would repel every debased thought and depraved desire.

If any man be in Christ, he is a new creature or creation. The infinite grace of God in the heart works a *creative change*. Old things are passed away; old debased thoughts, old depraved desires, old corrupt habits, and old evil practices flee away. The regenerating grace of Christ Jesus creates a new world, a new heart, within man, giving him a new name and a new nature. It is the new creation, the new heart, that by God's grace avails with God.

Thus, God is able to create things out of nothing, and He is able to create new things. By sanctifying old things and by adding to them and rearranging them, He makes something new.

Before God created the original earth in the very beginning, He *created* (*baw-raw*) the heaven (Genesis 1:1) with all its light. Each dispensation of the earth's existence, before its fall into the different pits, had some form of solar system comparable to the particular size of the earth in order for plant life and animal life to have existed. On the fourth creative day (Genesis 1:14-18), God said to let the luminaries or "light bearers" appear (as it is said in Hebrew). It also says in Genesis 1:18 that God *made* (*aw-saw*) the sun, moon, and stars. The Hebrew word *aw-saw* has a diversity of meanings, but it never means *create* (*bar-raw*). *Aw-saw* means to *do* by accomplishing, advancing, appointing, bestowing, bringing forth. After God raised the earth up out of the *teh-home* pit, He made the light bearers, the heavenly luminaries (which He had previously created) to appear.

Although the LORD God is immutable and changeless in His person and power, He is able to create and to make all things new according to His purposive will.

True Biblical facts and true scientific facts are in complete harmony with each other. True scientific discoveries merely affirm the creative work of Almighty God.

We do not know how many aeons God may have left the earth in the *teh-home* pit, but present-day man is a living witness that the earth was lifted out of the deep grave of the *teh-home* judgment.

God never forsook the earth, although He had cast it down into the third pit of judgment. After God punished the earth for a season, cleansing and purifying it, He came and hovered or brooded over it, preparing to lift it up to its present restored state in order to make a dwelling place for the present world of created new inhabitants.

God's work of creation did not involve the process of evolution, the slow, gradual process of one kind of life or non-life evolving into another kind of life or non-life. As we stated earlier in this book, it is because scientists do not know the history of the earth as God reveals it in His Word that they try to link the separate creations into one continuous evolvement. Modern scientists hold fast to the theory of evolution, even though there is much more evidence to prove the Biblical account than there is proof for man's guesses.

On one hand, the world's scientists claim ignorance—"We do not know everything. On the contrary, strange as it may seem, we know hardly anything,..."*

From the field of physics, Dr. James S. Trefil wrote an opening paragraph in his book *Space Time Infinity* that said: "In the many pages to follow, you will be led through a fine introduction into how astronomers and other celestial workers view our universe today. We must say "today" because tomorrow other researchers may have a significantly different picture to paint."

In an article, "Quest for the Missing Link," written for *Science Digest*, March, 1984, Andrea Dorfman reported from the paleontological field and had this to say, "As for the fossil's being a missing link, Walker recommends taking a more balanced view. 'If we think of all the generations of animals and ask how many fossils we've got, practically all the links are still missing. That's the perspective you've got to have.'"

Scientists speak of "gaps in their understanding," "missing links," "possibilities." Perhaps the clearest statement about the certainty of science's uncertainties is made by Mario Rigutti in *A Hundred Billion Stars*. He said: "Once in awhile it happens that a theory is invalidated by the realization that certain pieces that appeared to fit well together do not allow others to fit in. As a result, progress comes to a halt. There are times of crisis and revision, during which the scientists strive to find a new design, by more or less drastic modifications of the old, that will allow them to fit together all the pieces—the old pieces that fit already (though they may have to be fitted in new ways) as well as the new pieces that did not fit before. Sometimes the modifications are so radical that the new design hardly resembles the old. Physics has gone through a number of these periods of transition and change, and some of them have altered the scientific edifice to its very foundations."

On the other hand, amid their many controversies, they doggedly hold to their unproven theories, such as evolution. In this instance, they are trying to fit the wrong pieces together when they link present creation with previous creations, except for the common denominator of their having the same Creator.

Geologists and paleontologists have indisputable evidence of there having been mass extinctions of life in the past history of the earth and of new species appearing. How evolutionists could encounter such set-backs as knowing that 70-90 percent of life disappeared at a time and still believe that life would have had time to reach the advanced stages we see it in today is a miracle. According to Dr. Trefil, the whole

---

*Rigutti, Mario, *A Hundred Billion Stars* (MIT Press, Cambridge, Massachusetts 1984).

question of species extinction is the subject of intense work in fields from astronomy to paleontology. And the question will remain unanswered to scientists until they fit the pieces together according to God's Word.

First of all, God began creation by revealing His Son, the Light of the earth and the world. Christ, the Word, the *Ore* Light, assumed the responsibility for becoming the foundational support for the whole creation and proceeded gradually from the lowest to the highest—to man, who is the most excellent and noble of all God's creation because man, when he was first created, bore the glory and the image of God.

The events in the earth's history, which we have been examining up to this point, bring us to the time of our present earth. Genesis, the "book of beginnings," does not begin with our present earth. The first verse of chapter one of Genesis refers to the creation of the original earth.

> *In the beginning God created* the heaven and the earth (Genesis 1:1).

Then the first part of the second verse gives an account of the second restored earth and its inhabitants as they lay in the *teh-home* pit of judgment.

> And *the earth was without form, and void*; and *darkness was upon the face of the deep.* . . . (Genesis 1:2).

The dispensations through which the earth already had passed between verses one and two covered untold billions of years. The earth had experienced its original creation and its judgment in the *shakh-ath* pit; its first restoration and its judgment in the *bore* pit; its second restoration and then its judgment in the *teh-home* pit. Three separate worlds of inhabitants had lived on these prehistoric earths and were destroyed totally when the earths were cast into their different pits of judgment.

The last part of verse two begins the restoration of the earth for the third time, which is the beginning of our present earth. ". . . And *the Spirit of God moved* upon the face of the waters" (Genesis 1:2).

God's Spirit moved or hovered above the chaotic waters of the *teh-home* pit before God completely restored the earth for the third time since its original creation. The Hebrew word for *water* is *mah-yim*, signifying water, juice, urine, semen, watercourse, flood, spring.

The very contents of the water confirm the destruction of the second restored earth with its third created world of inhabitants. The presence of urine and semen in the water proves that a world of inhabitants had indeed existed on the second restored earth before our present earth was inhabited by present-day man.

God's mysterious, invisible and irresistible presence moved or brooded over the chaotic confusion and darkness of the earth to quicken and transform its condition so that the earth again would be a suitable dwelling place for a new world of inhabitants—present man.

The Hebrew word that is used to describe the Spirit's "moving" upon the waters is used again in Deuteronomy 32:11, which, in this case, describes an eagle "hovering over" her eaglets to care for them and to protect them. The Spirit of God, like a mother eagle, hovered over the "eaglet earth" that was buried under the face or ice of the deep (the *teh-home*).

It is obvious that both the waters and the darkness already had been created prior to God's Spirit moving upon them.

The description of the total restoration of the earth and the creation of its new world of inhabitants continues from verse three to the end of chapter one in the Book of Genesis.

God used four methods to bring the heavens, the earth, and its wonderful world of inhabitants into existence: He *created*; He *commanded by His Word*; He *made*; He *formed*.

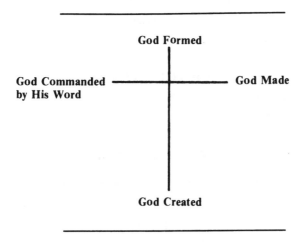

The Hebrew words for each of these terms indicate that each way God worked to bring His creation into visibility involved a different process. First, He created.

> In the beginning God *created* the heaven and the earth (Genesis 1:1).

The Hebrew word for *create* is *baw-raw*, meaning to cut down, select, feed as a formative process, choose, dispatch, do, make fat. All the cognate roots of *baw-raw* have the meaning of striving to get out, or getting out of a constrained and bound state. The word *create* (*baw-raw*) gives the underlying conception of bringing an invisible thing out into the open, or bringing it from the inside to the outside. Therefore, *baw-raw* really means to bring something into reality which hitherto had existed only in thought, inside the mind.

God *created* by selecting and cutting down the thoughts of His master plan from within His own mind and His own will. He *created, baw-raw*, all things purely and solely out of His own mind and His own will and out of nothing else. Before the worlds existed materially and visibly, they existed as an invisible, internal, divine thought inside the infinite, unbegotten mind of God. God cut down, as it were, the thoughts of His master plan and gave them to His Son Who, in turn, implemented His Father's master plan, making it into visible forms. The act of creation by the Son gave the unbegotten Father's thought or master plan an external, concrete existence. **The whole creation is nothing but the materialized thought of the eternal power of the Godhead.**

> For the invisible things of him *from the creation of the world* are clearly seen, being understood by the things that are made, *even his eternal power and Godhead*; so that they are without excuse: (Romans 1:20).

A limited, finite being cannot know perfectly the infinite, limitless, divine Being of God. Although as finite creatures we cannot comprehend fully the infinite Being of God, we can apprehend His Being, to a measure, through the LORD Jesus Christ. There is a measure of the invisible unbegotten God which can be understood through His divine Word and through His Works of creation.

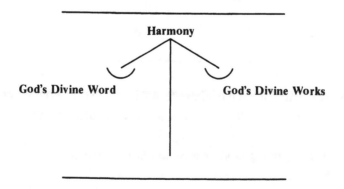

God's divine Works can be understood through His divine Word, and His divine Word can be understood through His divine Works. God's Word and Works are in complete harmony with each other since they have proceeded out of the same divine Person.

The invisible things of God and the invisible master plan of His eternal power and Godhead are seen clearly and visibly manifested by the things that are created, made, and formed. Created matter is powerless to make itself fall into faultless order, perfect harmony, and exact balance through a casual hit-or-miss process. All creation is a witness of a Mastermind Who has produced a perfect plan of order, harmony, and balance. The eternal power of the divine Godhead is the eternal "first Cause" of all things. The divine Workman is known by His creative Works.

The Hebrew word *baw-raw* also implies being plump, corpulent, and healthy, and it has its origin in a Hebrew root word meaning to become visible, concrete, and tangible. God selected and cut down from His invisible, infinite substance that which He purposed to bring forth into the visible realm. God brought forth His substance and placed it in many diverse and beautiful forms of matter.

The truth that God is the first Cause of all things and that He is the Creator of all things is the foundation stone of wisdom, understanding, and knowledge.

The second method that God used to bring things into existence was by His Word (*aw-mar*), meaning to appoint, bid, call, certify, charge, command, consider, declare, demand, desire, determine, require.

> And God *said, Let there be* light: and there was light (Genesis 1:3).

Finite man can make nothing unless he works hard to bring it to birth. But God, through the mere breath of His Almighty Word, brings things to birth.

God *said (aw-mar),* . . . "Let there be . . ." And whatever His purposive will desired came into being.

The third method that God used to bring things into existence was the "making" process.

> And God *made* the firmament, . . . (Genesis 1:7).

The Hebrew word for *made* is *aw-saw,* meaning to do, to accomplish, bring forth, appoint, finish, dress.

Then the fourth and last method that God used to bring things into existence was through the "formation" process.

And the LORD God *formed* man of the dust of the ground,...
(Genesis 2:7).

The Hebrew word for *form* is *yaw-tsar,* meaning to squeeze into shape, to mold into a form as a potter, to determine, to form a resolution, fashion, frame, potter, purpose.

God *created, spoke* (commanded), *made,* and *formed* all things, both visible and invisible. As we progress in the Biblical account of the restoration of our present earth, we shall see that God used all these methods in creating our present earth and its world of inhabitants.

I. The First Day or Aeon of the Third Restoration of the Earth

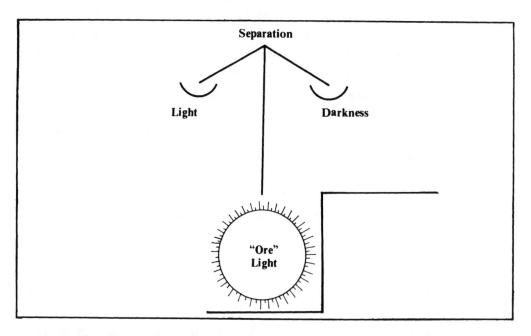

In the first "day" or aeon of time, God, in the midst of all the darkness, called for the Light to appear, and He divided the Light from the darkness. God did not *create* Light because He already had *begotten* the Light, Who was His Son, the Word.

> *And God said, Let there be light: and there was light.* And God saw the light, that it was good: and God divided the light from the darkness. *And God called the light Day, and the darkness he called Night.* And the evening and the morning were the first day (Genesis 1:3-5).

The fact that many things already were in existence when God began the restorative work that produced our present earth proves that God previously had created or begotten them. *Light* and *darkness*, *waters* with all their content, and the *earth* buried in the *deep* (*teh-home*) — all these already existed on the first "day."

The Light (*Ore*) that existed was none other than the Son of God, the Christ. Jesus Christ stated that He is the Light (*Ore*) of the world.

The Hebrew word for *light* is *ore*, meaning illumination or an illuminary.

> Then spake Jesus again unto them, saying, *I am the light* [*ore*] *of the world*: he that followeth me shall not walk in darkness, but shall have the *light* [*ore*] of life (John 8:12).

God is Light, and Christ, His only begotten Son, is also Light. God begot Christ in His own invisible image. Christ is the Messiah of Israel, and His Name is called the *Light* by the Prophet Daniel.

> He revealeth the deep and secret things: he knoweth what is in the darkness, and *the light dwelleth with him* (Daniel 2:22).

In His great master plan, God provided two great "suns" for the earth and its world of inhabitants: one created, natural sun, and one begotten, spiritual Sun of Righteousness. The spiritual Sun, with His begotten rays of Light, the Word of God, was given *first*. This teaches that the eternal LORD God and His divine begotten Word are to supersede all creatures and to become first in everyone's life.

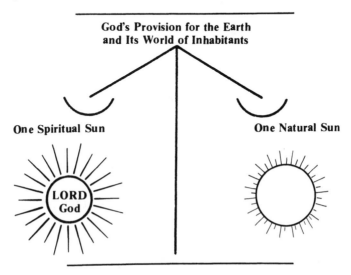

God's Provision for the Earth
and Its World of Inhabitants

One Spiritual Sun

LORD God

One Natural Sun

The Prophet Malachi gave witness to the existence of the spiritual Sun of Righteousness, the LORD God, and Christ, the Light of the world.

> But unto you that fear my name shall the *Sun of righteousness arise with healing in his wings*; and ye shall go forth, and grow up as calves of the stall (Malachi 4:2).

'When the Sun of Righteousness arises, He spreads out His light-giving rays like wings, radiating life and healing to all brokenness, gloom, and confusion.

God 'called for the appearance of the spiritual Sun of Righteousness before the restoration of the present earth was begun. Before this present earth's natural sun was remade or renewed on the fourth creative day to accommodate the size of the newly restored earth, the spiritual Sun was shining on the first day as the source of all light and life.

The Sun of Righteousness, the *Ore* Light, the great spiritual Luminary for the earth and world, began to spread the wings of His healing rays over the chaotic earth, restoring it once again into a habitable earth.

The Hebrew word *ore* also means to be awake and to be receptive to external impressions. Spiritual Light is the awakening force that awakens all elements for development. God saw that the Light was *good*, and He separated it from the darkness.

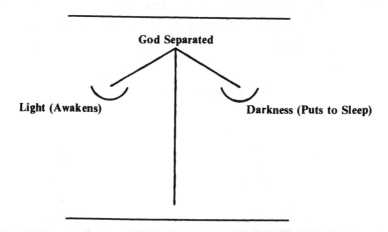

Darkness puts things to sleep and clothes them so they are not exposed to the awakening influence of external light.

God separated the light and the darkness, establishing a perfect balance between the two from the beginning. Light is needed to awaken everything to individual life and to stimulate growth. The darkness is needed to give opportunity for forces to relax from external stimulation so they can work internally. This darkness referred to in Genesis 1:4 is *not* Lucifer's wicked darkness.

God called the light Day (*yome*, in Hebrew), meaning to be hot, a day (as the warm hours), bright, a natural day, and an eternal day for ever.

God called the darkness *Night*. The Hebrew word for *darkness* in Genesis 1:4 is *kho-shek*, meaning to be dark, misery, woe, affliction; it comes from the primitive root *khaw-shak*, meaning to be dark as withholding light, to be dim, hide, obscure.

The Word of God says that He dwells in darkness.

> And he made *darkness* [*kho-shek*] pavilions *round about him,
> dark waters,* and thick clouds of the skies (II Samuel 22:12).

The darkness of God's Name is used to conceal His glorious presence and His mysterious will from the curious, sinful eyes of His fallen creation.

God gives His Word in the midst of darkness. He gave the Light of His oral law out of the midst of the *darkness (kho-shek).*

> And it came to pass, when *ye heard the voice out of the midst of
> the darkness* [*kho-shek*], (for the mountain did burn with fire,)
> that ye came near unto me, even all the heads of your tribes, and
> your elders; (Deuteronomy 5:23).

He makes darkness His secret place.

> *He made darkness* [*kho-shek*] his secret place; his pavilion round
> about him were dark waters and thick clouds of the skies (Psalm
> 18:11).

The glorious presence and Light of God are disguised by a veil of darkness. The dark veil to which God subjects His children is always a witness that His immediate glorious presence is on the other side of the veil.

So, the earth, lying sunken in a pit with a thundercloud of darkness hanging over its waters, was a witness that the radiant light of the Sun of Righteousness was soon to break through.

The Light, the Christ, Who was the divine Wisdom of God, was begotten, and then God *created* the darkness.

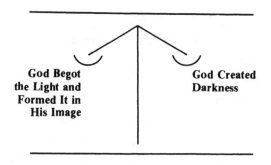

God Begot
the Light and
Formed It in
His Image

God Created
Darkness

> I am the LORD, and there is none else, there is no God beside
> me: I girded thee, though thou hast not known me: That they
> may know from the rising of the sun, and from the west, that
> there is none beside me. I am the LORD, and there is none else.
> *I form the light, and create darkness:* I make peace, and create
> evil. I the LORD do all these things (Isaiah 45:5-7).

The LORD God *begot* His only begotten Son, the radiant *Light* of the world, but He *created darkness*, and He set the darkness over against the Light. Light is infinite and divine; darkness is part of God's finite creation. The darkness was created from the beginning as a part of the original creation. This is why darkness already was in existence when God restored the earth for a third time.

God called the name of the darkness "Night." The Hebrew word for *night* is *lah-yil* or *lah-yel-aw*, meaning to twist (away of the light), midnight (season), adversity. God uses the expression *day and night* to express the turning of the great wheel of His Name. Day is the masculine side through which the wheel of the LORD's Name turns, and night is the feminine side through which the wheel of the LORD's Name turns.

The wheel of the LORD's Name turns through light and darkness in order to join the infinite with the finite.

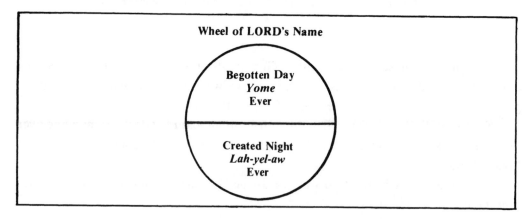

Wheel of LORD's Name

Begotten Day
Yome
Ever

Created Night
Lah-yel-aw
Ever

Day (*yome*) and night (*lah-yel-aw*) are used to express one revolution of the eternal Name of the LORD. The expression "day and night" is used frequently to signify *spiritual space* in heaven. For example, the Bible says the living creatures in heaven do not cease praising God *day* or *night*.

> And the four beasts had each of them six wings about him; and
> they were full of eyes within: *and they rest not day and night*,
> saying, Holy, holy, holy, Lord God Almighty, which was, and is,
> and is to come (Revelation 4:8).

The four living creatures, who are continually before God's throne in heaven, offer praise to God *day* and *night*.

This cannot be a solar day and night because the scene is in heaven, far above the solar system. Furthermore, God established this wheel of *day* and *night* before the solar system was created.

For another example, the Scriptures say that fallen Lucifer accuses God's people *day and night* before God's throne.

> And I heard a loud voice saying in heaven, Now is come salvation,
> and strength, and the kingdom of our God, and the power of his
> Christ: for the accuser of our brethren is cast down, which *accused*
> *them before our God day and night* (Revelation 12:10).

Fallen Lucifer (Satan, Devil, Serpent, and Dragon) is said to ascend before God's face to accuse the brethren *day* and *night*. Again the scene is in heaven, far above the earth and its solar system; therefore, it cannot be referring to a natural day and night.

Other Scriptures prove that the expression *day and night* also refers to *for ever and ever*.

> And the smoke of their torment ascendeth up *for ever and ever,*
> and they have no rest *day nor night*, who worship the beast and
> his image, and whosoever receiveth the mark of his name
> (Revelation 14:11).

God declared that those who receive the mark of the Antichrist and worship his image, during the tribulation period that is soon to come upon the inhabitants of the earth, shall be tormented *for ever and ever* (day and night) or for one turning of the great wheel of the LORD's Name.

The Devil, the Beast, and the False Prophet will be tormented in the lake of fire while the wheel of the LORD's Name makes a complete revolution (*for ever and ever*).

> And the devil that deceived them was cast into the lake of fire and brimstone, where the beast and the false prophet are, and shall be *tormented day and night for ever and ever* (Revelation 20:10).

The Devil, who will deceive the people at the end of the millennial reign, ultimately will be cast into the lake of fire to be punished for ever and ever or for one great revolution of the LORD's mighty Name.

In view of all these Scriptures, it is very clear that the six restorative and creative "day and night" periods were not solar day and night periods. God is the only One Who knows the amount of eternal space involved in the revolving of the wheel of His eternal Name in its relation to solar time on earth.

II. The Second Day or Aeon of the Third Restoration of the Earth and the Creation "Making" of the Firmament

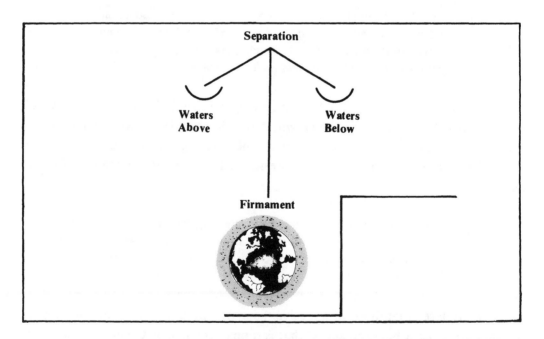

On the second day, God restored the above and below waters to their original places, and He *made* (one of God's methods of working) a firmament in between.

And God said, Let there be a firmament in the midst of the waters, and let it divide the waters from the waters. And *God made the firmament*, and divided the waters which were under the firmament from the waters which were above the firmament: and it was so. And God called the firmament Heaven. And the evening and the morning were the second day (Genesis 1:6-8).

God first revealed His master plan by saying words to this effect: "Let there be a firmament to divide between the waters above and the waters below." God knew, from the beginning of the earth, that our present earth would need a firmament with clouds and mist which would provide water, so He made the firmament and established His law of circularity within it to provide water for the land.

God *spoke (aw-mar)*; He said, ". . . *Let there be*," and a firmament or expanse came into existence, and then He *made (aw-saw)* the firmament. He hammered out, as it were, the firmament after He had spoken it into existence. God solidified the firmament, spread it out, stretched it out into a mighty dividing arched vault between the waters above and the waters below.

Scientists tell us that the earth's atmosphere and hydrosphere work together. "The first is our evolving gaseous envelope, the second our total water supply system including oceans, ice, surface water, and vapor providing clouds and precipitation. Both systems interact with each other and have gone through important and irreversible changes since the formation of our planet."*

God commanded, and the Word, the Son of God, *made* the firmament.

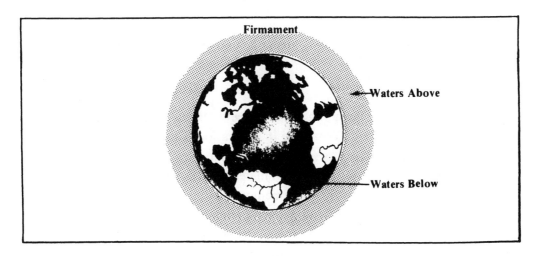

*Trefil, James S., *Space Time Infinity* (Smithsonian Institution, Washington, D.C., 1985).

153

God fixed the arched vault or firmament in heaven as a great reservoir to receive the vapors from the oceans, seas, and rivers, forming clouds which would give precious "liquid life" back to the thirsty earth and its thirsty inhabitants.

God's purpose in using the firmament to separate or divide was to establish the revolving wheel of receiving and giving.

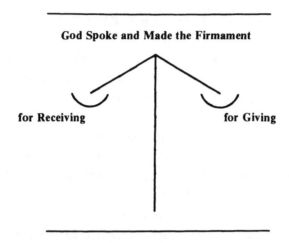

God did not say that the firmament was "good" on the second creative day because, on that day, the firmament could not begin fulfilling its purpose for existing (which was receiving and giving) until *all* the creation had been finished on the sixth creative day.

> And God saw *every thing* that he had made, and, behold, it was *very good*. And the evening and the morning were the sixth day (Genesis 1:31).

God saw everything, including the firmament, which He had made to separate, and it was "very good." God's purpose in separation is for receiving and giving or sharing. Nothing can be called "very good" until the wheel of sharing has been set in motion. God set the separating firmament in between the waters above and the waters below. "It was so" means that the firmament was set in an unchanging state from the day God *spoke* it into existence. God *made* the firmament into an absolute, perpetual arch from the day He spoke it into existence. "It was so" means God willed it to be so. God said that the firmament was very good after it had begun its ministry of sharing on the sixth day.

III. The Third Day or Aeon of the Third Restoration of the Earth, the Separation of the Waters from the Dry Land, and the Creation of Grass, Herbs, and Fruit Trees

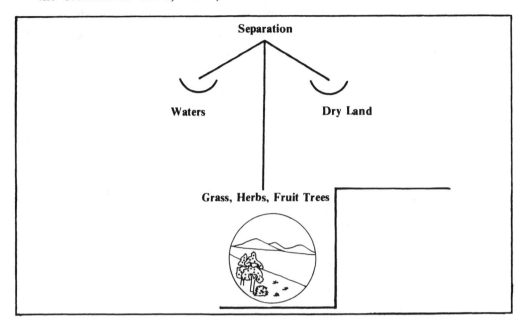

On the third day, God increased the principle of sharing when He divided between the waters and the dry land, causing more separation.

> *And God said, Let the waters under the heaven be gathered together unto one place, and let the dry land appear:* and it was so. And God called the dry land Earth: and the gathering together of the waters called he Seas: and God saw that it was good. *And God said, Let the earth bring forth grass, the herb yielding seed, and the fruit tree yielding fruit after his kind, whose seed is in itself, upon the earth:* and it was so. And the earth brought forth grass, and herb yielding seed after his kind, and the tree yielding fruit, whose seed was in itself, after his kind: and God saw that it was good. And the evening and the morning were the third day (Genesis 1:9-13).

God *spoke* and commanded all the waters to be gathered together or concentrated in one place, and He commanded that the dry land appear.

God continued the separation of things that are diametrically different. First, He had separated light and darkness. Second, He had separated the waters above from the waters below. Third, He separated the waters from the dry land.

That which was the same in nature had to be separated from unlike things, things that were different. The water which was a soft, dissolving liquid had to be separated from the dry land which was rigid and compressed.

God did not create the earth on this occasion. He simply commanded it to be lifted up from the bottomless pit and separated from the water. When God saw the separation of the waters and saw the dry land appear, He said it was good. Fossil history clearly indicates that the oceans have not always been where they are now.

So God saw that the earth and the seas were ready to share their substance with the life that He would bring forth in them; they were ready to fulfill God's purposive will for them. Without separation and division, the earth and seas could not have attained God's purposive will, which consisted of their being a dwelling place for the new life He intended to create for each of them.

Through God's separation and division, the earth and the seas entered into a mutual sharing of His law of circularity. All the waters of springs, brooks, streams, and rivers were to hurry to the seas. Then they were to rise up in vapours, forming the clouds so the clouds could pour down water upon the dry land. After the waters had nourished the thirsty earth and its thirsty inhabitants, they were to rush back to the seas to start their cycle once more. Thus, the seas and the land were to maintain a constant succession of receiving and giving or sharing.

On the third day, in addition to the appearance of the dry land, God spoke and commanded the grass, the herb, and the fruit tree to spring forth after its own kind. The Hebrew word for *kind* is *meen*, meaning to portion out, a sort, (referring to the family or the class), species (which deals with the appearance, shape, quality, and distinct kind within the family).

God covered the earth with a "garment" of grass, herbs, and fruit trees at this time. The original vegetation sprouted solely because of God's command to bring forth or to sprout. The earth was granted the unique productive power, by its Creator, to bring forth grass, herbs, and fruit trees.

Almighty God definitely has fashioned the *forms* of all plant life. His irrevocable law of the species was clearly working from the first, in the tiniest seed and the greatest tree.

God's law of separation was manifested in the dividing of the dry land from the water, and it was extended through to His infinite, divine law of the species, which applied to life on land and in the water.

Within His fixed boundary lines, God's law of the species allows each seed total freedom of expression in growth.

God's law that everything must reproduce after its own kind means that He has fixed a boundary line, which is evident by the way He has created and formed every creature with many elaborately interrelated, interconnected parts and peculiar characteristics of kind so they cannot be joined to another kind. God has made provision for each kind to produce a multitude of varieties or species, but the variety stays within its own kind. For example, dogs are a kind of animal, but there is a multitude of varieties of dogs. God's law of separation for each *kind* is the fence around each kind. Dogs do not breed with cats because God's law of separation is around both the dogs and the cats.

However, changes can and do occur within the various species due to inheritance, environment, and experience, but God's law of separation in nature continues to rule over all organic existence. Every organic seed belongs exclusively to the particular kind that its ancestors did. For this reason, man never has found either a seed or a creature in a stage of evolving from one kind to another kind.

God also used the law of separation on the third day, by dividing the waters from the dry land; and He saw it was good. When God instituted the law of fruitfulness after its kind, by giving each blade of grass, herb, and fruit tree seed after its own kind, He saw that it was good.

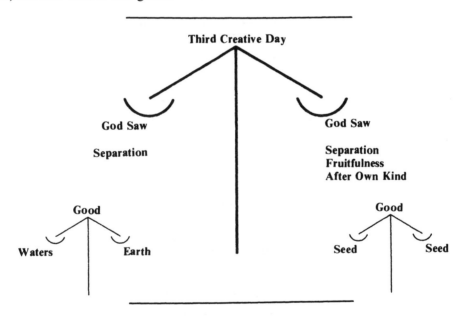

God pronounced a double portion of goodness on the third day of His restorative and creative work on this present earth. It was good for the waters and the earth to be separated, and it was good for every seed to be separated into its own species or kind. As the earth and its fruitfulness progressed toward God's purpose and perfection of it, God saw that it was very good or *good, good.*

God prepared the earth for the maintenance and support of its world of inhabitants that were to be forthcoming.

The restoration of the earth and the new creation of life and world of inhabitants had to be planned and accomplished by a Mastermind and an Omnipotent Power. What if the world of inhabitants had been produced first, before the necessary food for maintenance and support had come into existence? Life soon would have ceased to exist. However, in the beginning, God, in His wise design, established the orderly sequence of creation needed to preserve life on the original earth. Each time God has restored the earth out of a pit, He has followed the same orderly pattern of creation. On the third day or aeon of creation of the original earth, God commanded the grass, herbs, and fruit trees to clothe the land. Likewise, on the third day or aeon of the restoration of our present earth, God again commanded the grass, herbs, and fruit trees to clothe the land, and they have continued to bring forth after their own kind or species for the benefit and use of the inhabitants of the earth.

IV. The Fourth Day of Creation—Lights in the Firmament

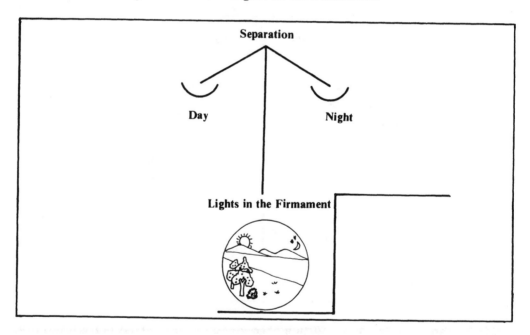

The lights in our galaxy were *made* by God through a process of doing, accomplishing, bringing forth, appointing, finishing, and dressing them for His intended purpose. God *made* chandeliers to hang in the firmament to be the light bearers for the earth.

And God said, *Let there be lights in the firmament* of the heaven to divide the day from the night; and let them be for signs, and for seasons, and for days, and years: And let them be for lights in the firmament of the heaven to give light upon the earth: and it was so. And God made two great lights, the greater light to rule the day, and the lesser light to rule the night: he made the stars also. And God set them in the firmament of the heaven to give light upon the earth, And to rule over the day and over the night, and to divide the light from the darkness: and God saw that it was good. And the evening and the morning were the fourth day (Genesis 1:14-19).

These verses give the history of God's working to bring forth the sun and moon of our solar system and the billions of stars in our universe. From their knowledge of physics, scientists have ascertained that our sun is a little less than 5 billion years old, and that it has about another 5 billion years to go before it burns itself up. In a given star (and our sun is a star), there are only so many hydrogen atoms, and when they are all used up the fusion of hydrogen into helium will stop.* (Of course this will not happen because God's Word prophesies that the new sun for the new earth will be seven times brighter than our present sun.)

God will accomplish this by causing some of the stars in our galaxy to fall. This process of growth by accretion goes on today. (Who has not seen a falling "star"?) But when God commands the stars to fall in order to accomplish His purpose, the process will involve massive numbers of stars being moved from their present orbits.

Remember, no one knows, as far as time is concerned, how many aeons were involved in each creative day. (Scientists claim our universe is 20 billion years old.) But no matter how long the creative acts and creative Works took, God brought these lights into existence by His Word (*aw-mar*) and by His Works.

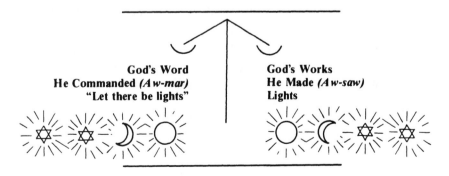

God's Word
He Commanded *(Aw-mar)*
"Let there be lights"

God's Works
He Made *(Aw-saw)*
Lights

*Trefil, James S., *Space Time Infinity* (Smithsonian Institution, Washington, D.C., 1985).

The Hebrew word for the lights God created is *maw-ore*, meaning a luminous body, a luminary, light, brightness, cheerfulness, chandelier. The *maw-ore* or chandeliers of lights obtained their light from the *Ore*, the Word of God, the Wisdom of God, the Son of God.

The light-bearing chandeliers, in their immeasurable plurality in the heavens, obey God's law of circularity, forming one harmonious system of light. The chandeliers of heaven radiate the light and glory of God's Word.

> *The heavens declare the glory of God*; and the firmament sheweth his handiwork (Psalm 19:1).

To a thinking, rational soul, the whole firmament, with its multitude of stars travelling in their measured, immutable circuits and cycles, reveals the existence of the one great Mastermind Who is the Cause of all the chandeliers of light in the universe. The whole firmament is a witness to the omnipotence, omniscient wisdom, and greatness of God Who brought the universe into existence. That the universe is not infinite is a relatively new idea. It was not until the early years of the twentieth century that astronomers decided from their studies that the universe is finite. It has a beginning. Scientists now know that the stars (suns) have a life cycle.

The chandeliers of light in the firmament are not the source of light, but they are bearers of the light. Their sole purpose in relation to the earth is to be a light bearer.

The sun, moon, and stars are the rulers which make a distinction between natural day and night and the seasons of the year. They are for the purpose of regulating life and the actions of the inhabitants of earth. By the periodic cycles they make in obedience to God's law of circularity, they serve as the most accurate means of fixing time in relation to the earth. Man can divide time into years, months, days, hours, and minutes by monitoring the faithful cycles of the sun, moon, and stars.

The Psalmist spoke of God's great wisdom that shaped the heavens.

> To him that *by wisdom made the heavens*: for his mercy endureth for ever. To him that stretched out the earth above the waters: for his mercy endureth for ever. *To him that made great lights*: for his mercy endureth for ever: *The sun to rule by day: for his mercy endureth for ever: The moon and stars to rule by night*: for his mercy endureth for ever (Psalm 136:5-9).

God's great wisdom took into consideration the position and orbit of each chandelier of light and planned for each of them to be influenced by its interaction with all others.

The ultimate purpose of God's brilliant heavenly chandeliers is to receive and to give. They receive their light from the *Ore* light of God's Word, the Son of God, and they give their light to govern and guide the life of earth's inhabitants.

The Prophet Jeremiah bore witness that the supreme Sovereign LORD is the Creator of the lights in the heaven, and he told of their ruling power.

> Thus saith the LORD, *which giveth the sun for a light by day*, and the ordinances of *the moon and of the stars for a light by night*, which *divideth the sea when the waves thereof roar*; The LORD of hosts is his name (Jeremiah 31:35).

As the Creator of the universe, the eternal God has ordained the laws of nature, including the laws that govern the heavenly chandeliers.

God declared that *it was so* and that it was *good* when He finished His work on the fourth creative day.

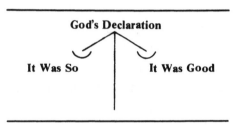

God's Declaration

It Was So   **It Was Good**

"It was so" signifies that God has established and fixed the cycles of the lights of heaven. "It was good" signifies that they were all working together in receiving and giving in order to accomplish God's purposive will.

V. The Fifth Creative Day - Sea Animals and Fowls of the Air

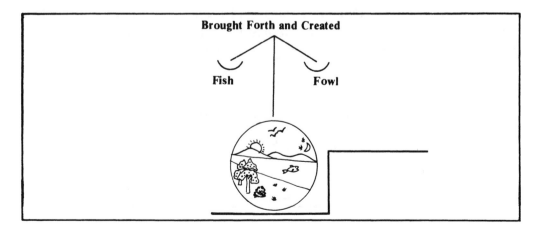

Brought Forth and Created

Fish   **Fowl**

Each previous day, God created good and excellent things, but He did not bring forth any living creatures until the fifth day when He brought forth the fish and the fowl.

> And *God said, Let the waters bring forth abundantly the moving creature* that hath life, and *fowl that may fly* above the earth in the open firmament of heaven. And God created great whales, and every living creature that moveth, which the waters brought forth abundantly, after their kind, and every winged fowl after his kind: and God saw that it was good. And God blessed them, saying, Be fruitful, and multiply, and fill the waters in the seas, and let fowl multiply in the earth. And the evening and the morning were the fifth day (Genesis 1:20-23).

Although there is one class of flesh of fowls and another class of flesh of fish, God brought forth both on the same day and out of the same water.

God, in His wise design, shaped, formed, and fashioned the fowl with the kind of flesh that it was necessary to have in order to live in the atmosphere of earth *above*, and He gave the fish the necessary kind of flesh to live *below*, in the waters of the seas.

On the third day God created *life* in the form of grass, herbs, and trees. Then on the fifth day, He brought forth independent "moving life," which was a different form of life, a form with a *nephesh* soul. *Nephesh* is one Hebrew word for *soul*.

In His command, God told the waters below the firmament to swarm with living creatures. The Hebrew word for *living* is *nephesh*, meaning the innate, intangible soul that is in every living creature. The inner "cause" for all innate movement in all living creatures is the *nephesh* (soul), which gives every creature a will, movement, motion, and personality. The *nephesh* (soul) remains constant in the midst of the ever-changing material body.

All living creatures retain impressions and have memory. These innate abilities prove the existence of a permanent *nephesh* (soul) within the changing material body.

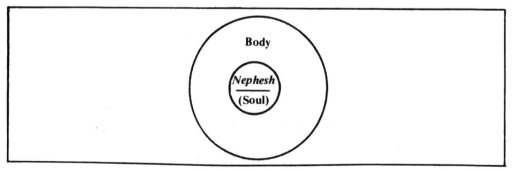

The *nephesh* (soul) is the center upon which the whole physical existence of every creature depends. A creature dies when its center of existence is removed.

The wisdom and power to receive and to assimilate that which is homogeneous to the creature is contained in the *nephesh* (soul), which also rejects and expels that which is heterogeneous to it. The *nephesh* (soul) has the free will and movement of life to receive suitable elements for rebuilding the life of the body and to reject the unsuitable elements that would try to destroy the body. The underlying principle of life in the physical is in the *nephesh* (soul).

By His Word and His power, God brought forth and created the great family of fish according to their species, and every winged fowl according to its species. God also created great whales. He blessed all organic creatures with life, giving them the power to fulfill His command to reproduce and multiply. God's Word of blessing works on and on in His creatures.

God's commanding Word and creating power produced the fish below and the fowl above, and His maintaining Word and power preserves them. Fruitfulness in the creation is the effect of God's blessing upon it. Therefore, let us give God the glory for the existence of all creatures and for the continuance of their existence.

The evening and the morning, or the turning of God's great wheel of humility and exaltation, formed the fifth creative "day" of our present earth.

VI. The Sixth Day of Creation—Land Animals and Man

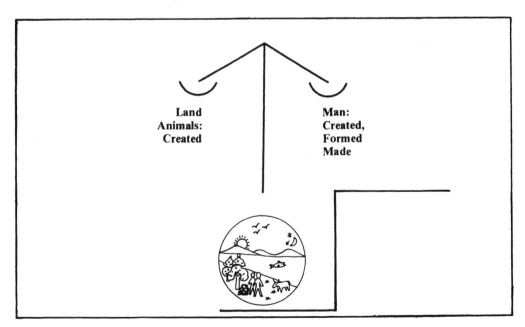

When God commanded Mother Earth to bring forth her seeds of grass, herbs, and trees, they remained bound to Mother Earth through their root system. When God brought forth free-moving water creatures, they still were bound within the elements God had used to produce them. However, on the sixth day, God created living land creatures, which were set *outside* the earth from which God had brought them forth. Thus, the land animals experienced a greater independence than the earth-bound plants and the water-bound creatures.

> And God said, *Let the earth bring forth the living creature after his kind*, cattle, and creeping thing, and beast of the earth after his kind: and it was so. And God made the beast of the earth *after his kind*, and cattle *after their kind*, and every thing that creepeth upon the earth *after his kind*: and God saw that it was good (Genesis 1:24,25).

A. Creation of Land Animals

While the living land-creatures enjoyed more freedom of movement and more independence on one side, subjection was still part of God's master plan for them. They were to be in subjection to man in order to form important stepping-stones upon which man could walk, making it possible for him to ascend into the spiritual heights of God's high calling for him. Oxen, for example, have served man by plowing for him, releasing him from his hardest work and his heaviest loads. Because of the help man has received from animals, his mind has been able to be delivered from the weight of physical exhaustion. With such help, man could be free to meditate on God's Word and to pray unto Him. Sheep and goats work, feeding and grazing, in order to grow skin and wool with which to clothe man. This is another way man has been freed from a certain amount of bodily exhaustion. Then his mind, freed from exhaustion, could meditate on the things of God. The living land-animals have given and do give their lives as a sacrifice to feed, nourish, and maintain man's natural life so he can live and be free to study God's holy Word, which makes it possible for him to achieve his spiritual education and moral development.

God commanded everything, from plants to animals, to bring forth *after their own kind*. God, the divine, infinite Lawmaker and Lawgiver, has limited everything to bring forth after its own kind.

Although there are great varieties within every species or kind, such as various shapes, sizes, and colours, these characteristics do not denote organic evolution. For example, there is great diversity within the species of cats and of dogs, but cats and dogs do not mate. There is not a single thread of evidence that basic kinds have evolved from a common ancestor.

Henry M. Morris commented on the species in his book, *Science and the Bible*: "Within all human history, there has never been documented one single example of any kind of organism evolving into a more complex kind of organism or even into a truly new 'species' at the same level."

God has created each kind of animal with organic diversity and definite physiological differences which make it impossible for the seed cells of one kind to unite with the seed cells of another kind and produce fertile offspring. A horse stays forever a horse, a cow stays forever a cow. There can be a uniting within a *kind* to produce offspring, but union between different *kinds* is not possible.

Science clearly has verified God's irrevocable law of the fixity of *basic kinds* or species of living things. God's divine laws cannot be revoked by man's theories, guesses, assumptions, and speculations. The LORD God created the great family of fish and all the life of every living creature that moves, with which the waters swarmed, each one according to its species, and every winged bird according to its species; and God saw that it was good. God commanded that everything bring forth "after its kind" or its species. Thus, when God created, He established the *law* of the species.

B. The Creation, Formation, and Making of Man

Last, but greatest of all, God created man—man, in God's own image and after His likeness, to rule over the earth and all the creation—a man whom God could instruct in all His wisdom, understanding, and knowledge—a man who could fellowship and praise the wonderful Creator and be God's representative on earth!

> And God said, *Let us make man in our image, after our likeness*: and let them have dominion over the fish of the sea, and over the fowl of the air, and over the cattle, and over all the earth, and over every creeping thing that creepeth upon the earth. So God created man in his own image, in the image of God created he him; male and female created he them. And God blessed them, and God said unto them, Be fruitful, and multiply, and replenish the earth, and subdue it: and have dominion over the fish of the sea, and over the fowl of the air, and over every living thing that moveth upon the earth. And God said, Behold, I have given you every herb bearing seed, which is upon the face of all the earth, and every tree, in the which is the fruit of a tree yielding seed; to you it shall be for meat. And to every beast of the earth, and to every fowl of the air, and to

every thing that creepeth upon the earth, wherein there is life, I
have given every green herb for meat: and it was so. And God saw
every thing that he had made, and, behold, it was very good. And
the evening and the morning were the sixth day (Genesis 1:26-31).

And *the LORD God formed man* of the dust of the ground, and
breathed into his nostrils the breath of life; and man became a
living soul (Genesis 2:7).

This is the book of the generations of Adam. In the day that *God
created man*, in the likeness of God made he him; Male and female
created he them; and blessed them, and called their name Adam,
in the day when they were created (Genesis 5:1,2).

God *created* man with a frame corresponding to the proportionate measure of his
high moral calling. God *fashioned* man's body, urges, forces, and organs according to
his destiny as God's servant. The body of man was created by God to be dedicated
exclusively to the high moral calling of His *Torah*. He *made* (aw-saw), *created* (baw-
raw), and *formed* (yaw-tsar) present-day man in His own likeness and image.

All other living creatures were introduced into God's living world solely by His
creation of each of them in turn, as He progressed upward in His creation. However,
after God had made, created, and formed Adam male and female, He halted all of the
process of His creation because man, made in the image and likeness of God, was the
highest form of all of His creation; He could progress no higher than His own image
and likeness. God's purposive will was for Adam to be the ruler and master over all of
God's earthly creation. The earth and its world of inhabitants were prepared and
waiting for the entrance of Adam male and female, their lord and master.

Adam male and female were to be the human sovereigns over God's creation for
the sole purpose of proclaiming God's divine will for all of His creation. They were to
carry out God's interest for the benefit of the entire present creation. (In the beginning,
God created man in His own likeness and image; He created them male and female and
called *their* name "Adam" [Genesis 5:22]. Both the male and the female shared the
name Adam. After sin entered, fallen Adam male named his fallen wife "Eve" [Genesis
3:20]. Thereafter, the first man and woman became known as Adam and Eve.)

Man was created with a spirit, soul, and body. His spirit and soul originated from
God's breath and Word, and his body had its origin from the dust of the ground.
Therefore, man belongs to the earth with only one-third part of his being. Two-thirds
of man's being (spirit and soul) came from God's own Being. And the other third

(man's body) came from the earth. God's breath and Word and creative acts made man into a special living creature.

Man's name, Adam, reveals his higher nature and his higher calling. The Hebrew word for *Adam* means to be red. Red is the least broken ray of the spectrum, a pure ray of light, which signifies the radiant and perfect health that Adam had in the beginning before he sinned.

Adam was to be the nearest creature on earth to the divine revelation of the Creator. He was to be the transmitter and bearer of God's glory on earth. Adam was to be God's footstool on earth. He was to have the privilege of sparing the supreme, superior Being from having to place His holy feet upon the earth. Even in the natural realm, the subjects of royalty always roll out a "red carpet" for their king or queen; Adam was to be the "red carpet" for the divine King. Through Adam, God desired to fulfill His purposive will of His love, benevolence, and truth for the earth and its world of inhabitants. Adam, through his divine likeness and his image of God, was to rule and reign over God's creation as a supreme lord and master. This was God's intended purpose for Adam. Adam was to rule under God's headship; he was not to usurp God's place of rulership, but he was to be a transmitter of God's will and a kingly instrument to execute God's will on earth. However, when man sinned, he lost his union with his Sovereign LORD and his right and power to rule and reign over God's creation.

The likeness, image, and visible form that God gave Adam encased God's truth, love, compassion, and holiness.

The Hebrew word for *Adam* is connected to a Hebrew word which means *silence*, signifying the truth that Adam was to be silent as far as his having any opposition to God's mind and will. In other words, Adam was in no way to contradict the truth, love, compassion, justice, and holiness of God's nature and purposive will. Man was to be like God in that he was not to tolerate anything within himself which was contradictory to God's truth, righteousness, and holiness. God intended for man to grow in the empirical knowledge of truth, righteousness, and holiness.

God intended that man grow in grace and knowledge of Him and that man rule over all of God's creation by raising and elevating all creation into the sphere of free-willed, God-serving purposes.

Contrary to God's purpose, however, (since man fell into sin), man forcefully exercises his dominion over God's creation by driving it away from every spot on earth that he demands for himself and for his dominion. As a result, sinful man has destroyed and eradicated many of God's created species.

In the beginning, God created man in a form (a spirit, soul, and body) worthy of Himself.

God formed the human body with its organs, urges, and forms to be kept holy and to be dedicated exclusively to the holy calling of His purposive will. God intended that man's spirit cause his soul and mind to soar upward to the moral heights of God's truth which would make man able to govern his body in the ways of righteousness and holiness. God's purposive will did not include man's body being left to indulge in unbridled, unrestrained, animal-like sensuality and moral degeneration.

The higher the spiritual and mental greatness the creation attains, the greater the demand that is placed on the body for control and dedication to God.

God created, made, and formed Adam male and female, equally, and in equal likeness to Himself. It took both the male and female sides of Adam to portray the likeness and image of God. It took the male and female sides to express the complete conception of the "one" Adam.

God blessed them both and commanded them to fulfill His purposive will on earth. Adam male and female were to be fruitful and produce children or human "fruit," just as the plants were to produce plant "fruit" and the animals were to produce animal "fruit." To Adam, God gave the task of seeing that the earth was filled with a world of human beings. God desired that the children be replicas, not only of the bodily traits of their parents, but also of the spiritual, intellectual, and moral integrity of their parents.

The manner in which God created, made, and formed man raised and elevated man to the highest level of all His creation. Man was different and separate from all other creation on one side of the scales, but he was joined as a part of the whole creation on the other side of the scales.

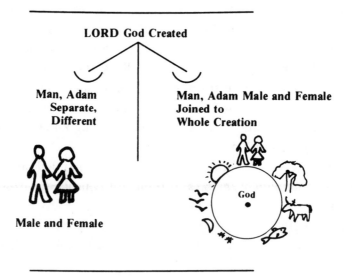

On one side of the scales, man is separated from all creation, inasmuch as he is above all other creation, but on the other side of the scales, he is joined to the whole creation.

When God saw all of the creation fitting together harmoniously and revolving around Him as the Creator, He pronounced it "very good." All creation had to be joined as one whole complete harmony before God esteemed it very good. Therefore, when one thing is separated from the whole, it becomes imperfect.

God restored the earth and turned it into a paradisiacal palace, designed completely as a suitable dwelling for God's representative upon earth, Adam the first. More honour was put on man; therefore, man was obligated to bring more honour and glory to God through his obedience to God's purposive will.

God graciously provided food for all flesh, both man and beast. He made man's body out of the earth, and He made provision for man to be maintained from the things that come out of the earth.

> Who giveth food to all flesh: for his mercy endureth for ever
> (Psalm 136:25).

God's goodness gives food to all living things, sustaining all flesh which He has created.

The creative Works of God's hands are under His inspectoral eyes. When He reviewed His creative Works, He saw they were very good. When God compared His Works to His master plan, He saw that His visible Works were exactly the same as His master plan. God's creative Works were very good because they were fit for His purposive will.

When God's creative Works were joined into one harmonious sharing, they were *very good*. The glory, goodness, beauty, and harmony of God's creative Works made them *very good*.

Thus, God restored the earth and made and formed a whole new world of inhabitants to live upon it so that His creation might praise and serve Him.

VII. The Seventh Day, the Sabbath Day of Rest

God finished all of His creative Works during the six creative days; then He rested on the seventh day.

> Thus the heavens and the earth were finished, and all the host of
> them. And on the seventh day God ended his work which he had

made; *and he rested on the seventh day from all his work which he had made. And God blessed the seventh day, and sanctified it*: because that in it he had rested from all his work which God created and made (Genesis 2:1-3).

The heavens, the earth, and its world of inhabitants are *finished* pieces of God's handiwork. Nothing can be added to or taken away from them. Although God continues preserving, governing, and guiding all His creatures, **He is not making any new kinds in the present time**.

The eternal, supreme God rested from His Work, not because He was weary and worn, but because He was infinitely happy and well pleased with the finished Works of His own hands.

God took divine satisfaction in the visible manifestation of His master plan which was adorned with His eternal goodness and everlasting glory. The heavens and the earth came into existence as a result of God's thought. He is the Originator of all things.

In the beginning, nothing was in existence except the master plan in the mind of the Originator. The cause of the existence of heaven and earth does not lie in either heaven or earth, but in the Originator, the supreme Sovereign God. Heaven and earth cannot be the cause of their own existence. This would be a most contradictory, incogitant, and unimaginable thought!

The heavens and the earth did not come into existence by some force working blindly or by some inorganic speck of matter that decided to expand itself into an infinite amount of diverse forms. Nor did matter set up an infinite amount of complex laws by which it decided to govern its expanded self. The cause of the existence of the heavens and the earth lies external to them and is found in the omniscience and omnipotence of the divine Originator. In his discussion of the First Law of Thermodynamics, Dr. Gange made the following statements: "According to the First Law, no natural process can bring into existence something from nothing . . . Natural processes neither annihilate material things out of existence, nor do they bring into existence observable things out of nothing. . . . Thus, recent scientific discoveries argue for a creation that was supernatural."

God, the divine Originator, brought matter and force into existence, and then He developed, fashioned, and formed it according to His master plan. Finally, He set a limit of development around these forms. God said in essence: "It is finished; it is sufficient." Otherwise, the creation would still be in a continuous state of progressive development today.

God has restrained, limited, and fenced in all creation. There may be changes taking place *within* a kind, but there are no new kinds or formations emerging since

God ended the creation and instituted the Sabbath day of rest. God rested from creating because His Works were finished and complete. Therefore, since He is the only Creator, it is impossible for new creations to be taking place.

If the origin of the heavens and the earth and its worlds of inhabitants were due to physical causes, why has there been a Sabbath, a rest, in creation for thousands of years? Why have physical forces ceased to work, develop, and produce new, great, and mighty things? **If these great creative physical causes existed, then they must still exist! If the great creative physical cause exists today, why is the effect missing?**

Scientists think they can find the answer to this queston by unraveling the secret of the moment of creation. Because man has discovered that God's physical laws are the same throughout His universe, man thinks he can explain, eventually, the moment of creation by the laws of physics. If this were to be so, then God is limited by His own laws and is not supreme at all; or else we are saying that the physical laws we see in operation in the universe are God. But this brings us back to the questions just asked, "Why have these creative forces ceased to work?"

If existing forces of evolution were responsible for the existence of the earth and its inhabitants, who put these existing forces in operation, and who brought these existing forces to an end? The reigning of the Sabbath rest in creation proves that the Sabbath rest in creation was preceded by the thinking of Almighty God, Who placed His Almighty fence, the *El Shadday* fence, around every atom in creation.

The heavens, the earth, and the worlds of inhabitants are not the result of blind forces of nature working out of blind necessity. Rather, **creation is the result of the organized work of Almighty God Who has created out of His purposive will and out of His perfectly arranged master plan.**

The marked fence or limit of Almighty God, *El Shadday*, is stamped upon the whole creation, upon each species, upon the diametrically different forms, and the definitive shapes within the same species.

If we look at the heavens, we see the multitudes of stars that are diametrically different in the time frame of their cycles that are fixed by *El Shadday*. Some stars complete their course in a few days, some in a few years, and some take many centuries.

If we look upon the earth, we see the same principle of the rulership of *El Shadday*. Some seeds grow and produce fruit every year, while other seeds take different periods of years to grow to maturity and become fruitful.

Almighty God, *El Shadday*, has brought all things into existence by His purposive will and His master plan, and He has set His fixed fence upon all His creation. Almighty God has limited sizes, shapes, and the nature of all His creation, according to the purpose that He has chosen for everything. Through His infinite purpose and power, Almighty God has brought all things into existence. Therefore, is it the blind force in an inorganic speck of matter that caused things to come into existence? No! ALL creation was brought into existence by the "all-wise" design and the "all-power" of Almighty God.

All things are important and are a significant part of God's master plan. There is nothing superfluous and insignificant in His master plan. Man is unwise to feel unimportant and insignificant. Each creation is part of God's great, eternal master plan. On the other hand, man has no right to feel arrogant and egotistical, as though he were the "whole" of God's creation.

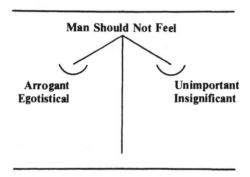

Created man does not exist by his own forceful power, and he does not stand alone as a supreme one by his own governmental authority, whether a man be great or small. Everyone, both small and great, is an important part on God's mighty "wheel" of creation.

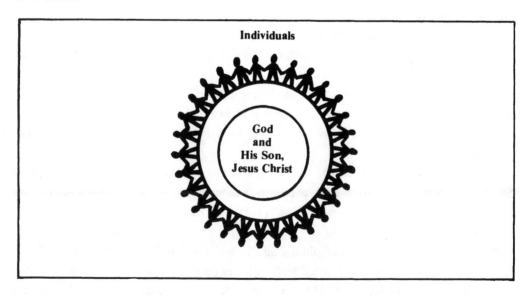

All mankind is a part of God's great circular host, whose center and hub is Almighty God and the Son of God, the Creator, the Owner and the Master.

God has given everything its place, part, and power on His great wheel. Therefore, man has no excuse for not accomplishing the portion of God's purposive will which has been allotted to him.

Remember, the most that each one can accomplish is only a fraction of God's whole master plan. Thus, it behooves all men to remain intelligently humble and modest, not allowing a diseased perception of reality to overtake them and coerce them into believing that they are the *whole* instead of the *fraction* that they really are. God's great inspectoral eye does not overlook the smallest one nor the largest one in His great circular host because each individual is of equal importance to Him.

By placing a fence around all the forces and forms that He had made, God completed His Works on the seventh day, the Sabbath day of rest.

The Hebrew word for *Sabbath* is *shaw-bath*, meaning to desist, to cease, to leave off an activity that has been previously going on until that time. It does not mean complete inactivity. God ceased from the works of the previous six days because no further addition or alteration to them was necessary.

Likewise, God requires that, on the seventh day, man cease what he has been doing the previous six days of the week, laying the work of his six days in complete surrender and homage at God's feet.

The Sabbath day was blessed so that a *new* kind of work could begin on the seventh day. The Sabbath day was blessed with power and fruitfulness to lead mankind and all creation into God's lofty purpose and high calling for them. God ordained the seventh day with holiness and power to accomplish the spiritual education and the moral development of mankind.

In six creative days, God completed His natural Work, but His spiritual Work was just begun on the seventh day. Had man remained faithful and obedient in God's "Sabbath School," he would have been inviolably insured against all confusion, shame, nakedness, and death.

God gave man a free will, and He desired to educate man spiritually through choices made from his own free will so that man might grow up to the full stature of spiritual truth; and then man could practice all goodness and grace out of his own free will.

However, because of his sinful choice, Adam the first (male and female) temporarily hindered God's plan for man's spiritual education. Notwithstanding God has sent His only begotten Son, the LORD Jesus Christ, Who is called the *last Adam* (I Corinthians 15:45), to continue man's spiritual education and moral development under the blessing and holiness of the Sabbath day.

The eternal, infinite God will not cease working in the whole of man's spiritual education until every knee bows in holy Sabbath rest and surrender to Jesus Christ to the glory of God the Father (Philippians 2:10,11).

Thus, after six restorative and creative days of natural Work, God blessed, hallowed, and separated the seventh day for His spiritual, educative Work of mankind.

Summary

In this part of the book, we have given the essential truths from God's Word that explain why the Christian world has been baffled by many facts scientists have discovered in relation to prehistoric man and the age of the earth. Staunch believers in the Bible have often felt that scientific discoveries had to be ignored or labeled as erroneous because they seemed to contradict traditionally held Biblical beliefs. In reality the Word of God does not refute true facts, but the revelation of the truth in God's Word must be sought diligently, humbly, and prayerfully. Then God will give understanding of the truth because His Word, as it is revealed in the Holy Scriptures, *is* true and man can rely on it. God did not give man part truth and part error. If Christians and scientists both trusted the infallibility of God and His Word, they would know that in God are the answers to all things because *all* things were created by Him and for Him.

In a booklet, "The Bible or Evolution," William Jennings Bryan said, "We do not object to truth; there is no truth that can disturb Christianity; I am not afraid that any truth will ever be discovered that will disturb Christianity. Why? Because God stands back of all truth; therefore, whether truth is revealed by God's Word or by nature, no two truths can conflict. . . ."

This brings us to our next section in which we wish to elaborate more fully, with facts from the scientific world, on the Biblical truths which we already have covered. We could fill a book with example after example of truths from God's Word that agree with scientific research. However, we have selected just a few. Some of these truths we have already mentioned and have quoted proof from scientific books and journals, but other sources give even more evidence of the accuracy of the Bible and are, therefore, worth incorporating in this book.

Part Three

Facts From the World of Science That Agree With Truths in the Bible

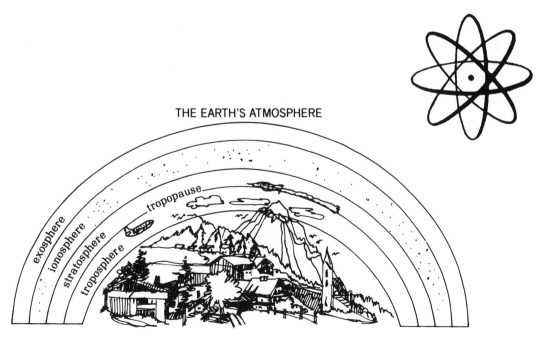

THE EARTH'S ATMOSPHERE

exosphere
ionosphere
stratosphere
troposphere
tropopause

Chapter One

Facts from the World of Science That Prove the Biblical Account of Creation

TRUE scientific facts and the Bible agree. They must. God is the Creator of the facts and the Author of the Book, so God's Works of creation and the Words in His Book are going to bear witness of each other.

When scientists have made discoveries that have appeared to negate the religious world's traditional interpretations of the Scriptures, battles have ensued, names have been called, and opinions have been labeled as heresies. There seems to be total separation between science and the church. Both groups feel there can be no common meeting ground, that each has to remain at opposite ends of the pole, with the scientists slinging accusations such as prejudice, superstitious, bigoted, while the church world says fake, hoax, untrue, anti-God. Each group is so busy trying to prove the other wrong that they never seek God for understanding to see how to fit the facts with the truth. If it has happened and the facts prove it, then the truth in God's Word is not going to deny it.

(Man's archenemy, Lucifer, delights in keeping everyone so stirred up against each other that peace and agreement never can be achieved. We should recognize his tactics by now.)

Uncovering the physical records contained within the earth and discovering the laws governing the creation are means of identifying the truth that the Bible corroborates. In the foregoing sections of this book, we have established from the Bible certain truths: (1) the heavenly lights had a beginning, and they are billions of years old; (2) the earth is billions of years old; (3) plant life appeared before animal life; (4) there is a boundary line over which different species cannot cross; (5) there were prehistoric people and animals; (6) there were sudden catastrophic judgments that changed the earth and destroyed its worlds of inhabitants. This part of the book will furnish proofs from the scientific world which agree with the truths found in God's Word.

I. Scientific Proof That the Heavenly Lights Had a Beginning and That They Are Billions of Years Old

Scientists know that the sun, moon, and stars that illuminate our sky are billions of years old and that they are finite. All creation had a beginning. In his book *A Hundred Billion Stars*,* Mario Rigutti said:

> If you look around, you will not find anything that lasts forever. Even things that embody the idea of permanence and immortality, such as the mountains or the oceans, are neither unchanging nor eternal. Today we know this for a fact. But even the ancients sensed that it had to be so, that nothing could have existed forever and that everything must have had a beginning. . . .

> Let us reason in modern terms and consider the sun. We know that it has been there for a very long time. And we know that it keeps on radiating a huge amount of energy. There is no doubt, therefore, that the sun is consuming itself, day after day, like a burning log. Since it has no other source of energy than itself, it follows that at a certain moment the sun will come to an end. Working backward, it follows that unless it was infinitely large, the sun cannot ever have been what it is today. It must have started somehow. It does not take much imagination or thought to conclude that the same must be true for every other star, our galaxy, and perhaps the universe as a whole. . . .

In *Time Space Infinity*, by Dr. James Trefil, we read that our sun is called a relative newcomer in the universe, since it was born a mere 5 billion years ago.

There is no contradiction between what scientists have discovered and what God has recorded in His Holy Word. The natural lights that shine in our universe are ancient in comparison to the age of our present restored earth because they were created in God's original creation. Obviously, God created even the *original* earth

---

*Rigutti, Mario *A Hundred Billion Stars* (The MIT Press, Cambridge, Massachusetts, 1984).

many billions of years after the universe was in existence. Each time God cast the earth and its sinful world of inhabitants down into a pit of judgment, the earth experienced a time of extended darkness. So great was this darkness that no natural light from the existing sun, moon, and stars was able to penetrate it. Thus, each time God lifted the earth out of a pit and began His Work of restoration, He again had to bring forth these natural lights and rearrange them in the sky above the restored earth. God's sequence of working is always the same. His Word says He is the same yesterday, today, and forever.

Because of the great age of the universe, the question has arisen in the past of whether or not the earth and its heavenly luminaries have existed forever; or did they have a beginning? This is an important question to resolve because the answer means the Bible's opening statement is true or not true. Let us see what the latest scientific information tells us.

According to Dr. Robert Gange, ". . . Some have taught that the world had a beginning; others that it is eternal. But what do the facts teach? Today we have many new facts, and, in the last thirty years, knowledge has increased sixfold. What does the new knowledge teach concerning origins?"*

Dr. Gange went on to make the following statements:

> . . . the older idea of an eternally existing world is now known to have a problem. These measurements of what scientists call the background radiation that fills the universe tell us that *the world is not eternal*, but that it actually had a beginning.

> Today, virtually every scientist working in the fields of cosmology or particle physics is convinced that *the world had a beginning*. And, as a practical matter, this conviction is now shared by scientists in other disciplines. In other words, there has been a growing confidence over the past several decades in the scientific community that the world actually had a beginning.

*Gange, Dr. Robert A. *Origins and Destiny* (Word Book Publisher, Waco, Texas, 1986).

In conclusion, it seems that the trial is over and the verdict is in. *The Bible was correct all the time—the world has not been here forever.* What new trial looms in the future we cannot say. But this much is sure: *Based on today's knowledge and data, 'In the beginning' has become scientific truth—there was a beginning.* (Emphasis by Author)

Another proof Dr. Gange put forth to prove that the universe had a beginning is this fact:

The problem with this idea [the idea that the world is eternal], however, is that as the universe expands, we are seeing the stars destroying themselves and creating energy in the process. If the universe has been expanding forever, these stars would have had 'forever' to destroy themselves. If this were true, then no stars would exist today. Since the stars *do* exist, it means that the present expansion of the universe has not been going on forever.

Dr. Gange noted that "There are also other evidences that our universe had a beginning. For example, the fact that three independent measuring techniques all yield finite ages for the universe is itself proof that it isn't infinitely old."

By using the newest, most modern knowledge and technology available today, even scientists who may not believe in God as the Creator have come to accept the truth that heaven and earth had a beginning.

II. Scientific Proof of the Earth's Age

In about every source one can examine, the age of the earth is estimated to be approximately 5 billion years. In his book, *A Hundred Billion Stars*,* Mario Rigutti made a comparison between the age of the earth and humanity's time on the earth. He said: "The earth was formed approximately 5 billion years ago. The first traces of life date back 3.5 billion years, but human beings appeared only about 3 million years ago.

*Rigutti, Mario, *A Hundred Billion Stars* (Massachusetts Institute of Technology, Cambridge, Massachusetts, 1984).

In mathematical terms, 3×10^6 is to 5×10^9 as 6×10^{-4} is to 1. In other words, humanity's time on earth is only 0.0006 of the earth's life, which is like 50 sec in a day."

Science reckons geological time in a megayear (1 million years) and in gigayears (1 billion years). Geologists estimate that the age of the earth is about 5 gigayears. The oldest known mineral has been dated at 4-5 gigayears. It probably came from the mantle of the earth deep down below the crust. It was found on St. Paul Island in the South Atlantic. Primative plants have been found that are more than 3 gigayears old.

An article by Gonzalo Vidal in the February, 1984, issue of the *Scientific American* magazine gave nearly the same estimated age of the earth since this information is generally accepted by modern scientists as being true. Mr. Vidal said: "According to the modern interpretation of the fossil record, the first traces of life appeared on the earth about 3.5 billion years ago, within a billion years or so of the planet's formation."

The discoveries made by scientists affirm the preexistence of the earth before its present restoration. There is no conflict, then, in man's discoveries that show the earth's antiquity and what the Bible teaches about the creation of the original earth and its three restorations. The fact that the Bible records *present* mankind's existence upon this *present restored* earth at approximately 6,000 years does not deny the fact that the earth upon which he lives was originally created billions of years ago.

III. Scientific Proof That Simple Plant Life Appeared First

On the third day God began His creation of life by creating the simple plant life that was to be used for the maintenance and support of the higher forms of life that were to come later in His creation.

> And God said, Let the earth bring forth grass, the herb yielding seed, and the fruit tree yielding fruit after his kind, whose seed is in itself, upon the earth: and it was so. And the earth brought forth grass, and herb yielding seed after his kind, and the tree yielding fruit, whose seed was in itself, after his kind: and God saw that it was good (Genesis 1:11,12).

God made perpetual provision for the higher realms of life by first creating the lower realms of life. God has provided numerous, various, and curious herbs and plants, each having its seed in itself, so that animals and man might have food for their use and benefit.

God began His creation with the lowest forms of life, then proceeded to the highest form in His creation—man—who was crowned with the dignity and honour of being created in God's own likeness and image.

Starting with the simple and progressing to the most complex is one of God's infinite, divine principles, both in the natural and in the spiritual realms. He begins in the lowest place of humility and works to the highest place. The wise scribe confirms this truth in the Book of Proverbs.

> The fear of the LORD is the instruction of wisdom; and before honour is humility (Proverbs 15:33).

God's immutable law is that before honour is humility. Thus, humility, the lowest place, is the foundation upon which all high things rest, whether they be things in the natural realm or things in the spiritual realm.

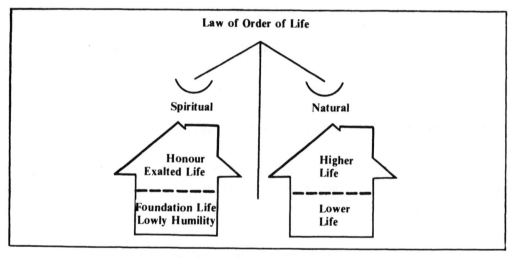

God practiced His divine law of humility in His creation by first creating and establishing the lowest forms of life before He created and set in place His higher forms of life.

This divine order of creation is confirmed by scientists of our day. In his book *Space Time Infinity*, Dr. Trefil's description of how the earth's present atmosphere was formed shows that God used this principle in His creation of life on this planet.

> . . . it is sufficient to realize that when the Earth was about a billion years old the new ingredient [life] was present. We postulate at that time the existence of primitive single-celled

systems which we would one day grace with the title "living." Although we are not sure how they came to be, we know of their spread because of fossils in the Australian rocks.

For billions of years, these cells and their descendants, the primitive blue-green algae, floated in the world's oceans. They took in carbon dioxide and put out oxygen as a waste product. About two and a half billion years ago, this particular pollutant had reached such a high level that a massive turnover occurred in the atmosphere. The oxygen produced by the plants reacted chemically with the methane and ammonia in the atmosphere. This process resulted in an atmosphere made up almost completely of nitrogen (derived from the ammonia) with a small mixture of oxygen. The increase in the oxygen content to its present 20 percent may have taken place about 600 million years ago.

Scientific facts agree—God created the lower forms of life first. After the simple oceanic plants, came vegetation on the land, grass, herbs, land plants, and trees. Then God created the higher forms of life—fish, birds, whales, land animals—and finally Adam, the first man, who was the highest form of life in all God's creation.

Thus, all forms of life were created by God's Sovereign, supernatural power, according to His divine master plan.

V. Scientific Proof That "Kinds" Are Bound by Uncrossable Lines

In the very beginning of His Work of creation, God established the boundary line that separates one kind of seed from another kind of seed and one kind of animal from another kind of animal. Now, at last, scientists have come forth with valid proof of the existence of this very real boundary line. This proof was not available until the 1960's, when living cells could be studied under an electron microscope.*

Scientists call their discovery DNA, which is an abbreviated name for deoxyribonucleic acid. DNA is a living microscopic computer with an intelligent built-in memory. It stores a vast number of blueprint codes or plans, and at the proper time

*Gange, Robert A. *Origins and Destiny* (Word Books, Waco, Texas, 1986).

183

and place, DNA gives the commands to build all the cells and structures of every form of both animals and plants. It contains the intelligence that changes chemicals into living cells.

DNA is like a tape recording that preserves all forms of life within their basic kind; it is the substance of which genes are made.

God has created man with tens of thousands of genes, with each containing a thousand or more units, making a marvelous potential of variety within a kind. This explains why, even within a family, one will not find two people who look exactly alike. In spite of this variety among the billions of persons in the world today, they all remain within the basic human kind.

DNA is the *established law* of Almighty God, El Shadday, Who said "Let every living thing bring forth after its own kind." The mechanism of DNA is so exact and explicit that it permits no alterations within, *unless they are imposed from without* by accidents, radiation, or man's interference, for instance. The fantastic DNA keeps the boundary lines or fence that El Shadday established for living organisms in the beginning.

Scientists have made discoveries about DNA that reveal amazing facts about heredity. These discoveries help to establish the fact that, from a scientific point of view, neither mutations nor natural selection could result in fashioning and forming a different species of life from a previous species of life. However, evolutionists continue to hold to their theories in spite of acknowledging that they cannot explain exactly how evolution works.

Their determination to avoid recognizing the Sovereign Creator is unbounded, and causes them to make rather ridiculous statements. One has to try awfully hard to accept the line of reasoning that Dr. John Gribbin promotes in his book *Genesis* when he writes about "the Origin of Species." He credits—". . . the development of life from single-celled organisms to the variety of the present day, including human animals with many billions of living cells cooperating to produce one distinct living organism, endowed with mobility, a perception of the surrounding world, and, not least, a self-awareness which leads directly to the question 'where do we come from?'"—to the ". . . natural processes of selection operating among replicators" [cells capable of reproducing themselves], He said:

> . . . Over 3,000 million years, natural selection has led to the
> diversification of species and to the production of
> multicellular organisms; but the 'old' biological systems are
> not replaced when they continue to reproduce effectively in

their own ecological niches, and alongside the 'modern' multicellular organisms we can still find types of single-celled species descended almost unchanged from the first colonists of the Earth 3 thousand million years ago.

This indicates the dichotomy of the 'struggle for survival': nothing *wants* to evolve, and the basic life process is that of replication, as accurately as possible, of existing molecules. The success of replication at this level is shown by the 'living fossil' single-celled species that remain unchanged since the beginning of the story of life on Earth. *Changes only happen by mistake, and very few of the copying mistakes are beneficial.* Most imperfect copies of replicators do not survive, but end up as chemical 'food' for successful replicators. . . .But the process happens willy-nilly, and in the replicating game the single-celled varieties that have been unchanged for thousands of millions of years could, from one point of view be regarded as more 'successful' than the collection of *bizarre mistakes that has produced you and me.**

Later in the same chapter, Dr. Gribbon added these two statements:

. . . Once complex creatures with long chromosomal DNA molecules appeared on Earth, copying mistakes—evolution—became more likely, and this is precisely what we find in the fossil record of life on Earth, although there are many hiccups in the evolutionary path that have not been fully explained.

. . . We don't know how the first replicators evolved, or how they came to 'invent' cells. But we know that cellular living organisms existed on Earth more than 3,000 million years ago, . . .

*Emphasis by Author

We can conclude from Dr. Gribbon's statement that evoution is a mistake and that mankind is the result of mistakes. How strange that such divine order in nature could be the result of "mistakes."

Some scientists claim to have discovered a crossing over or a sharing of DNA information between different species. But in his book, *Origins and Destiny*, Dr. Robert Gange explained where the proponents of molecular phylogeny have failed to rightly interpret their findings.

> . . . Moreover, the vastly higher information content along human DNA attests to a labor of *intellect rather than primeval confusion.*

> Some have argued that the evolution through natural processes of one species from another have been proven by data from a field of science know as "molecular phylogeny," the study of the chemical history of the amino acid sequences. This false belief about molecular phylogeny comes from the failure to distinguish between the amino acid *count* along protein strands, and the information *content* resident within the actual sequence of the residues.

> When one considers that a typical human cell contains almost seven feet of DNA, and that its information continues to be resolvable down to distances of well under ten-millionths of an inch, one can well understand the confusion that exists regarding alleged similarities between the protein of humans and apes. For example, just to assimilate the content of this amount of information for study requires a computer whose storage capacity exceeds 10 billion bits. And were we to attempt to examine the short- and long-range interactions in and among the triplet centers throughout each of the twenty thousand DNA folds, it would require a computational capability that exceeds all of the computers that exist on earth now or that we can hope to produce in the foreseeable future.*

* Emphasis by Author

Dr. John Gribbin described the DNA molecule in this way:

Each single strand of the life molecule DNA can be thought of as a backbone to which the side branches A,G,C, and T are attached. The full double-stranded DNA molecule is most probably a double helix, with the opposite side branches joined up to make the 'rings' of a 'spiral staircase'. If we imagine the spiral untwisted to make a simple ladder, it is easier to see how the opposite sides join up. A can pair only with T, and G can pair only with C. When this happens, although each of the four branches is a different size, each of the two possible rungs (AT or GC) is the same size, and all of the bits of the ladder fit together.

In order to control the workings of the cell (and the body), a section of DNA separates and untwists. The broken rungs of the ladder then act as a template on which a strand of messenger RNA is built. This exactly mimics the mirror image of the DNA strand, except that a base U replaces the base T. The messenger RNA then acts as the basis for construction of amino acids, while the DNA zips itself back up.

A group of three 'letters' in the DNA alphabet is called a condon, and specifies the construction of one particular amino acid.

. . . The DNA is arranged in chromosomes (forty-six in man, . . .), and chromosomes are made up of subunits called genes. Genes are made of DNA and carry specific messages in the four-letter A,T, C, G alphabet of DNA. Every cell in the human body carries the DNA plans which describe the building, care, and maintenance of that whole human body, although we do not yet know just how the control of production and release of certain proteins makes the difference between a single cell developing into a human being, a mouse, or a potato.

The forty-six chromosomes in man are made up of twenty-three chromosomes from each parent.

According to Dr. Gribbin, ". . . the four compounds which make up the four-letter DNA alphabet (A,T, C, G) only form bonds in two ways: A always with T, and C always with G. So if the double helix is unzipped, one broken bond may leave A at a particular site on one molecule and T at the corresponding site on the other. The A will only recombine with another T, and the T only with another A, so that the two single strands, each opposite halves of a whole, rebuild themselves as two new DNA molecules, each identical to the whole original. . . . in . . . DNA . . . hundreds of thousands of coils, containing millions of nucleotids, have to be untwisted, unzipped, paired up, and put back together again."

Does not a spiral staircase reveal a master plan of a master Architect? Does not the magnetic recording tape show a divine design of an omniscient Designer? The DNA of the *nephesh* soul is endowed with creating power to produce its *own kind*! Mutation and natural selection cannot produce this miraculous feat!

After relating scientific evidence to support his statement, Dr. Gange, in his book *Origins and Destiny*, said: ". . . one thing is sure: Scientific data do not support the thesis that life arose by chance. The calculations could have come out differently, but they didn't, so the likelihood of life having occurred through a chemical accident is, for all intents and purposes, zero," He stated: "Despite all that one hears and reads, no one has ever produced life from nonlife. . . . No one anywhere has ever created life from chemicals."

The astonishing intelligence that God has placed within the DNA, with its complex blueprints for all future development, is a miraculous, divine piece of organization in the *nephesh* soul.

When one beholds the modern skyscrapers, the complex freeways, or the amazingly complicated computers, one immediately knows that a wise designer developed blueprints for all these things. Why, then, is man so slow to give God the honour as the rightful, intelligent Designer of the far more complex and complicated blueprints of the DNA, which are implemented through the *nephesh* soul working in the body? Although, in all living things, the amazing DNA molecules are composed of the same basic elements, they produce diametrically different living creatures, according to their God-given blueprints. The potential for variation in the DNA is tremendous.

The sameness of the DNA molecules in all creatures is not sufficient reason to *assume* that they evolved one from another. For example, houses can be made of the same substances (brick or wood), but they can be entirely different, depending on the blueprint of the wise builder. Likewise, God has used the same building blocks in all creation. Nevertheless, He has ordained a different blueprint in the DNA for each kind, according to His purposive will.

God's special blueprint for each creature, according to His purposive will, makes a gulf between each *kind* of creature, and particularly between human and animal societies.

Recent discovery of how to generate a picture of the DNA by way of the computer is added confirmation that God's natural creation types His spiritual creation.

Terence Mommaney, in the *Smithsonian* of July, 1985, reported on Robert Langridge's computer graphic works. He said:

> . . . A seasoned guide, Langridge was among the first to explore DNA's structure, and he's a pioneer in the field of computer graphics, which opens up the strange territory of molecules for others to explore.
>
> Smiling mischievously, Langridge, the director of the Computer Graphic Laboratory at the University of California, San Francisco, says that this computer-generated picture of DNA also conjures up the inside of someplace else. "When I first saw the DNA end view, it reminded me of a rose window." The dots of blue, red, green, and yellow do look like tiny chinks of stained glass. And viewed from the end, the colored dots and lines do take the shape of a rose window, *a kind of high-tech daisy with ten petals.* Yet rose windows generally have eight or 12 or 16 panels — rarely ten, like DNA. *But Langridge found such a window at the National Cathedral in Washington, D.C. "The window has exactly the tenfold symmetry of DNA,* which is the genetic material of all living things,. . ."

In the natural realm, the DNA is God's tenfold symmetry for all genetic material in all living things. In the spiritual realm, God's tenfold symmetry for all spiritual genetic material is His Ten Commandments.

God intended for man's soul and spirit to be structured by the perfect symmetry of the holiness of His tenfold Commandments, God's purposive will is for man's soul and spirit to be illuminated and his life to be ordered by the tenfold symmetry of His Commandments.

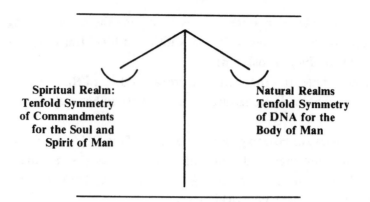

Spiritual Realm:
Tenfold Symmetry
of Commandments
for the Soul and
Spirit of Man

Natural Realms
Tenfold Symmetry
of DNA for the
Body of Man

The tenfold symmetry of God's Word controls the structure and character of the soul and spirit. Likewise, the tenfold symmetry of the DNA controls the physical structure, character, and nature of the body.

True scientific facts verify the Biblical truth that Almighty God has put a fence around every species.

In the beginning, when God told everything to bring forth after its own kind or species, He assigned boundary lines to each species. God allows each species to develop with the greatest freedom within His boundary lines.

The Hebrew word for *kind* is *meen*, meaning to portion-out, a part, form, shape, offspring, according to kind, image, likeness, and similitude. *Meen* (kind) signifies the complex characteristics and law by which one species keeps itself separate from other species in such a manner that, when it is left to itself, will not unite with another species. *Meen* (kind) signifies the form of the species which presents the essential characteristics that are common to all of the different members of that species; it indicates the principal outline for any kind of species. *Meen* (kind) is God's law that visibly governs and guides the whole world of organic life.

This does not mean that man cannot chose, if he so desires, to break God's law and cross the boundary lines. Obviously, if the crossing of the boundary line of a species were impossible, God would never have given a law to govern the boundary line. God's laws of nature rule over organic species, closing them up to another species so that one species does not desire to unite with another species. Each species, when left to itself, keeps its reproductive powers for its own species.

Apart from man's intervention, every organic germ of life remains basically and exclusively within its own species. The capricousness of man forces species to be unnatural.

The law of separation of the species always has been highly important to God. In the Book of Leviticus, God forbade mixtures in the breeding of animals, mixtures of seeds used in agriculture, and mixtures of substances used to make clothing. The distinct wording in the Hebrew reveals clearly that God was not giving a new law at that time, but was reminding them of a law that had been in existence for a long time.

God has forbidden man to interfere with the laws of nature by the unnatural mixing of species of plants and animals. God forbade His people to sow and plant their field with a mixture of different kinds of seeds. He also forbade them to wear a garment that was made of linen and wool, a mixture of substances from the plant world and the animal world.

> Ye shall keep my statutes. *Thou shalt not let thy cattle gender with a diverse kind: thou shalt not sow thy field with mingled seed: neither shall a garment mingled of linen and woollen come upon thee* (Leviticus 19:19).

All of the countless diverse species have been assigned a separate purpose and a separate form in which to obey God's particular purpose. Therefore, when an unnatural mixture is forced, it destroys both the God-given separate purpose and the God-given form in which to fulfill its purpose.

God's law of separation of the species in nature was for the pure continuation of each species. Hence, the continued existence of a species depends on their keeping the purity of the species. Every forced, unnatural reproduction is digging a grave for the species. The weighty seriousness of forced, unnatural reproduction is apparent in the frequency of the sterility of hybrid seeds and animals. For example, when a mare is interbred with an ass, the offspring is a sterile mule, although there have been some rare exceptions recorded.

The ability to cross over the boundary lines of the species, by the outside force of man or some infrequent mishap in nature, is not evidence of evolution. This is simply the breaking of God's laws of nature, or an accident which is most often detrimental to the organism.

The word *genus* is a catagory of organisms containing several species; genus is a more extensive classification than species; it denotes a universal trait which is predictable of several different species. Genus is an assembly of species or a sub-genera closely agreeing together in all essential characteristics not found in any other of the sub-family or family to which they belong.

For example, there is a genus called *Mus* containing, among other animals, both the domestic mouse and the rat, which differ in size, and which make up clearly distinct species within the genus. Likewise, the various species of the rose constitute the genus Rosa; the horse and the zebra are both of the genus *Equus*.

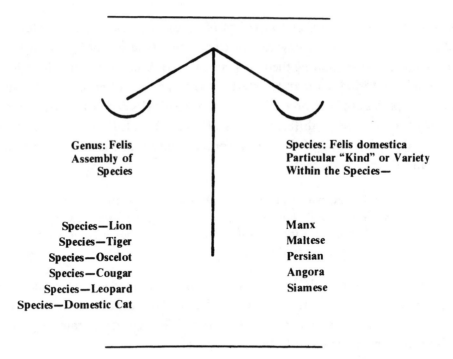

Genus: Felis
Assembly of
Species

Species: Felis domestica
Particular "Kind" or Variety
Within the Species—

Species—Lion
Species—Tiger
Species—Oscelot
Species—Cougar
Species—Leopard
Species—Domestic Cat

Manx
Maltese
Persian
Angora
Siamese

In his book, *The Collapse of Evolution*, Scott M. Huse said:

> The Biblical statement, *after its kind* not only is verified by
> the paleontological record but also is confirmed by modern
> scientific observation and experimentation. Practical
> breeders and geneticists have experimentally verified the
> great stability of kinds.
>
> Boundaries between kinds are very real and stubborn
> biological facts. When abnormal crosses are attempted,
> sterility is always the result.

Mr. Huse gives Gish's definition of the Biblical term *kind* as "A generally
interfertile group of organisms that possess variant genes for a common set of traits
but that does not interbreed with other groups of organisms under normal
circumstances.

Instead of being supports for the theory of evolution, hybrids are, in fact, proofs
of God's divine law in Genesis for everything to bring forth after its own kind.

Hybrids have their origin in a union of living things already closely related and of the same kind. Hybrid corn, for example, still *remains corn*. It does not evolve into some other kind or species of plant. There are all types of variations within a basic kind. However, man's efforts to change a basic kind to some other species always will prove futile because Almighty God already has placed a fence around every species.

This God-given boundary line to every kind ultimately can never be crossed. This divine law of separation always has preserved the basic species.

Living organisms have the power to adapt to different circumstances and to different environments, but this does not mean they have changed their species. The DNA within each organism specifically limits the extent to which a species can change. Scientists know that horizontal variation is possible. For instance, there are different breeds of cats, horses, and different species of flowers, but vertical transformation is not possible. Cats do not change into dogs. Forced interbreeding between species oversteps the boundaries God instituted when He placed the blueprints for each creation in its DNA; and it results in sterile offspring.

Yes, God's boundary lines are phenomena. Interbreeding by man must be continued in order to prevent deterioration of the breeds. If man is ever able to cross the boundary lines of God, you can imagine what a "zoorific" world we will have! As man probes into the mysteries of DNA, he may someday artifically produce weird animals, but whether he does, and what the outcome will be is still in the future. We do know that merely crossbreeding animals does not produce new species, only varieties within the species. Whatever man does by interfering with God's plans still will not prove evolution—it will only prove his foolishness in trying to implement his own plans in place of his Creator's plans.

V. Scientific Proof of Prehistoric Man's Existence

Scientists have found evidence of prehistoric man's existence, which agrees with the Biblical record of previous inhabitants on the earth. Scientists' mistake, however, is in *assuming* that these men were evolutionary predecessors of present-day man. Man's findings of prehistoric bones do not discredit God's Word; they simply confirm the truth that present man is a member of the fourth created world of inhabitants on the earth.

All the scientific facts relating to the discoveries of prehistoric man are incomplete and always will be incomplete because so much needed evidence has been destroyed permanently in past aeons. Nevertheless, sufficient evidence has been found to confirm the existence of prehistoric man.

Such discoveries have shaken both the world of science and the religious world. Uncovering the facts of God's creation should not shake one's belief in God's Word or in God as the Creator. The lack lies in man's understanding of either the scientific facts or of God's Word. In no way is the infallibility of God and His Word ever at stake. God alone is omniscient; man is finite and what man knows about God and His creation, though great on one hand, is minuscule on the other hand.

No one knows better than the scientist how limited his knowledge is. Dr. Trefil devotes several pages of his book to "unsolved problems," and throughout his text he mentions problems that face the scientist. Many times researchers must say, "We simply do not know—we do not know the moment of creation—we do not know what exists at the hub of our Galaxy or on its fringes—we do not know how to make a living cell—we do not know what ignited the fires in the suns."*

Yet man has learned an exceedingly great amount in the last five or six centuries. Man, in just about every field of scientific study, has made tremendous strides in learning about man and the universe in which he lives.

As man searches, he uncovers more and more evidence that confirms the Bible's record.

In the *Smithsonian* of August, 1984, John Pfeiffer affirmed the existence of prehistoric man. He said:

> A decade or so ago workers in a quarry near Rabat, Morocco, noticed a bone imbedded in a limestone block. It was the skull of an adult, perhaps 40 years of age, and originally classified as a "progressive" specimen because of its rounded modern appearance in the back portion. According to Jean-Jacques Hublin of the University of Paris, however, this feature and others point not to an advanced evolutionary status, but to pathology dating back an estimated 400,000 years.

Another article, "The Search for Our Ancestors," printed in the November, 1985, issue of the *National Geographic* magazine, was written by Kenneth F. Weaver who reported several recent findings which confirm the existence of prehistoric men:

---

*Trefil, James S., *Space Time Infinity* (Smithsonian Institution, Washington, D.C., 1985).

Suddenly a primate that stands, walks, and runs on two legs is discovered in a three-million-year-old stratum—with a skeleton so strikingly like our own that it is classified in our unique bipedal primate family, the Hominidae. Identified as an adult female of about 25 years and nicknamed Lucy, the partial skeleton was found by Dr. Donald C. Johanson and an international team at Hadar, Ethiopia, in 1974. Lucy, along with subsequent finds of bits of more than 60 other individuals there and at Laetoli, Tanzania, led to the naming of a new species: Australpithecus afarensis.

Lucy and her kind adapted to the dry open uplands of Laetoli and the wooded lakeshores of Hadar and survived for about one million years before disappearing from the fossil record.

Lucy created intense excitement on several counts. She was the most complete and—except for a few questionable fragments found elsewhere—the oldest hominid known up to that time, dated by the radio-metric potassium-argon method at about three million years ago.

Other bipedal hominid fossils date back to four million years, the article points out.

This article by Mr. Weaver is very lengthy, so we are quoting a very scant portion, but one thing stood out in the report—that scientists are not exactly sure about what the evidence they have uncovered tells them. Mr. Weaver quoted F. Clark Howell of the University of California at Berkeley as having said, "'Most of what researchers know about early hominids has been learned in the past 25 years.'"

Footprints of prehistoric men were found in 1978, buried under layers of volcanic ash where they had been preserved as a record. Mr. Weaver said:

Fossil bones found in the same ash layers as the footprints show resemblances to the Australopithecus afarensis hominids of Hadar, in Ethiopia. But the Laetoli individuals have been dated at about 3.7 million years, more than half a million years older than Lucy. Are they the same species?

This question provokes one of the most spirited controversies in paleonanthropology today.

In reference to all the ideas projected about classifying fossil discoveries, the author pointed out, "Perhaps all these ideas will be superseded because of future discoveries. Fossils, after all, do not come with labels. Many a proposed classification has later been dropped."

The picture that early discoveries seemed to paint is now revised by today's scientists. For instance, the fossil bones which have given rise to the term "Neanderthal man" are given a different image today from the one originally portrayed. Mr. Weaver's article stated:

> Marcellin Boule, an authority on fossils, undertook to reconstruct the skeleton [of the Neadertal man]. He created the image of a hulking, dim-witted brute, who shuffled with the bent-knee gait of an ape.

> Today, with specimens from more than a hundred sites, we know that Boule was wrong. The neandertals were not so different from us, although decidedly more robust. Thick, heavy bones with markings of powerful muscles reveal a people capable of enormous exertion and endurance.

Scientists say that the Neanderthals just disappeared, as did indeed all other prehistoric men.

In 1984 an entire Homo erectus skeleton 1.6 million years old was discovered in Kenya on the shore of Lake Turkana.

Another article in the same issue of *National Geographic*, this one by Richard Leakey and Alan Walker, described the finding of the Turkana boy. The authors made this statement: "This spectacular find dramatically confirms the antiquity of the human form."

Once more, we see that the scientific discoveries that push the existence of man back to prehistoric days are just confirmations of the truthful record of God's Word. And again we see the perfect harmony that exists in God's Works of creation and His Words in the Holy Bible. After God created the original earth, He created a world of inhabitants with the type of body they needed to live upon the original earth. Then each time He lifted the earth out of one of the pits of judgment, God created a new world of inhabitants, with the inhabitants of each world having the type of body needed for their particular earth.

VI. Scientific Proof of Catastrophic Events That Have Occurred on the Earth

God's Word and the discoveries of scientific researchers corroborate that catastrophes, which at a given time have obliterated up to 90 percent of the world's inhabitants, have occurred periodically on the earth. These catastrophes not only have affected the life on the earth, they also have changed the earth's crust.

Richard A. Muller in an article in *Reader's Digest*, September, 1985, (which was condensed from the *New York Times* magazine [March 24, 1985]) said:

> At various times in the past, whole life forms have simply disappeared from the earth. One of the largest of these mass extinctions occurred 65 million years ago, when a huge assortment of plants and animals — including the dinosaurs — abruptly vanished. What caused the catastrophe?

The preceding excerpt is from only one article of many which says the same thing. In the June, 1984, issue of the *Scientific American* magazine, an article, "Mass Extinctions In the Ocean," written by Steven M. Stanley, said:

> At various times, however, there have been sharp peaks in the number of vanishing species. Such mass extinctions have affected terrestrial as well as marine organisms, but the fossil record documenting their occurrences is more abundant in the marine realm. During geologically brief intervals of several million years some of these events have eliminated most of the species in the ocean and as many as half of the families. Devastation of this magnitude could have been inflicted only by radical changes in the environment, on a regional or even global scale. . . .

Along with mass extinctions of plant and animal life, there also have been vast changes in the earth's crust. Many scientists in the past have contended that the earth's crust has remained basically unchanged since the appearance of living things upon it.

But the earth's crust *has not remained unchanged*. Gigantic catastrophes have buried fossils deep under rocks and soil which are far more ancient than the fossils they cover.

Although modern scientists do not always recognize divine judgment as a source of the upheaval and change in the earth's crust, they do recognize and admit to cataclysmic change in the earth's geology. Dr. John Gribbin, of Cambridge University, described the results of past catastrophic events in his book *Genesis*:

> . . . To some extent, the oldest rocks of the crust today ought to be the ones which lie deepest beneath our feet, buried by successive layers of younger rocks. But the crustal material has been bent, broken, and distorted by the forces involved in tectonic activity, with whole mountain ranges being thrown up in some places at some times, while elsewhere and at other times crustal material is ripped apart by tectonic forces, this is hardly a reliable guide. Instead, the main guideline for establishing the order in which rock layers formed and the boundaries between different periods of geologic time (eras, periods, and epochs) depends upon the fossil remains of once-living creatures that the rock layers contain.

A few pages later, Dr. Gribbin referred to the "distortion" that ". . . appears for more recent divisions of geological time, since we know most about more recent times, for which the geological strata are easy to identify and still plentiful, whereas older strata have been broken up by erosion and *other processes*,* and revoked into new formations."

One of the foremost scientists of his day, the father of comparative anatomy and an important contributor to the studies of paleontology and geology, Georges Cuvier, who lived from 1769-1832, wrote an essay entitled, "Theory of the Earth." To this work, Professor Jameson added mineralogical notes and an account of Cuvier's geological studies. Although this work was published as a book in the year 1817, Cuvier's discoveries and theories have not been proven wrong by scientists today, although many scientists have disagreed and do disagree with many of Cuvier's

*Emphasis by author.

conclusions. Still, Cuvier's theories about the earth were the widely accepted ones until Darwinism took the forefront in the present century.

Cuvier did err in that he maintained, from his belief in the currently held views of the church, that no man had been present in the earth long enough for his skeleton to have fossilized. In spite of his errors and the error of the scientific world in discarding many of his views, Cuvier did find evidence of global catastrophes. Because his findings were so extensive in the fields of paleontology and geology, we feel that the evidence he found should be presented in this book. Therefore, the following excerpts from his essay are repeated because they offer proof of the Bible's accuracy in relating the catastrophes that have happened to the earth.

As the following quotes are read, one will note that M. Cuvier's findings cannot relate to Noah's flood since marine life was not destroyed at that time. The presence of rocks without petrifactions, which he lists in his description of the earth's four strata, proves the original formation of the earth before God's first catastrophic cataclysmic judgment. The kinds of life that are found in the different strata, which are distinct from each other, prove the restorations of the earth and the three catastrophic cataclysmic judgments that have occurred to the earth and its different worlds of inhabitants.

The following is a reprint of the earth's four strata as outlined by Cuvier:

First System of Strata

The lowest series of strata, or first system of strata, of the coarse limestone formation, is very sandy, and sometimes contains a substance resembling green earth; it is still better characterised by containing a great variety of well preserved shells, many of which still retain the pearly lustre, and differ more from the present existing species, than those in the upper strata of this formation. It is particularly characterised by the nummulites it contains.

The following are the petrifactions enumerated by Cuvier and Brongniart, as occurring in it.

Nummulities laevigata	These always are
scaba	found in the lowest
numismalis	part of the bed.

Madreopora	At least three species
Astraea	Three species at least
Carophyllia	Three simple, and one branched species

Fungites
Cerithum giganteum
Lucina lamellosa
Cardium porulosum
Voluta cithara
Crassatella lamellosa
Turritella multisulcata
Ostrea flabellula
    cymbula

Second System of Strata

The limestone of these strata is of a greyish yellow colour, is in part oolitic, or composed of small roundish grains, and contains remarkable cotemporaneous cavities, that traverse the strata, and which are filled with loam, sand, and flint. It is still very rich in shells; nearly all the bivalves found by M. Defrance at Grignon belong to it. It also contains a few impressions of leaves and stems of vegetables, and *single fresh-water shells*. The most charactistic petrifactions of this system of strata are the following.

- Cardita avicularia
- Orbiotolites plana
- Turritella imbricata
- Terebellum convolutum
- Calyptraea trochiformis
- Pectunculus pulvinatus
- Citheraea nitidula
    elegans
- Miliolites—It is very abundant
- Cerithium—Probably several species; but neither the lapidam and petrocolum, nor cinctum and plicatum, which latter belong to the second marine formation which covers the gypsom.

Of these petrifactions, the most characteristic is the certies.

Third System of Strata

The third system of strata is already less abundant in petrifactions, and contains fewer species than the two preceding. The following have been observed:

Miliolites—Very rare
Cardium Lima, et obliquum
Lucina saxorum
Ampullaria spirata
Cerithium tuberculatum— Almost all the
    mutabile   other species
    lapidum   with the
    petricolum   exception of
                         the giganteum.

Corbula anatina?
    striata

Also impressions of the leaves of a fucus.

The strata of the second and third systems sometimes contain beds of sandstone, or masses of hornstone filled with marine shells. In some cases the sandstone takes the place of the limestone. Land shells and fresh-water shells (Limnaa et Cyclostoma) have also been observed in this sandstone. The sandstone and the hornstone, containing marine shells, rest either immediately on the marine limestone, or are contained in it. The following list contains the names of those species of petrifactions which occur most frequently in the sandstone.

Calyptraea trochiformis?
Oliva laumontiana
Ancilla canalifera
Voluta Harpula
Fusis bulbiformis
Cerithum serratum
                    tuberculosum
                    coronatum
                    lapidum, mutabile

Ampullaria acuta, or spirati

                  patula

Nucula deltoidea

Cardium lima

Venericardia imbrieata

Cytherea nitidula

                  elegans

                  telliaarin

Venus callosa?

Lucina circinaria

                  saxorum

Two species of oyster still undetermined; the one appears allied to ostrea deltoidea, the other to ostrea cymbula.

Fourth System of Strata

This set of strata consists of hard calcareous marl, soft calcarious marl, clayey marl, and calcareous sand, which is sometimes agglutinated, and contains horizontal layers of hornstone, crystals of quartz, and rhomboidal crystals of calcareous spar, and small cubical crystals of fluor spar. Petrifactions occur very rarely.

Fourth Formation

Siliceous Limestone Without Shells

This formation occurs alongside the coarse marine limestone, on the same level with it, and in no instance either above or below it. It rests immediately on the plastic clay. It consists of strata, not only of a white limestone, but also of a grey, compact, or fine granular limestone, which is penetrated in all directions with silica; and its numerous cavities are lined with siliccous stalactites, or quartz crystals. It is destitute of petrifactions. A species of millstone sometimes occurs in it, which appears to be the siliceous limestone deprived of its calcareous ingredient by some agent unknown to us. This rock is scarcely entitled to the rank of a distinct formation: it appears to be one of the members of the preceding series without petrifactions. It may be remarked that it is not uncommon to observe in the same formation beds with and without petrifactions.

Fifth and Sixth Formations

Fresh Water and Marine Origin
Gypsum Formation,
and the
Marine Marl Formation

This formation is not entirely of gypsum, but contains also beds of clay marl and calcareous marl. These are arranged in a determinate order when they all occur together, which, however, is not always the case. They lie over the coarse marine limestone; and the gypsum, which is the principal mass of the formation, does not occur in wide extended plateaus, like the limestone, but in a single conical or longish masses, which are sometimes of considerable extent, but always sharply bonded. Montmartre presents the best example of the whole members of the formation, and there three beds of gypsum are to be observed superimposed on each other.

M. Cuvier also made the following observations about the various strata and the fossils they contain:

If we institute a more detailed comparison between the various strata and those remains of animals which they contain, we shall soon discover still more numerous differences among them, indicating a proportional number of changes in their condition. The sea has not always deposited stony substances of the same kind. It has observed a regular succession as to the nature of its deposits; the more ancient the strata are, so much the more uniform and extensive are they; and the more recent they are, the more limited are they, and the more variation is observed in them at small distances. Thus the great catastrophes which have produced revolutions in the basin of the sea, were preceded, accompanied, and followed by changes in the nature of the fluid and of the substances which it held in solution; and when the surface of the seas came to be divided by islands and projecting ridges, different changes took place in every separate basin.

Amidst these changes of the general fluid, it must have been almost impossible for the same kind of animals to continue to live:—nor did they do so in fact. Their species, and even their genera, change with the strata; and although the same species occasionally recur at small distances, it is generally the case that the the shells of the ancient strata have forms peculiar to themselves; that they gradually disappear, till they are not to be seen at all in the recent strata, still less in the existing seas, in which, indeed, we never discover their corresponding species, and where several even of their genera are not to be found; that, on the contrary, the shells of the recent strata resemble, as it respects the genus, those which still exist in the sea; and that in the last-formed and loosest of these strata there are some species which the eye of the most expert naturalist cannot distinguish from those which at present inhabit the ocean.

In animal nature, therefore, there has been a succession of changes corresponding to those which have taken place in the chemical nature of the fluid; and when the sea last receded from our continent, its inhabitants were not very different from those which it still continues to support.

Finally, if we examine with greater care these remains of organized bodies, we shall discover, secondary strata, other strata that are crowded with animal or vegetable productions, which belong to the land and to fresh water; and amongst the more recent strata, that is, the strata which are nearest the surface, there are some of them in which land animals are buried under heaps of marine productions. *Thus the various catastrophes of our planet have not only caused the different parts of our continent to rise by degrees from the basin of the sea, but it has also frequently happened, that lands which had been laid dry have been again covered by the water*, in consequence either of these lands sinking down below the level of the sea, or of the sea being raised above the level of the lands. The particular portions of the earth also which the sea has abandoned by its last retreat, had been laid dry once before, and had at that time produced quadrepeds, birds, plants, and all kinds of terrestrial productions; it had then been inundated by the sea, which has since retired from it, and left it to be occupied by its own proper inhabitants.

Near the beginning of his essay M. Cuvier made the following remarks about the earth as it might appear today:

When the traveler passes through those fertile plains where gently-flowing streams nourish in their course an abundant vegetation, and where the soil, inhabited by a numerous population, adorned with flourishing villages, opulent cities, and superb monuments, is never disturbed except by the ravages of war and the oppression of tyrants, he is not led to suspect that *nature also has had her intestine wars, and that the surface of the globe has been much convulsed by successive revolutions and various catastrophes.*

In point four of his essay, he offered proof of the past revolutions on the surface of the globe which have brought about its present state:

The lowest and most level parts of the earth, when penetrated to a very great depth, exhibit nothing but horizontal strata composed of various substances, and containing almost all of them innumerable marine productions. Similar strata, with the same kind of productions, compose the hills even to a great height.

Sometimes the shells are so numerous as to constitute the entire body of the stratum. They are almost everywhere in such a perfect state of preservation, that even the smallest of them retain their most delicate parts, their sharpest ridges, and their finest and tenderest processes. *They are found in elevations far above the level of every part of the ocean, and in places to which the sea could not be conveyed by any existing cause.* They are not only inclosed in loose sand, but are often incrusted and penetrated on all sides by the hardest stones. *Every part of the earth, every hemisphere, every continent, every island of any size, exhibits the same phenomenon.* We are therefore forcibly led to believe, not only that the sea has at one period or another covered all our plains, but that it must have remained there for a long time, and in a state of tranquillity; which circumstance was necessary for the formation of deposits so extensive, so thick, in part so solid, and containing exuviae so perfectly preserved.

The time is past for ignorance to assert that these remains of organized bodies are mere *lusus natura*,—productions generated in the womb of the earth by its own creative powers. A nice and scrupulous comparison of their forms, of their contexture, and frequently even of their composition, cannot detect the slightest difference between these shells and the shells which still inhabit the sea. *They have therefore once lived in the sea, and been deposited by it: the sea consequently must have rested in the places where the deposition has taken place.* Hence it is evident that the basin or reservoir containing the sea has undergone some change at least, either in extent, or in situation, or in both. Such is the result of the very first search, and of the most superficial examination.

M. Cuvier also offered proof that these revolutions have been numerous and that they have been sudden:

These repeated irruptions and retreats of the sea have neither been slow nor gradual; most of the catastrophes which have occasioned them have been sudden; and this is easily proved, especially with regard to the last of them, the traces of which are most conspicuous. In the northern regions it has left the carcases of some large quadrupeds which the ice had arrested, and which are preserved even to the present day with their skin, their hair, and their flesh. If they had not been frozen as soon as killed they must quickly have been decomposed by putrefaction. But this eternal frost could not have taken possession of the regions which these animals inhabited except by the same cause which destroyed them;* this cause, therefore, must have been as sudden as its effect.

*The two most remarkable phenomena of this kind, and which must for ever banish all idea of a slow and gradual revolution, are the rhinoceros discovered in 1771 in the banks of the *Vilhoui,* and the elephant recently found by M. Adams near the mouth of the *Lena.* This last retained its flesh and skin, on which was hair of two kinds; one short, fine, and crisped, resembling wool, and the other like long bristles. The flesh was still in such high preservation, that it was eaten by dogs.

Next M. Cuvier examined the causes which act at present on the surface of our globe and stated his conclusion that no presently occurring action in nature explains the radical geological changes seen in the unfolding of the earth's past.

. . . But we shall presently see that unfortunately this is not the case in physical history; the thread of operation is here broken, the march of nature is changed, and none of the agents that she now employs were sufficient for the production of her ancient works.

Volcanoes have never raised up nor overturned the strata through which their apertures pass, and have in no degree contributed to the elevation of the great mountains which are not volcanic.

Thus we shall seek in vain among the various forces which still operate on the surface of our earth, for causes competent to the production of those revolutions and catastrophes of which its eternal crust exhibits so many traces: And if we have recourse to the constant external causes with which we have been hitherto acquainted, we shall have no greater success.

The pole of the earth moves in a circle round the pole of the ecliptic, and its axis is more or less inclined to the plane of the ecliptic; but these two motions, the causes of which are now ascertained, are confined within certain bounds, and are much too limited for the production of those effects which we have stated. Besides, *as these motions are exceedingly slow, they are altogether inadequate to account for catastrophes which must necessarily have been sudden.*

The same reasoning applies to all other slow motions which have been conceived as causes of the revolutions on the surface of our earth, chosen doubtless in the hope that their existence could not be denied, as it might always be asserted that their extreme slowness rendered them imperceptible. But it is of no importance whether these assumed slow motions be true or false, for they explain nothing, since *no cause acting slowly could possibly have produced sudden effects.*

Admitting that there was a gradual diminution of the waters; that the sea might take away solid matters from one place and carry them to another; that the temperature of the globe may have diminished or increased; *none of these causes could have overthrown our strata; inclosed great quadrupeds with their flesh and skin in ice; laid dry seashells in as perfect preservation as if just drawn up alive from the bottom of the ocean; or utterly destroyed many species, and even entire genera, of testaceous animals.*

These considerations have presented themselves to most naturalists: And, among those who have endeavoured to explain the present state of the globe, hardly any one has attributed the entire changes it has undergone to slowly operating causes, and still less to causes which continue to act, as it were, under our observation. The necessity to which they were thus reduced, of seeking for causes different from those which we still observe in activity, is the very thing which has forced them to make so many extraordinary suppositions, and to lose themselves in so many erroneous and contradictory speculations, that the very name of their science, as I have elsewhere said, has become ridiculous in the opinion of prejudiced persons, who only see in it the systems which it has exploded, and forget the extensive and important series of facts which it has brought to light and established.

As M. Cuvier pointed out in his essay, God's sudden catastrophic judgments upon the earth and its world of inhabitants have buried many forms of life under gigantic torrents of water which became frozen, preserving the different forms of life in icy graves for millenniums.

We cannot devote space here to mention all the suppositions that men have given over the years to explain these riddles. But we do know that all the true discoveries made by man about the history of the planet Earth concretely confirm the Biblical and historical record of Earth as revealed in God's Word.

Although there is the physical evidence that sudden catastrophic judgments from God have altered the earth's crust, changed climates, and buried many preexisting forms of life, it is impossible to assess completely what has gone on in the past because there is no written record left by previous inhabitants as to what actually happened. What is happening in the present is not the whole story of what went on in the past, the facts from which are now buried deep under tons of ice, earth, and rock.

So, scientists prove by their discoveries the same truths that are recorded in the Bible: that catastrophic cataclysmic changes have happened on the earth; that prehistoric men and most of all other life have disappeared during these times; that the earth's crust has not remained the same always.

Summary

In this chapter we have presented just a sampling of the available scientific proof that agrees with and supports truths that God has revealed in His Holy Word.

Scientists have now devised instruments that can measure the mass of the sun, the moon, and the stars and calculate their age and life expectancy. They know that stars, for example, are born and that they die. The lifespan of the heavenly lights seems infinitely long in comparison to that of mortal man. Nevertheless, these heavenly bodies are finite; and this is proved by the very fact that man now knows there was a time that these heavenly lights did not exist and by the fact that men can project their calculations into the future and know that each of these lights will cease to exist. These finite lights had to have an infinite Creator, then, Who had power and light within Himself to bring them forth and set them in their particular place in the sky.

Scientific discoveries prove beyond doubt the antiquity of the earth upon which we live.

From their observation of the universe today, scientists can tell much about the processes that happened in the past that helped form our present, inhabitable earth. They also know from the efforts of paleontologists that simple plant life existed on the earth before animal life appeared.

In the beginning, God established the fence that separates one kind of seed from another kind of seed and one kind of animal from another kind of animal. Now man has discovered this uncrossable fence; he calls it DNA, an abbreviated name for deoxyribonucleic acid. The DNA is a living, microscopic computer with an intelligent built-in memory. Stored in the memory of the DNA of each seed and each animal is the particular blueprint for its particular species. And apart from man's intervention and the forcing of unnatural unions, each species always keeps its reproductive powers within its own species. Hybrid seeds and hybrid animals, products of man's meddling, are sterile if man does not work to restore their fertility. This is simply proof that the blueprint within the DNA has been so marred by man that it cannot carry out the divine commands given to it by God.

The fossils that have been discovered by present-day man are silent witnesses that men as well as plants and animals lived upon the earth in prehistoric days.

In his "Essay on the Theory of Earth," George Cuvier, the French geologist and naturalist, reported his findings of four different strata of earth and the different catastrophic cataclysmic changes that have happened on the earth in past ages.

Findings, such as the frozen mammoths discovered in Northern Siberia, provide clear proof that catastrophic events have occured. Men are still searching for answers to explain the riddles that surround these giants that were frozen so quickly that their flesh was still fresh and able to be eaten by other animals after it was defrosted thousands of years later. What happened so suddenly to the mammoth found sticking out of the bank of the Lena River? It certainly could not have been the slow advance of an ice age. How could slow freezing preserve, in an uncorrupted state, the flesh of a huge warmblooded animal?

Thus, we see that true scientific findings do not contradict the infallible truths in the Bible, not will they ever be able to do so.

Scientists have made other discoveries about the universe in which we live, which are *not* about God's *past judgments* of the earth, *but* about the *laws* He has established to govern it. Some of these laws are the subject of our next chapter.

Chapter Two

Scientific Facts and Laws That Were Recorded in the Bible Prior to Their Discovery by Modern Man

GOD'S Works in the natural realm and the laws that govern them are pictures and types of His Works in the spiritual realm and the laws that govern them. This principle of truth is revealed in the Holy Scriptures.

> For the invisible things of him from the creation of the world are clearly seen, *being understood by the things that are made*, even his eternal power and Godhead; so that they are without excuse; (Romans 1:20).

God has chosen to make Himself known by the things which He has made. The eternal invisible things of the Godhead are seen clearly and understood through the things that God has made in the visible realm. Thus, by His Works, He makes known His eternal power and Godhead.

We can know the invisible, eternal power of the Godhead by beholding the things that He has made visible in such exact order and perfect harmony. These things could not and did not make themselves by some casual hit-or-miss process. A workman is always known by his works. Thus, all of God's infinite designs, manifold varieties, divine order, perfections of beauty, and all the pleasing harmonies of the proportionate parts of nature abundantly prove the eternal power and Godhead of the Creator.

For everything in the spiritual realm, God has set its natural counterpart in the visible world. For example:

- There is the spiritual water of God's Word and God's Spirit (Ephesians 5:26; John 7:38,39), and there is natural water.

- There is the spiritual seed of God's Word (I Peter 1:23), and there is natural seed.

- There is spiritual milk of God's Word (I Peter 2:2), and there is natural milk.

- There is spiritual meat of God's Word (I Corinthians 3:2), and there is natural meat.

- There are spiritual fruits of the Spirit (Galatians 5:22), and there are natural fruits.

I. The Spherical Form of the Earth Was Revealed in the Bible Before Modern Man Discovered This Truth and Confirmed It

A primary example of knowledge which was first revealed in the Bible and which harmonizes with man's subsequent discoveries is God's revelation that the earth is round or spherical. The Prophet Isaiah unveiled this knowledge.

> It is he that sitteth upon *the circle of the earth*, and the inhabitants thereof are as grasshoppers; that stretcheth out the heavens as a curtain, and spreadeth them out as a tent to dwell in: (Isaiah 40:22).

Isaiah was not a scientist in his day. Yet because he was the anointed prophet of the LORD God, and because his words were inspired by the LORD's Spirit, he was able to say that the earth was round. This truth was spoken long before the earth's spherical form was asserted by Pythagoras and Aristotle. Before Columbus proved in A.D. 1492 that he could sail across the ocean without dropping off the end somewhere, and long before Magellan proved the earth was round by circumnavigating the globe (between 1519 and 1521, according to *World Book Encyclopedia*), the Prophet Isaiah referred to the spherical form of the earth.

The supreme, infinite God sits on the circle or the globe of the earth. The Hebrew word for *circle* is *khoog*, meaning a circle, a compass. God sits upon the circle of the earth. His residence is in the upper world, but He maintains His Sovereign dominion over the lower world, giving laws to nature, guiding, and directing all the motions of the earth to His own glory.

God said that the earth is round. Through discovery and knowledge, man has learned that this is true.

II. The Course or Rotation of the Sun Was Revealed in the Bible Before Modern Man Discovered This Truth and Confirmed It

Another truth that God revealed in the Bible before it was discovered and confirmed by man is the course or rotation of the sun.

The LORD God in His gracious mercy has spread out the starry heavens which contain our sun and moon so that the earth and its inhabitants have a house or tent of light in which to dwell. The lights of the heavens are a glorious canopy drawn over all the heads of the earth's dwellers. Thus, God's creatures are *encircled* in light both day and night. This circle of light in the natural realm pictures the divine light of God's truth and God's Name with which He desires to encircle our heads and to govern us in our spiritual day and night seasons.

> The heavens declare the glory of God; and the firmament sheweth his handywork. Day unto day uttereth speech, and night unto night sheweth knowledge. There is no speech nor language, where their voice is not heard. Their line is gone out through all the earth, and their words to the end of the world. In them hath he set a tabernacle for the sun, Which is as a bridegroom coming out of his chamber, and rejoiceth as a strong man to run a race. His going forth is from the end of the heaven, *and his circuit unto the ends of it:* and there is nothing hid from the heat thereof (Psalm 19:1-6).

The Hebrew word for *circuit* is *tek-oo-faw*, meaning a revolution of the sun, a course. The sun is the great central luminary which gives light to our earth and to the other planets of our solar system. The planets move in elliptic orbits around the sun as a center. *The New Book of Knowledge* says: "The sun rotates on an axis. The two imaginary points where the axis goes through the sun's surface are called poles. An imaginary line that circles the sun midway between the poles is called the Equator. It takes about twenty-five days for the equatorial part of the sun to turn around once on the sun's axis. The parts of the sun above and below the equator *rotate* more slowly."

What can be seen in the sky with one's naked eye is sufficient to proclaim a Sovereign Creator Who is a Master Architect and a Master Mathematician Who works with infinite designs, master plans, quantities, magnitudes, and forms beyond the ability of man's finite mind to comprehend in its fullness. The invention of astronomical instruments has helped us appreciate, with reverential astonishment and amazement, the grandeur of God's creative handiwork.

The sun and the starry heavens reveal the ineffable wisdom and the infinite glorious power of God's wondrous Work.

Each day utters the speech of God's omnipotence through the revolution of the sun, as it appears to rise and to set on the earth.

Each night reveals the might of the Creator through the orbits of the moon and the stars. The message of light in the night season is conveyed to man without the use of audible sound.

The sun is like a bridegroom and a warrior full of joyful strength and wise expertise, rising early, as it were, at dawn, to overcome and dispel the foe called the darkness of night. With its inaudible voice, the power of the sun's heat and light penetrates everywhere in the earth, proclaiming the God of nature. God first revealed the revolutions of the sun in His Word; since then astronomers have discovered and learned this truth scientifically.

III. The Truth That the Stars Are Innumerable as Far as Man Is Concerned Was Revealed in the Bible Before Man Developed Instruments Powerful Enough To Confirm It

Before man invented the powerful astronomical instruments with which he could observe the heavens and see that the stars were indeed too numerous for him to count, God revealed man's lack of power to count the host of heaven.

> As the host of heaven *cannot be numbered*, neither sand of the sea
> measured; so will I multiply the seed of David my servant, and the
> Levites that minister unto me (Jeremiah 33:22).

The lights in the heavens are not uncountable to God. He can number the stars; He knows them all by name and commands them.

> *He telleth the number of the stars*; he calleth them all by their
> names (Psalm 147:4).

God, the Master Mathematician, has counted all the number of the starry hosts of heaven and called them by their names. Only the omnipotent, omniscient Creator of the universe could determine how many stars it would take to illuminate the heavens. Such a task is beyond the finite power and the finite intelligence of a creature.

216

> Lift up your eyes on high, and behold who hath created these
> things, that bringeth out their host by number; *he calleth them all*
> *by names* by the greatness of his might, for that he is strong in
> power; not one faileth (Isaiah 40:26).

The LORD God calls the stars by their names. He bids them to appear for service when called upon. Each star is known individually to God, and not one fails to perform his daily task according to the will of God.

> I have made the earth, and created man upon it: I, even my hands,
> have stretched out the heavens, and *all their host have I*
> *commanded* (Isaiah 45:12).

God has commanded or ordained, arranged and appointed the host of stars to their special ministry of lighting the heavens.

IV. The Law of Circularity in the Circuits of the Earth's Wind Currents Was Revealed in the Bible Long Before Man Discovered and Learned About the Whirls and Eddies of the Wind

The wind travels in circuits or circles, according to God's law of circularity. The Hebrew word that is used for *circuits* in connection with the motion of the wind is *sawbeeb*, meaning to circle, to compass around about on every side.

> The wind goeth toward the south, and *turneth about* unto the
> north; it *whirleth about continually*, and the wind returneth again
> according to his *circuits* (Ecclesiastes 1:6).

The law of circularity is essential for the progress of nature. God has revealed in His Word that the wind moves in circuits. Wind is a current of air moving in the atmosphere in any direction or with any velocity. Wind currents are set in motion by variations of temperature in different latitudes. Heated air tends to ascend; so in order to prevent a void from arising in the lower portion of the atmosphere from which the heated air has ascended, a current of colder and, therefore, denser air takes its place.

This phenomenon is most obvious in the tropics, from which hot rarefied air is ever ascending, one part toward the northern pole, and the other part toward the southern pole. From these two regions, cold currents of air proceed near the surface of the ocean to supply the threatened void. If the earth were at rest, the hot currents would depart from and the cold currents would strike the equator at right angles; but owing to the earth's rotation from west to east more quickly than its friction can carry the atmosphere with it, the latter is somewhat deflected westward, the hot current leaving the cold current striking the equatorial line at an oblique instead of right angle.

The *World Book Encyclopedia* gives a simple diagram and an easily understood explanation of the wind's circulation.

General Circulation Of Air Around The Earth

Prevailing winds result from the general circulation of air around the earth, shown at the right. In this drawing, the circulation has been greatly simplified. At the equator, air is heated by the sun and rises, as shown by the blue arrows. In the upper atmosphere, this air flows away from the equator. When the air returns to the earth's surface, it flows across the surface, as shown by the black arrows. This moving surface air produces the six belts of prevailing winds around the earth. The turning of the earth causes the prevailing winds to blow toward the east in belts where the air moves away from the equator. In belts where the air moves toward the equator, the prevailing winds blow toward the west.

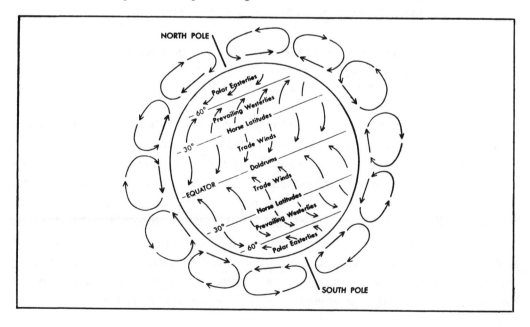

As the circles to be traversed by the rotation sphere vary in magnitude in every latitude, cyclones tend to be generated which rotate in one direction, when they arise to the north, and in another when they are generated south of the equator. Cyclones that arise to the northern hemisphere blow in a counterclockwise direction, and those that arise to the southern hemisphere blow in a clockwise direction.

On one side of the scales, wind is fickle and changeable; on the other side of the scales, wind is joined to the fixed law of circularity in nature.

Diagrams in the *New Book of Knowledge* clearly explain and confirm the law of circularity of the currents of the winds as stated in the Word of God.

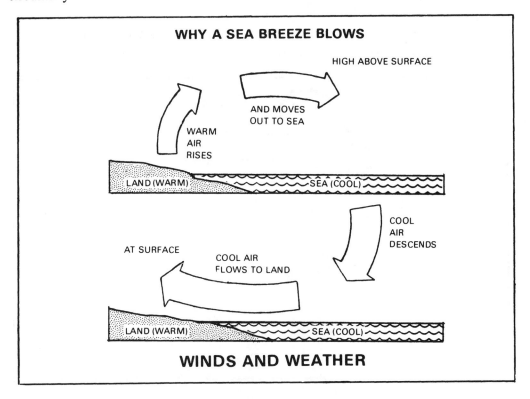

WHY A SEA BREEZE BLOWS

HIGH ABOVE SURFACE

AND MOVES OUT TO SEA

WARM AIR RISES

LAND (WARM) — SEA (COOL)

COOL AIR DESCENDS

AT SURFACE

COOL AIR FLOWS TO LAND

LAND (WARM) — SEA (COOL)

WINDS AND WEATHER

The wind blows in many different patterns. Some are large patterns—for example, the vast rivers of air, thousands of miles wide, flowing eastward or westward around the earth. Others are small patterns—for example, the air swirling about a building or a tree. In between are wind patterns of all sizes—sea breezes, mountain winds, tornadoes, hurricanes, squalls, cyclones, anticyclones, jet streams, and many others.

Why Does Air Move?

Air moves because forces are acting on it. Perhaps the best way to understand what happens is to compare the movement of air with the movement of water in a pipe. Water moves through a pipe because the water pressure is higher at one end of the pipe than at the other. The water flows from high to low pressure. Air also tends to flow from high to low pressure.

The flow of air from the equator to the poles is broken up into smaller units, or cells.

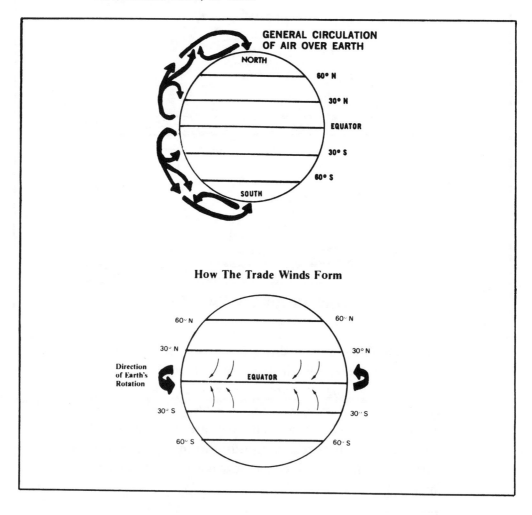

GENERAL CIRCULATION OF AIR OVER EARTH

How The Trade Winds Form

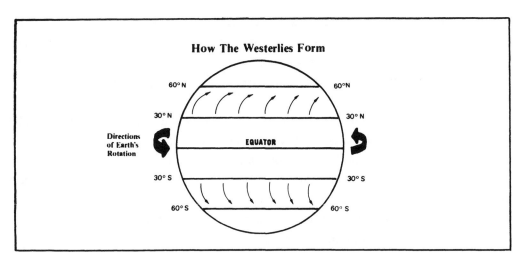

How The Westerlies Form

General Circulation Of The Air

Great wind currents flow around the earth. This pattern is known as the general, or planetary, circulation. Like the sea breeze and the monsoon, it is caused by temperature difference. It is mainly the result of the temperature differences between the equator and the poles. As you will see, however, this process is much more complicated than the others.

The earth receives heat from the sun and itself gives off heat into space. At the equator the earth receives more heat from the sun than it gives off to space. Therefore the air at the equator is constantly getting warmer. At the poles the earth gives off more heat than it receives, and it therefore becomes colder. (In fact, this is true everywhere north of about latitude 35 degrees north and south of latitude 35 degrees south.) The temperature differences between the equator and the pole causes a flow of air to develop. The flow carries heat from the equator to the poles.

These are sufficient examples to confirm that the discoveries of science are completely congruous with the truth revealed in God's Word.

The circle in the spiritual realm signifies the unending power, perfection, and harmonious pattern of the Name of the LORD. Therefore, the ultimate end of all nature is through the round-about way of the circle. Much of nature's created objects, both organic and inorganic, assume a somewhat circular form. The trees, although endless in their elegant diversity, have round circular stems that reach upward in their progressive development until they reach maturity, putting forth their curved or circular fruit in the top.

The LORD God has used the circular form of His Name in all His creation. The curved, circular formation is seen in seeds, stems, leaves, and fruits. It is seen in the invisible world of the atom. The body of man originates from one circular cell in the womb. And when the one cell ultimately matures, it is crowned with the circular head in which resides the *nediybah* soul of man.

This circle of progress and development continues to repeat itself over and over as the generations of mankind come and go.

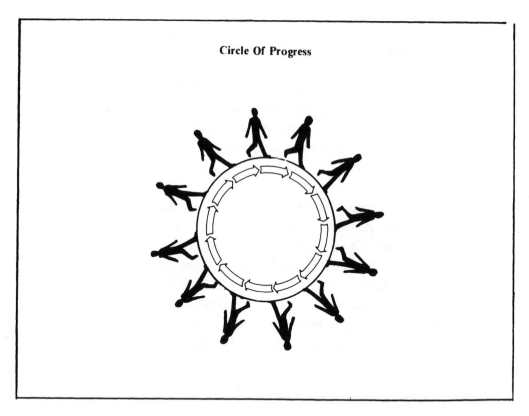

Circle Of Progress

Each generation of mankind has trodden the circle of progress and development either naturally or spiritually. God's first desire is for man to move onward and forward in his spiritual education and in his moral development, advancing upward toward the higher spiritual state of completion and perfection.

V. The Law of Circularity That Governs the Earth's Waters Was Revealed in the Bible Long Before Modern Man Discovered the Circuitous Route the Water Takes as It Ascends into the Clouds to be Dropped Back Down on the Earth at a Later Time

All rivers run into the sea or the ocean, and yet the sea or ocean never overflows because the sun lifts the water again in the form of vapors which make clouds.

> All the rivers run into the sea; yet the sea is not full; unto the place from whence the rivers come, thither they return again (Ecclesiastes 1:7).

Clouds are God's visible floating reservoirs which wait to dispense their liquid life upon the earth. In that way they can continue their circuitous journey as water, flowing into the ocean, and then reforming into clouds to continue their cycle all over again.

> For he saith to the snow, *Be thou on the earth*; likewise to *the small rain*, and to the great rain of his strength (Job 37:6).

The providence of God sends the small rain in seed time, governing the water by His laws of nature so the rains come down in gentle drops and not all at the same time.

He sends the great rain in the winter season to replenish the water level of the earth. Although God is so great that He commands the hosts of heaven, He is so gracious and merciful that He satisfies the thirst of the smallest weed in His earthly kingdom. How much greater is His mercy and grace that constrains Him to satisfy the spiritual thirst of the children of men when they call upon Him.

> *Who hath divided a watercourse* for the overflowing of waters, or a way for the lightning of thunder (Job 38:25).

God has divided the water course. This means He guides and directs the water to the place it should fall on the earth. He has provided pipes, as it were, to guide every drop of water upon the earth to satisfy the desolate and waste ground, causing the tender herb and grass to spring forth. God's law of circularity keeps the earth watered and fruitful.

VI. The Law of Circularity That Governs the Ways and Paths of the Water Currents in the Seas and Oceans Was Revealed in the Bible Long Before Modern Man Discovered the Gulf Stream and the Rivers That Run Through the Seas and the Oceans

There are "ways" and "paths" in the seas and oceans that are established and governed by the circulatory law or the divine Sovereignty of God.

> *Thy way is in the sea*, and *thy path in the great waters*, and thy footsteps are not known (Psalm 77:19).

The circulatory law of nature was described in God's Word more than two thousand years before Benjamin Franklin discovered its existence. *The New Book of Knowledge* shows the Gulf Stream currents which confirms what the Scriptures say.

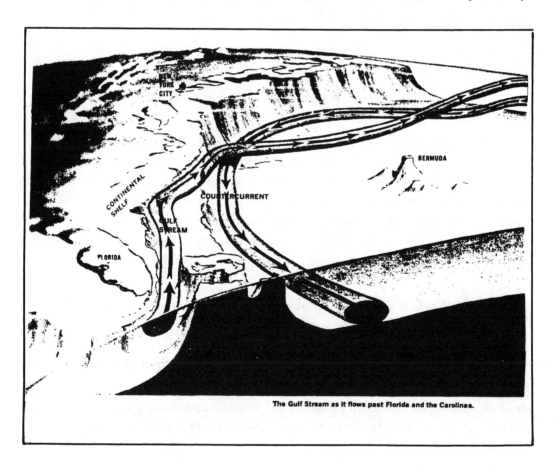

The Gulf Stream as it flows past Florida and the Carolinas.

The law of circularity is then described, and we find that God's Word is the most up-to-date science book.

Sometimes the winds and the shape of the coastline push the circulating water together. Then the water has to flow much faster and becomes a current. *Currents are like rivers in the sea. The most famous current is the Gulf Stream*, discovered by Benjamin Franklin. The Gulf Stream starts in the Atlantic Ocean near the equator. It pushes the warm, salty water past the Caribbean islands into the great bay made by Florida and the east coast of the United States. The water then flows northward past Cape Hatteras. Here the Gulf Stream is narrow and flows swiftly. Its speed is several miles an hour. The current is less than ten miles wide and is almost 1,800 feet deep. Like a river on land, the Gulf Stream does not flow straight; it winds its way over the ocean. But unlike a river, the Gulf Stream is not always found in the same place, for it has no fixed banks.

Swallow floats have shown scientists many startling things about how water flows in the deep ocean. *Many surface currents*, such as the Gulf Stream, *have current flowing beneath them*. These are called countercurrents. They flow in an opposite direction but in the same path as the surface current. The floats have also shown that circulation in the deep ocean is not steady. Sometimes the water goes round and round in a huge eddy or whirl, which slowly drifts along.

The *World Book Encyclopedia* also gives a map that shows the circular ocean currents.

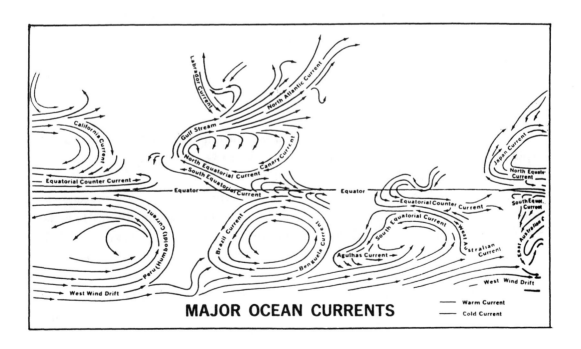

MAJOR OCEAN CURRENTS

God's law of circularity is seen in motion everywhere in nature, which includes the curving currents and rivers in the ocean and seas.

God's way and paths were also in the Red Sea for the destruction of His enemies, when He led His people like a flock out of Egypt.

VII. There Is No Variableness or Shadow of Turning With the Nature of Light. Light Travels in Straight Lines and Curves in Order to Accomplish God's Purposive Will. These Truths Are Confirmed by Science.

God, the Father of lights, the begotten Light, and the creative light never abandoned the creation as an orphan, leaving it without light.

> Every good gift and every perfect gift is from above, and cometh down from *the Father of lights, with whom is no variableness, neither shadow of turning* (James 1:17).

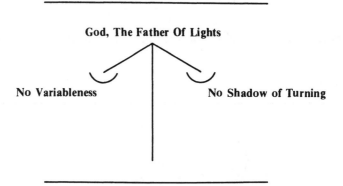

The Hebrew word for *variableness* is *khal-ofe*, meaning surviving; by implication orphans and destruction, from the Hebrew root word *khaw-laf*, meaning to slide, to hasten away, pass on, change, abolish, and alter.

God's gift of light perpetually goes out from Him and ceaselessly descends in unbroken streams of blessing and uninterrupted radiation of illumination. He is the Source of light of all love, joy, faith, hope, wisdom, understanding, and knowledge. It is God Who kindles the splendour of inspiration that causes any man to rise as a shining star in his generation.

God has commanded that the sun not abandon His creation, leaving it orphaned—neither shall the sun abandon the good seeds nor the evil seeds in the creation.

226

That ye may be the children of your Father which is in heaven: for *he maketh his sun to rise on the evil and on the good*, and sendeth rain on the just and on the unjust (Matthew 5:45).

Evil men disbelieve the existence of God, and good men are often ungrateful to Him for His manifold mercies; nevertheless, because there is no variableness in the Father's immutable nature of light, He continually gives His blessed sunlight to all surviving mankind, both good and evil.

There is also no shadow of turning or changing shadow with the Father of lights. He built the world with the straight lines of His square of faithfulness and with the curves of His compass of mercy. Light, in both the natural realm and the spiritual realm, moves in straight lines or in curves in order to accomplish the purposive will of God. Light has power to penetrate objects or to curve around them. Light does not turn into another substance and leave its course or circuit because an object arises in its pathway. Light always finds its way through or around an object.

God is the Father of lights, both naturally and spiritually. He is the Father of physical light, intellectual light, and spiritual light. Physical light makes the outer world visible. Intellectual light enables the mind to see truth about God's outer world. Spiritual light empowers the heart to see God's moral truth in the invisible world which surrounds man so he can walk in its light.

God is the Father of light, the Fountainhead of all conceivable modes of illumination. God pours down all good things, including light, in unceasing rains of blessing.

First, God begot His only begotten Son, Wisdom, Who is the Light of the world spiritually. Then, God's Son (Light) created the lights of this world and set them as chandeliers in the firmament above to give light upon the earth. Natural light is nature's glorious, brilliant robe, without which all the world would be clothed in gloom and darkness.

Likewise, spiritual light from God's Word is His glorious, brilliant garment for the soul, without which the soul is clothed in gloom and darkness.

Light empowers us to see, both in the natural and the spiritual realms. Light transports images to our eyes, informing and acquainting us with what is transpiring around us. In order to have light, there must be a source from which light emanates. In its relationship to the earth, the sun is the largest and most brilliant source from which light radiates. There are many different kinds of radiating light that come to us from the sun, such as infrared and ultraviolet light. Likewise, in the spiritual realm, the Word of God, the Son of God, the Wisdom of God, is the largest and most brilliant source that the Father of Lights has chosen to shine through.

Although there are many scholars in both worlds, man has not been able to exhaust the knowledge of the truth concerning light, neither in the natural world nor in the spiritual world.

The New Book of Knowledge confirms that light travels in straight lines.

Light Travels in Straight Lines

Light spreads directly outward from a source, moving in straight lines rather than in curved paths.

Then, the book, *The Universe and Dr. Einstein,** tells us that light also curves itself.

... Since light is a form of energy they will deduce that light has mass and will therefore be affected by a gravitational field. Hence the curvature of the beam.

From these purely theoretical considerations Einstein concluded that light, like any material object, travels in a curve when passing through the gravitational field of a massive body. He suggested that his theory could be put to test by observing the path of starlight in the gravitational field of the sun. Since the stars are invisible by day, there is only one occasion when sun and stars can be seen together in the sky, and that is during an eclipse. Einstein proposed, therefore, that photographs be taken of the stars immediately bordering the darkened face of the sun during an eclipse and compared with photographs of those same stars made at another time. According to his theory the light from the stars surrounding the sun should be bent inward, toward the sun, in traversing the sun's gravitational field; hence the *images* of those stars should appear to observers on earth to be shifted outward from their usual positions in the sky. Einstein calculated the degree of deflection that

*Barnet, Lincoln *The Universe and Dr. Einstein* (William Morrow and Company, Inc, New York, N.Y., 1957), pp. 89-91.

should be observed and predicted that for the stars closest to the sun the deviation would be about 1.75 seconds of an arc. Since he staked his whole General Theory of Relativity on this test, men of science throughout the world anxiously awaited the findings of expeditions which journeyed to equatorial regions to photograph the eclipse of May 29, 1919. When their pictures were developed and examined, the deflection of the starlight in the gravitational field of the sun was found to average 1.64 seconds—a figure as close to perfect agreement with Einstein's prediction as the accuracy of instruments allowed.

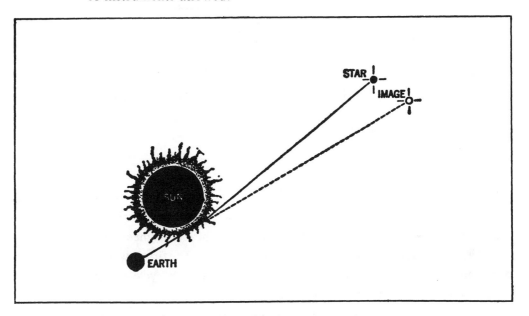

The deflection of starlight in the gravitational field of the sun. Since the light from a star in the neighborhood of the sun's disk is bent inward, toward the sun, as it passes through the sun's gravitational field, the image of the star appears to observers on earth to be shifted outward and away from the sun.

Since God is the Creator of all things, it should not appear a shocking surprise that He has recorded in His Word many of the secrets of the wondrous Works of His own hands, which include the truth that light travels in lines and curves.

VII. The Law of Entropy Was Revealed in the Bible Long Before Modern Man Discovered the First and Second Laws of Thermodynamics

God, as a Lawmaker and a Lawgiver, created the laws with which He controls and governs His creation. The natural laws that have been revealed in the Bible are in perfect harmony with the laws of nature that have been discovered and learned by man.

The laws of thermodynamics also exist in both the spiritual and the natural realms. By studying the first and second laws of thermodynamics that exist in the natural realm, first, we can better understand the invisible power of God's spiritual thermodynamics.

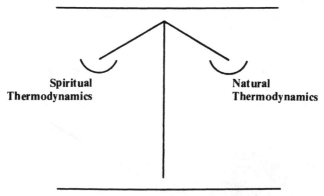

Thermodynamics is a Greek name that was given to motive power of heat, meaning "hot power," and the transformation of heat into mechanical energy.

There are two principle laws of thermodynamics. The first law is the conservation and constancy of energy. The second law is the reversible cycle or the dissipation or changing of energy which is called entropy.

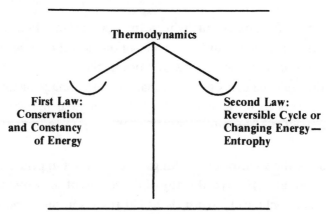

The first law of thermodynamics, the conservation of energy, consists of the principle that energy cannot be consumed, destroyed, or created, but it can be transformed into some other shape or form. The total energy of the universe can neither be increased nor diminished, which means that material things cannot be totally taken out of existence; nor can natural processes bring things into existence out of nothing.

The stuff from which things are made remains constant and changeless. God fixed the amount of energy in the universe at the beginning of creation, and it will remain fixed unto the end of the present creation.

This principle has existed since the beginning of God's original creation. There is nothing new under the sun.

> The thing that hath been, it is that which shall be; and that which is done is that which shall be done: and *there is no new thing under the sun*. Is there any thing whereof it may be said, See, this is new? *it hath been already of old time, which was before us* (Ecclesiastes 1:9,10).

The Hebrew root word for "old time" is *aw-lam*, meaning remote time, future or past ages, forever, everlasting. Every atom of energy that exists now, existed in the universe in the prehistoric ages that went before us.

We pridefully boast of our new contrivances, our new inventions, our new discoveries, our new compositions, our new fashions, our new hypothesis, and our new methods as though we had negated the first and second laws of thermodynamics. But, in reality, we have not created a new atom or any new energy.

However, we have and we do continue to use the second law by dissipating and wasting energy.

The second law of thermodynamics relates to the reversible cycle of energy called entropy. The word *entropy* simply means the measurement of the dissipation of energy or loss of usefulness. Energy is paradoxical. On one side of the scales, it is changeless and constant; on the other side of the scales, the declension of useful energy is seen everywhere. The entropy of matter increases as the useful energy that matter produces decreases. For example, let us consider what happens to steam in relation to this principle. When steam enters a turbine, it has a low degree of entropy because it is useful in moving the shaft of the turbine. However, the steam's amount of useful energy declines as it is used to turn the shaft of the turbine; therefore, its entropy increases.

There is a price to be paid every time energy is transformed from one form to another because there is a loss of a certain amount of usable energy. Entropy is the measurement of this loss. In any actual engine some of the heat energy received by the working fluid is *lost* before it can contribute its maximum quota of work, and some of the work that is done will be reconverted into heat by internal friction, which then will be ejected in the form of heat. Thus, in the whole process, entropy is increased because there are molecules of "hot power" that have left the center of operation and have "flown" off, as it were, in the form of useless energy. This energy is not destroyed, but it simply is transferred to somewhere else in the universe.

Entropy is the measuring of the degree to which energy declines into less useful forms until it is no longer capable of being converted into useful work.

Take a nail, for example. When the nail is shining and sharp, it can be used to function usefully. But left alone, outside, where it is subject to interaction with natural processes, it will mix with the air around it and eventually become a pile of shapeless, useless rust. Thus, the nail's entropy increases with the passage of time. This example is an illustration of "The New Generalized Second Law," which, in simple language, can be summarized as follows: On average, things mix. . . . This means that with the passage of time, natural processes will destroy patterns."*

Now let us compare the laws of spiritual thermodynamics to the laws of natural thermodynamics.

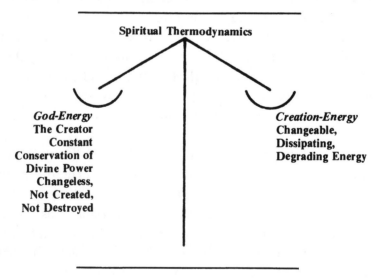

Spiritual Thermodynamics

God-Energy
The Creator
Constant
Conservation of
Divine Power
Changeless,
Not Created,
Not Destroyed

Creation-Energy
Changeable,
Dissipating,
Degrading Energy

* Gange, Robert A. *Origins and Destiny* (Word Books, Waco, Texas, 1986).

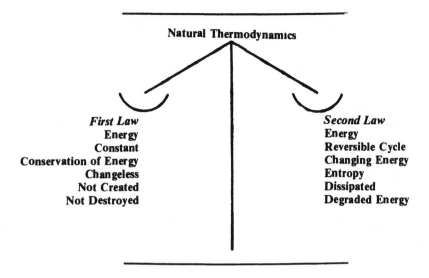

Natural Thermodynamics

First Law	*Second Law*
Energy	Energy
Constant	Reversible Cycle
Conservation of Energy	Changing Energy
Changeless	Entropy
Not Created	Dissipated
Not Destroyed	Degraded Energy

God is an immutable, changeless fire or omnipotent, infinite energy.

> For the LORD thy *God is a consuming fire*, even a jealous God (Deuteronomy 4:24).

> For our *God is a consuming fire* (Hebrews 12:29).

God is a consuming fire, and He is a God Who demands His rights. He is the Supreme One Who is above all and over all as the Owner and Master. He is the exclusively unique God, and He is zealous for holiness and justice. He is infinitely concerned about the doings and deeds of His creation.

When God created all creation, He encompassed it with His omnipresent, omnipotent, and immutable fiery breath.

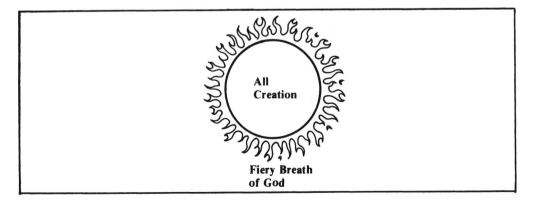

All Creation

Fiery Breath of God

233

In the beginning, when the creation remained in the midst of God's changeless, immutable, fiery breath, it remained constant and changeless. Hence, the creation experienced no loss or waste of energy in the beginning.

However, when the creation sinned by choosing to take itself out of the fire of God's personal presence, it began to experience both the spiritual and natural laws of entropy or the reversible cycle of energy; consequently, the creation began to undergo the dissipation and degradation of its energy.

One of the Hebrew root words for *sin* is *khaw-taw*, meaning in its basic conception and relation, to take something out of the realm to which it belongs. It means specially to take burning coals out of the fire. It also means to miss, to forfeit, to lead astray, trespass. When the creation took its existence out of God's fiery breath and the glowing, radiant rays of His personal presence, the source of life and wakefulness, its coals of fire began to be extinguished, turning into "cold clinkers," as it were. When the creation sinned against God, the second, spiritual and natural law of thermodynamics was set in motion. *Sin is energy in reverse.* Therefore, energy is abused, misused, dissipated, and wasted as a result of sin. God intended that the creation be filled with and surrounded by God's divine fire, which is constant and changeless.

In the beginning before sin, when the creation was filled with the divine fire of God, it was without the "cold clinkers" of changed, dissipated, and degraded energy. When the creation fell out of the divine fire of God's personal presence, it became cold, dark, dull, and degraded.

Although entropy is increasing in the world, with faster dissipation of energy, we need not despair because God will not cease working with His creation until He returns all "cold clinkers" to His changeless fiery presence—either to His fire above or to His fire below.

In spite of the fact that our universe is moving onward toward chaotic disorder and deathly decay, we can be hopeful and confident because God always has brought order out of chaotic disorder and life out of deathly decay. There is an eternal rest waiting for God's creation.

Part Four

The Theory of Evolution— Fact or Fiction?

Chapter One

How It All Began

EVOLUTION is a theory developed by scientists to explain the origin of life. Since the discoveries have been made which have proven the existence of prehistoric life, many scientists have attempted to connect the present creation with previous creations. Within the last two centuries the idea of organic evolution spread so among the scientific world that when the theory of evolution finally was put into a scientific statement, it very rapidly came to be accepted around the world as fact.

Even though no proof has been established that has verified this theory, it is taught in schools and written about in scientific journals as though it were indeed fact.

How did the unproven theory of evolution begin?

The man who is credited with the rudimental ideas that helped give birth to Charles Darwin's "Origin of the Species" was a contemporary of Cuvier, a Frenchman, Jean Lamarck. Cuvier and Lamarck more or less started the great debate over the origin of man which has raged ever since.

Jean Babtiste Pierre Lamarck (1744-1829) was the founder of the theory of organic evolution and of invertebrate paleontology. In *The New International Encyclopedia*, we read this about Lamarck's beliefs:

> A little book, published in 1822, entitled *Hydrogeologic*, preserves his [Lamarck's] reflections on geology, in antagonism to the 'catastrophic' ideas of Cuvier; and Huxley characterized it as containing 'sober and philosophic hypotheses; compared with those of Cuvier . . .'
> He utterly opposed Cuvier's views of sudden general extinction and creation of species, believing that the fossil forms were the ancestors of the animals now living; species to his mind being variable and undergoing a slow modification. He insisted on the following foundation principles of paleontology: (1) the great length of geological time; (2) the continuous existence of organic life through the geological periods; (3) the physical environment remaining

of the same general nature throughout, but with (4) continued gradual, not catastrophic, changes in the relative distribution of land and sea—changes which (5) caused corresponding modifications in the habitats, and (6) consequently in the habits, of living beings, so that there has been all through geological history a slow modification of life. . . . His idea of creation was evolutional rather than simply uniformitarian.

Lamarck tried to advance the theory of organic evolution by suggesting that acquired characteristics can be inherited.

Lamarck put his ideas and theories into a set of four laws. He stated seven factors of organic evolution and became the forerunner of the Theory of Evolution. However, his theory of organic evolution, though accepted by many contemporary scientists, was later proved to be incorrect. According to Lamarck, once a change occurred in a plant or animal, it could be passed on to the next generation. Lamarckism had Stalin's backing. The result was a setback in genetics in the USSR during the Stalinist era.

However, some of his ideas did give rise to the development of the modern Theory of Evolution. Lamarck failed to catch the idea of natural selection—the essence of Darwinism. Still the germ of the idea of evolution began with Lamarck's theory, and the idea of evolution was further expanded through the geological theories of Lyell who developed the concept of uniformitarianism.

Opposed to Lamarck's views, Cuvier took the creationist's view of the origin of life. By means of his knowledge of comparative anatomy, and his theory of the correlation of growth, Cuvier reconstructed a large number of extinct animals, proving that *every geological epoch* is represented by *distinct* animal forms, having a similarity well defined to animals in preceding or succeeding epochs. Nevertheless, he held to the Linnaean doctrine of the constancy of species, and looked upon the similarity of animal forms in successive epochs as a recurrence of types rather than a steady development of the same type.*

*The New International Encyclopedia (Dodd, Mead and Co., New York, NY, 1908, Volume 5).

238

Both Cuvier and Lamarck were right in some points of their theories—and both were wrong.

Everyone is right sometimes, and everyone is wrong sometimes. Even a broken clock is *right* twice a day. Therefore, it behooves us to walk humbly before our God. We may think we are great geniuses today, when in reality we may be the foolish fossils of the future.

In what ways were Cuvier and Lamarck right and wrong?

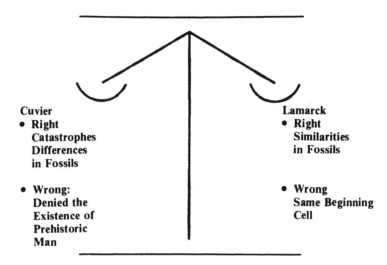

Cuvier
- **Right**
  Catastrophes
  Differences
  in Fossils

- **Wrong:**
  Denied the
  Existence of
  Prehistoric
  Man

Lamarck
- **Right**
  Similarities
  in Fossils

- **Wrong**
  Same Beginning
  Cell

In his book, *Before the Deluge*, Herbert Wendt quoted Cuvier's belief in catastrophic cataclysmic events:

> Life on earth has been frequently interrupted by frightful
> events. Innumerable organisms have become the victims of
> such catastrophes. Invading waters have swallowed up the
> inhabitants of dry land; the sudden rise of the sea bottom
> has deposited aquatic animals on land. Their species have
> vanished forever; they have left behind only sparse remains,
> which the naturalist is currently striving to interpret.

Although Cuvier, in his day, may not have been able to separate and classify all petrifactions of fossils, he was right in that he discovered *different* types of fossils in *different strata*—most of which are different from present-day species.

However, Cuvier was wrong in that he did not believe in prehistoric man.

Wendt also made this statement:

Cuvier did not believe in the existence of man in primordial times. But since the Bible represented man as well established on earth before the flood, Cuvier cautiously added to his dictum "L'bomme fossile n' existe pas!" a few explanatory comments: "To be sure, this is not to say that from four to six thousand years ago, in other words before the last catastrophic deluge, men could not yet have existed. Perhaps their dwellings plunged into abysses and their bones sank to the bottom of the present seas. . . . There remained only that small number of individuals who reproduced our race."

A few pages later, Wendt made the following statement, affirming *his* belief in prehistoric man.

The discovery of the different prehistoric animals from different geological periods proves that these prehistoric periods of the earth and its world of inhabitants did indeed exist.

Lamarck was right in that he discovered the threads of similarity in the organic world and in the fossil world, but he reached the wrong conclusion when he assumed similarities meant a common origin from a beginning cell.

Wendt quoted Lamarck as having said:

You must always proceed from the simplest to the most complicated; you thereby have the Ariadne's thread which runs through the entire organic world! You will thereby obtain a precise picture of progress in nature. And you will thereby also be convinced that the very simplest organisms gave rise to other living beings.

Not so! The thread of similarity in the creation is no sign that one form evolved into another form! It is, however, a sign of a *mutual Creator* in all forms of life.

240

Lamarck was wrong in asserting that fossil varieties are the predecessors of contemporary organisms. Lamarck *could not* furnish the required proofs for his theory.

The *New Encyclopedia Britannica* reported Lamarck's wrong views. It said:

> A similar view was reached quite independently by the naturalist Lamarck, who experienced such difficulties in distinguishing between species and varieties that he concluded that there was no real difference between them and that, if enough closely related species were studied together, they merged into one another and differences between them could no longer be made out. *In this he is known to have been wrong*; however difficult the barrier between the species may be to detect, *it nevertheless exists*. In 1809 Lamarck's views enabled him to propose a system of evolution and to draw up an evolutionary tree, from microanimals to man, with branches indicating community of ancestry between different groups. To explain evolution, Lamarck invoked two factors. The first was a supposed tendency to complexity and perfection (incompatible with the fact of evolution of degenerate forms), which meant that simple organisms alive in Lamarck's time must have arisen recently by spontaneous generation (which was disproved under the conditions of the time by the experiments of an Italian naturalist, Lazzaro Spallanzani, and the French microbiologist Louis Pasteur). *His second factor was an imagined sentiment interieur, which, he supposed, caused movements and introduced habits* that produced new organs that satisfied the animals' needs. *This was an unfounded speculation*, and, since Lamarck provided no evidence in support of his views, they found no acceptance. It is perhaps regrettable that the term Lamarckism is not applied to evolution itself. *However erroneous, his was the first systematic presentation of the subject.*

However wrong, Lamarck upheld the doctrine that all species, including man, are descended from other species.

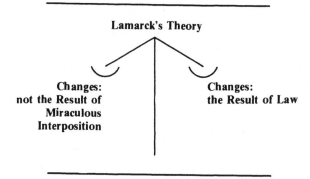

Lamarck's Theory

Changes:
not the Result of
Miraculous
Interposition

Changes:
the Result of Law

Although Lamarck denied the miraculous interposition of God on one side of the scales, he believed in the miraculous laws of gradual change and marvelous laws of progressive development.

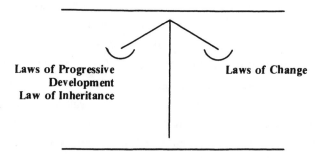

Laws of Progressive
Development
Law of Inheritance

Laws of Change

Charles Erasmus Darwin, one of the earliest promoters of evolutionary theories, was the grandfather of Charles Darwin. Drawing from Lamarck's studies in paleontology and geology and the ideas of uniformitarianism and gradual change, Charles Darwin, who was an English naturalist, added the new ideas of natural selection and survival of the fittest to form his theory of evolution. From the combination of these ideas, he wrote his essay on "The Origin of the Species." Darwin's theories have affected man's thinking more than anything since the life of Jesus Christ on earth. It is an anti-God theory, designed to separate the creation from the Creator.

Christian believers need to explore some of the fallacies of the theory of evolution for themselves so they will not be railroaded into believing the lies of fallen Lucifer, a created being himself, who desires to ensnare men's hearts and minds in order to separate them from their Creator.

Darwin's theory of evolution claimed that all species of plants and animals developed from earlier forms through hereditary transmission of slight variations to

242

successive generations. These stronger forms of life passed on their beneficial traits to their descendants. Thus, gradually, a new species was originated through natural selection and the process of mutation, those organisms surviving who were best adapted to the environment.

Darwin had great doubts about his own theories. D. J. Tice, in an article entitled "Life after Darwin," published in the August, 1986, issue of *TWA Ambassador Magazine*, said, "The problem of how the eye could have evolved through natural selection gave Charles Darwin fits. On one occasion he wrote that it caused him to 'shudder,' on another that it made him 'cold all over.'" (One could pose this question: Since the eye does not function until it is perfectly complete, how did all the first creatures manage to stagger in darkness while they were making their advantageous natural selections?)

Using a slightly different concept, Lamarck had proclaimed that acquired characteristics were obtained by the *internal driving force* produced by the needs of the organisms. He said that giraffes, for example, grew long necks because they ran out of vegetation in the low place and had to stretch their necks to obtain vegetation from high places in the trees. According to Lamarck, each generation passed on a longer neck to its offspring.

This hypothesis provokes a logical mind to ask this question: if conditions were so terrible that vegetation had ceased to grow in the low place, how is it possible that vegetation could continue to exist and flourish in the high places—in trees that were rooted in the ground?

It is impossible for a rational mind to conceive the idea that a drought would continue through successive generations, always affecting the low place while producing lush vegetation in the high place. One cannot help but wonder who planned this great miracle? Was the low place made barren just so the giraffe would stretch his neck into a longer form? Why was the giraffe the only creature to gain a long neck during this extended drought?

However, since the discovery of DNA, Lamarck's theory of acquired characteristics has been laid to rest permanently. Scott M. Huse wrote the following in his book, *The Collapse of Evolution*:

> It is now known, however, that change can only be transmitted to offspring through alterations in genes and their contained DNA. Discovery of this fundamental error of Lamarckism resulted in its ultimate rejection. By the 1930's, the theory of inheritance of acquired characteristics was fittingly discarded by the scientific commnunity.

The modern scientific world is absorbing a new generation of scientists who are diffusing more light on evolution, which in the process has cast dark clouds of doubt upon Darwin's venerated theory. They are acknowledging that they know much less than they thought they knew and are seeing that Darwin's theory is not congrouous with their new knowledge.

So the history of evolution is still evolving, and if truth ultimately is to be reached, the scientists' theories will evolve into the acceptance of God as the beginning, the Cause of all things. Life did not originate from non-life, but from the Source of life, God the Creator. No one will ever disprove "In the beginning God. . . ."

Chapter Two

Some Reasons for Not Believing in the Theory of Evolution

IN SPITE of all the work they have done trying to prove the theory of evolution, scientists still are unable to resolve all the questions they face.

Instead of the scientific world producing more and more factual evidence for its theories, the facts it is discovering cast new doubts and somber shadows of suspicion upon the validity of the theory of evolution. More scientists today seem to be willing to look for the truth as found in the creation instead of simply projecting some inconclusive evidence to justify a man-made theory.

As one examines the so-called "witnesses" to the theory of evolution, he finds that the ideas the scientific world projects as a sure basis for its beliefs in evolution are really very flimsy reasons for accepting the idea.

Consider the following reasons for **not believing** in the theory of evolution:

- The uncertainties in the minds of scientists about their theories
- The lack of evidence for evolution in the fossil records
- The lack of proof that similarities point to a common ancestor
- The impossibility of mutations having been numerous enough or beneficial enough to have produced man
- The immutableness of God's creation which refutes natural selection and adaptation as being the means of developing a new species
- The complexity of creation which argues against random selection
- The degeneracy of man and the destruction of his environment which argue against what should be the

final outcome of an evolutionary process—perfection of
the species in a perfect environment!

I. The Uncertainties in the Minds of Scientists About Their Theories

The fact is that *evolution is just a theory* which contains many uncertainties. In an article in "The Wall Street Journal," dated December 9, 1986, Tom Bethell, a media fellow at the Hoover Institute, pointed this out most clearly. He said, "We are repeatedly told that evolution is 'not a theory but a fact.' This is little more than whistling in the dark. There has been a persistent campaign by evolutionists to bully the lay public into accepting evolution by adopting an authoritarian posture inappropriate to science. The fact is that we know very little about evolution—far less than most educated people realize."

Mr. Bethell continued his article with this comment: "Colin Patterson, a senior paleontologist at the British Museum of Natural History, remarked at a public lecture in New York in 1981 that there was 'not one thing' that he knew about evolution. 'Question is,' he went on, 'can you tell me anything you know about evolution, any one thing that is true? I tried that question on the geology staff of the Field Museum of Natural History and the only answer I got was silence.'"

Is there indeed evidence that evolution is not true? Is the evidence for creation-science (evidence for the sudden appearance of highly developed forms of life) harder to believe than the unproven theory that man has evolved through random selection and mutations, determined through chance and not the creative power and force of an eternal God?

Mr. Bethell's article, "Creationists and Authoritarians," to which we have just referred, pointed out that many scientists even find creation a more suitable, believable explanation for the origin of life than evolution. He said, ". . . Dean Kenyon, a professor of Biology at San Francisco State University, has submitted an affidavit in which he attests to his belief 'that a scientifically sound creationist view of origins is not only possible, but is to be preferred over the evolutionary view.'"

Mr. Kenyon was reassigned to another position after he expressed his views on evolution, according to Mr. Bethell's article. Mr. Kenyon had been teaching undergraduate courses on evolution and the Darwinian theory.

According to Mr. Bethell, another professor who has raised questions about evolution is G. Lawrence Vankin of Williams College, in Massachusetts. Mr. Vankin also was reassigned to a new position ". . . after having assigned to his students two articles from the prestigious *Journal of Theoretical Biology* that questioned the plausibility of evolution by random process."

Mr. Bethell made this statement in his closing remarks in the "Wall Street Journal" article: "But the truth is that there is great uncertainty about what (if anything) is known about evolution. Those who embrace controversy should be fearless in pointing this out."

Contained in Mr. Bethell's statement is a reflection of the author's attitude toward the controversy surrounding creation versus evolution. We fearlessly say that truth bears examination, and we are free, praise God, to examine the truth as recorded in His Holy Word and state fearlessly what we perceive and know to be the truth: that God is the Creator and the Sustainer of all life and that He created man in His own image.

Let us look at other examples of uncertainty among the scientists.

In the *Smithsonian* of June, 1984, Paul Trachtman in an article "The Search for Life's Origins and a First 'Synthetic Cell,'" said:

> In the past few decades, researchers have demonstrated clearly that the necessary building blocks of the cell, including amino acids and nucleotides, can be made out of simple, ordinary compounds found in any chemistry lab and likely to have been present on the ancient Earth. Now, as their research goes beyond the building blocks, scientists are trying to demonstrate how the basic components could have evolved and organized themselves into the first cell. They are *trying to show* how, before there was life, molecules *could have* made copies of themselves through a primitive kind of reproduction, grown more complex and evolved through *accidental errors* like mutations—and also how conditions in their environment *could have* enforced a kind of "natural selection" to direct their evolution toward life.*

There is much assumption, hypothesis, and philosophy permeating the field of science.

*Emphasis by the Author

In his article, Mr. Trachtman also reported the theory of Francis Crick who *believed* that a spaceship landed in ancient oceans, releasing the first microorganisms on the earth. (Who, may we ask, prepared the earth and the ancient oceans for this great landing feat? Who built this mighty spaceship? Who created the microorganisms that were brought to earth?)

Many terms expressing uncertainty were used in Mr. Trachtman's article, such as probably, estimate, may have, surmise, and assume. For instance, he mentioned the uncertainty scientists have when they try to recreate the state of the earth when life first appeared.

> But there is much that remains *uncertain about the world* in which life arose. The day was shorter about four billion years ago, but no one really agrees on how short, says David Usher, who is trying to simulate that pre-biotic world.

Mr. Trachtman also quoted the suggestion of Alexander Oparin—"that evolution was at work even before life began." Obviously, then, according to Mr. Oparin's proposal, evolution is more than a theory, for it has a mind, can choose, and knows the difference between the simple and the complex.

The following facts are made very clear when one explores the writings of evolutionists: they are still very unsure of what their findings have revealed. Their conclusions are constantly being changed, so one can see they have not arrived at the true answer to the origin of life even in their own minds. It certainly makes one wonder why, among all their uncertainties, they are so certain that evolution is scientifically true!

II. Lack of Evidence for Evolution in the Fossil Records

It is impossible for present researchers to come up with anything but a theoretical picture of the stages of the history of the previously created worlds of inhabitants. They must glean most of their information from the small amount of witnesses left in the earth's crust in the form of fossils. Therefore, let us look at two *facts* that have been discovered in the fossil records.

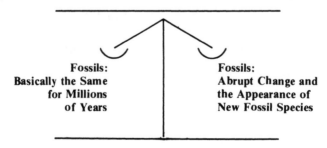

Fossils:
Basically the Same
for Millions
of Years

Fossils:
Abrupt Change and
the Appearance of
New Fossil Species

What a beautiful confirmation of the truth: creation, first, followed by catastrophic judgment, followed by the abrupt appearance of new creation! At first the evolutionists stoutly maintained that evolution was a gradual process. Now they are saying that it occurs by spurts and stasis. (One wonders who tells the creation when to "spurt" and when to "stasis.")

In *Newsweek* of November 3, 1980, the writer of the article "Is Man a Subtle Accident?" said:

> . . . the story of life is as disjointed as a silent newsreel, in which species succeed one another as abruptly as Balkan prime ministers. The more scientists have searched for the transitional forms between species, the more they have been frustrated. Paleontologist Patricia Kelley has traced a burrowing mollusk - Anadara staminea - over 2 million years of the Miocene Epoch, during which time the position of one muscle gradually shifted by 1.5 millimeters. Abruptly, A. staminea disappears, to be succeeded by the closely related species A. chesapeakensa - in which the muscle has suddenly shifted by 1.5 millimeters in the opposite direction. What kind of evolution is this, which seems to stand on its head the notion of gradual progress from primitive to more advanced species?
>
> Seventy years after quantum theory revolutionized physics, an oddly analogous change has occurred in the theory of evolution - and it is just beginning to filter down to public understanding. Evidence from fossils now points overwhelmingly away from the classical Darwinism which most Americans learned in high school: that new species evolve out of existing ones by the gradual accumulation of small changes, each of which helps the organism survive and compete in the environment. *Increasingly, scientists now believe that species change little for millions of years and then evolve quickly, in a kind of quantum leap - not necessarily in a direction that represents an obvious improvement in fitness**.

*Emphasis by author.

How can the beliefs of *evolutionists* be dependable, since they continually have to adjust their theories because scientific discoveries prove them to be unfit and untrue?

If things evolved from a speck of inanimate matter to a one-celled organism, and from the one-celled organisms into a higher form of animal and plant life, then one should see the evidence of such evolutionary processes in the fossil records.

However, the fossil evidence scientists uncover exposes the pernicious error of their theories. If the record is hopelessly incomplete, why make such grandiose statements as though the record is most complete?

Where is the evolving process today of the ape, seeing it is diametrically different anatomically from any monkey? If the monkey cannot evolve into an ape today, by natural selection and adaptation, and if an ape cannot evolve by natural selection and adaptation into a man today, why do they suspect it happened yesterday?

No transitional forms have been found between groups of animals and plants in the fossil record, and no transitional forms are found in the groups of living animals and plants.

The *lack* of this kind of evidence presented real mental confusion to Charles Darwin over a century ago. Scott M. Huse noted this in his book: "Even the great champion of evolution himself, Charles Darwin, acknowledged this fatal flaw." (The lack of fossil evidence for transitional forms.) Mr. Huse quoted Darwin:

> 'As by this theory, innumerable transitional forms must have existed. Why do we not find them imbedded in the crust of the earth? Why is all nature not in confusion instead of being as we see them, well-defined species? Geological reseach does not yield the infinitely many fine gradations between past and present species required by the theory; and this is the most obvious of the many objections which may be argued against it. The explanation lies, however, in the extreme imperfection of the geological record.'

Darwin hoped all the gaps in fossil information would be filled, but the more fossils that are found, the less evidence they produce for evolution.

If evolution were a truthful principle of operation in the primeval past, there would be evidences of its operation today. Scientists cannot prove that life evolves today from an inanimate speck of matter or that an animate speck of matter can evolve into a complex, complicated, living form. All life and forms have their origin and growth in the divine, intelligent mind and infinite power of Almighty God.

However, if we can speculate, assume, suppose, and surmise in order to interpret the dim past, we can accept the theory of evolution. And, if we can continue to dream about our assumptions, we can later call them proven facts. Then we will have the mental fortitude to defend our assumptions to the point of accusing all contrary thinkers of being emotionally unbalanced, irrational, narrow-minded, and biased.

We find that man's ego and emotions became hindering forces to his objectivity in the search for truth. Man thinks to exalt himself through his knowledge instead of humbly seeking God's wisdom and understanding, whether in the natural realm or in the spiritual realm.

Yet scientists know from past history that hypotheses often are proven to be wrong, and so entire schools of thought have had to be discarded in the light of more recent discoveries and facts.

One truth remains steadfast in all the changing theories. God's Word will not disagree with the facts.

Darwin's confusion would have been solved if he had looked within the pages of God's Holy Bible. His findings and lack of findings merely prove God's prehistoric creations and God's catastrophic judgments that fell on each of them.

The fossil records are *proofs* that prehistoric creation did exist, but *they do not prove* that these creations were linked to our present creation through the process of evolution. The only link between prehistoric creations and present day creation is that they all had the *same Creator!*

Therefore, based on the harmony that exists between the Biblical facts and the scientific facts, the basic logical conclusion is that God created the prehistoric worlds of inhabitants upon the original earth and the restored earths, and He created the present world of inhabitants upon the present earth.

III. The Lack of Proof That Similarities in Organisms Point to a Common Ancestor

According to The New Encyclopedia Britannica, the first indirect evidence for evolution is based on similarities that are found in different organisms.

> *The indirect evidence for evolution is based primarily on the significance of similarities found in different organisms,* which are explicable only *if* they have derived the features in question, structures or functions, from a common ancestor during descent with modification, for the laws of

probability insist that fundamental similarities can be traced only to one single origin.

Similarity is the close likeness or the partial resemblance that is found in all of God's creation. It is neither a direct nor an indirect evidence for the theory of evolution. However, it certainly points to a mutual ancestor, the LORD God, the Creator, as the common parent of all things.

All living things have one particular thing in common. It is called *life*. This life proceeds from one common parent—God, the Creator.

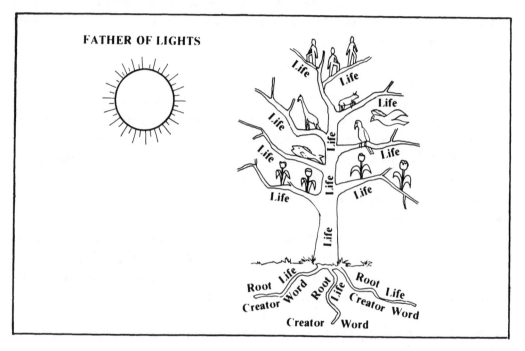

Life has flowed from God to His creation in both similar forms and structures and in distinctly different forms, according to God's purposive will. Yet, the promoters of the theory of evolution maintain that similarities are witnesses that give their theory substance.

The New Encyclopedia Britannica drew from the scientific disciplines of Comparative Anatomy, Embryology, Ethology, and Biochemistry in promoting the idea of evolution, but the conclusions the writers used lack evidence to prove them. Until ideas are backed by the irrefutable facts, they are still just ideas.

Comparative Anatomy is the first scientific field of study that the *The New Encyclopedia Britannica* dealt with in its attempt to prove evolution.

Comparative anatomy provides the first set of witnesses. There are a quarter of a million different species of flowering plants, but all of them (except for a few parasitic forms) share the basic structures of roots, stem-bearing branches, leaves containing the green pigment chlorophyll, and flowers composed of modified leaves, sepals, petals, stamens, and pistils. They differ in detail between different species, but all are built on the same plan and live in the same way, absorbing salts in water through the roots and fixing carbon dioxide in green plastids of the leaves in sunshine to synthesize more of their substance. *The similarity of plan is easily explicable if all descended with modification from a common ancestor, by evolution, and the term homologous is used to denote corresponding structures formed in this way.*

The similarity of plan in all flowering plants certainly points to one master plan: that of a common Creator or common Ancestor.

If a man's works, his paintings, sculptures, or buildings are easily identifiable by the similarity found in them, why should creation's Master Planner not show similarity in His Works?

God made all the quarter of a million different species of flowering plants to be natural examples of the spiritual principle of humility and exaltation. The nature and character of the Creator are seen in both worlds, the natural and the spiritual. This is why there is such a great similarity in all things and why the natural world is a picture of the spiritual world.

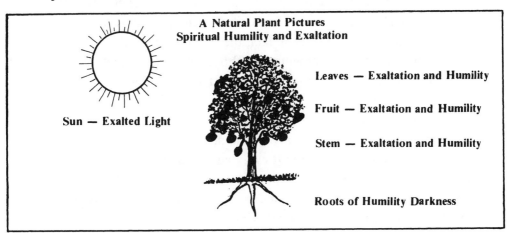

A Natural Plant Pictures
Spiritual Humility and Exaltation

Sun — Exalted Light

Leaves — Exaltation and Humility

Fruit — Exaltation and Humility

Stem — Exaltation and Humility

Roots of Humility Darkness

The life of the plant depends upon the root system which lives in humility darkness. Because of the mutual harmony and work that exist within the plant, it is able to live and to share its life in all parts of its stature. But suppose that one day the stems, leaves, flowers, and fruit decided to boast themselves against the root and pridefully declare their independence from the root of humility darkness and the exalted light. How long would the plant survive without the support of the root of humility or without the light of exaltation? God has placed within every part of each plant His intelligent mind and His purposive will so that each root, stem, leaf and flower, sepal, stamen, and pistil knows what its contribution is supposed to be. Within each plant is great similarity and great difference, which points to a common master plan and an infinite, wise Designer.

Likewise, in the spiritual realm, God's wise design and master plan calls for humility before exaltation. Without the support of God's humility Word, one's spiritual plant will not survive very long. So, in all situations of life, if we forget the "root people" who have helped us to achieve some form of exaltation, our exaltation will become an empty and dead thing. When we cease to remember to share the life and glory that are not ours alone, we will have destroyed our humility foundation, and our exaltation will crumble.

To offer more evidence from the studies of Comparative Anatomy, scientists have used what they term "abortive or degenerate" organs as signs of evolution. *The New Encyclopedia Britannica* mentioned the rudimentary wings of the ostrich and man's appendix as two examples.

> Some organs are called *abortive* or *degenerate* because they no longer serve a function. The possession of wings by ostriches, which cannot fly, is explicable if ostriches were *descended from flying birds*, in which the wings were functional. That this is, in fact, the case is evidenced by the structures of the cerebellum, the bones of the wing, and the tail, which show adaptations characteristic of flight.

First, it said *if* the ostrich *descended* from flying birds, its useless wings and tail could be explained. Then, in the following sentence the *if* has become a *fact*. The only evolutionary process seen here is the *if* evolving into a *fact*.

The basic concept of the theory of evolution declares that life evolved from a lower, one-celled creature to a higher, more complex one. But here are supporters of this same theory saying that the ostrich *descended* from a higher, more perfect bird! In the meantime, the ostrich does not know of its great humiliation, so it continues doing God's purposive will and making its contribution to the world. Its flesh is good for food, when properly prepared. Its feathers serve as quills and decorations. Its skin is used to make beautiful purses and shoes.

While it is true that the ostrich's wings are useless for airbourne flight, they are of great assistance to it. With the help of its so-called useless, degenerated wings, the ostrich, averaging forty miles an hour, can outrun the fleetest horse. God created the ostrich with the kind of wings and tail that it would need to assist its swiftness of foot.

The New Encyclopedia Britannica continued with the claim that the development of man's appendix is an evidence of evolution since it appears to resemble or be *similar* to the cecum of the alimentary canal of herbivorous mammals.

> The appendix of man has no useful function, but it corresponds to the cecum of the alimentary canal of herbivorous mammals (and of man's ancestors) in which it is a sac in which bacteria digest the cellulose cell walls of vegetable food.

When man's lack of understanding prevents him from perceiving God's purposive will in different parts of His creation, he pridefully renders the unknown part useless and degenerated. If man humbly will keep searching, he surely will find a very good reason for God's having created the appendix. Just because the appendix sometimes becomes diseased and has to be removed is no reason to say it is useless.

Doctors made this same mistake when they could find no apparent reason for the thymus gland. However, further research finally uncovered the reason and proved that man's ignorance can bring him to a wrong conclusion, even when he thinks he has exhausted every possibile reason.

Embryology is the second scientific discipline that *The New Encyclopedia Britannica* referred to in presenting its evidence for the idea of evolution based on similarities. It shared an article by Embryologist K.E. Von Baer who wrote that Embryology provides further examples of a common ancestor.

> In my possession are two little embryos in spirit, whose names I omitted to attach, and at the present I am quite unable to say to what class they belong. They may be lizards or small birds, or very young mammals, so complete is the similarity in the mode of formation of the head and trunk of these animals.

However, scientists have not *proven* that similarities of embryos are the result of descent from a common beginning.

The embryo of a new life consists of the germs of two new cells which are deposited within the ovum by an intelligent spontaneous movement. *The Universal Dictionary of the English Language* gives the following description of the development of the embryo. It says:

> They occupy only the pellucid centre of the germinal spot at first, but speedily increase in size, and develop new cells in their own interior, until they alone fill the whole germinal vesicle. Each cell gives birth to a new generation of two, making four, then eight cells, sixteen, and so on, doubling progressively, until a mulberry like mass is produced of innumerable cells. This in the animal embryo moves up to the side of the yolk, flattening against its lining membrane, in contact with the yolk bag. A second and third layer is then formed from the centre within the first mass of cells. The whole is known as the germinal membrane; the external pellicle is called the serous layer, the internal mucous layer, and the middle the vescular layer, giving rise to the first vessels of the embryonic structure. Thus the beginning of the embryo is a sac, enclosing the nutriment prepared for it prior to the permanent portion to be evolved from the centre of this mulberry-mass. The greater portion is then cast off, and nearly all the permanent embryonic formation is derived from one large cell, at first in the centre, but ultimately at the surface of the mass, when it undergoes the flattening described. This, with the cluster of cells round it, forms the germ spot, with a round transparent space in it, the area pellcida. The nucleus of this cell is first annular, then pear-shaped, then violin-like, being two long parallel lines, with a narrow space between them, but separating to enclose a wider space at one time.

> The parts first formed from this are the spine and spinal cord. Vessels at the same time are being formed within the substance of the germinal membrane, forming a network

known as the vascular area, and terminating in the embryo, at the point afterward becoming the umbilicus, at two large trunks. The formation of the heart takes place in the vascular layer, and at the same time the production of a digestive cavity begins by the separation of a small part of the yolk-bag, below the embryo, from the general cavity. The amnion and allentais are then formed, the chief office of the latter being to convey the vessels of the embryo to the chorion. Then comes the respiratory process.

What an unfolding picture this gives of a wise Creator Who has placed within organic matter some of His infinite intelligence that governs and guides the embryo. From its beginning, through all the stages up to the development of its spine, then onward until the embryo becomes a fetus, God's powerful laws of nature guide the embryo's growth!

It is an unparalleled mystery how one can behold such orderly movements, arrangements, and wise preparation and still not see the infinite wisdom and power of a Creator at work.

The similarity in the developmental process in all embryos in their earliest stages neither proves evolution nor negates the intelligent master plan and powerful Works of a Creator. (Some people appear to have been wiser in their embryonic stage than after their birth. At least as embryos, they followed the master plan of the Creator and worked to become what He had purposed for them to be.)

There is a vast difference between the embryo and the fetus. Everything begins as a germ or seed of life, which develops by amassing cells, but the divergence of the similar beginnings into the complex end-products, speaks of a master plan within the seed that has been designed by divine intelligence. We now know that this is the DNA, put there by God to determine the exact creature that will develop from each seed of life. Each seed ultimately becomes visibly conformed to God's purposive will for it.

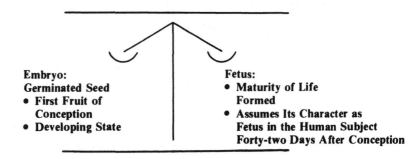

Embryo:
Germinated Seed
• First Fruit of
  Conception
• Developing State

Fetus:
• Maturity of Life
  Formed
• Assumes Its Character as
  Fetus in the Human Subject
  Forty-two Days After Conception

Again, similarity merely points to a mutual Creator, a mutual ancestor. If artists use the same media, their paintings have their origin in complete similarity. They begin with the same oils and the same canvas, for example. It is the picture and plan in the artist's mind that cause a different painting and a different form to appear on the canvas.

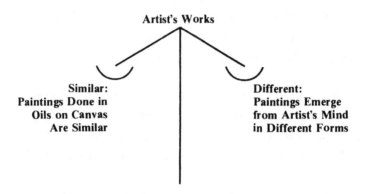

Artist's Works

Similar:
Paintings Done in
Oils on Canvas
Are Similar

Different:
Paintings Emerge
from Artist's Mind
in Different Forms

Neither similarities nor differences in the creation negate the existence of a Creator, a master Architect and a master Artist; rather, they prove a common Creator.

Ethology, the next scientific discipline that *The New Encyclopedia Britannica* used to support the theory of evolution, stresses the similarities of behaviour as evidence of the evolving process.

> Ethology (the study of behaviour) reveals similarities between different species that affirm their community of descent. This is the case, for example, in regard to the instincts in ants, bees, and wasps and to nest building among birds. Thrushes of separate species in Britain and in South America line their nests with mud in the same manner. Hornbills in Africa and in India both plaster up the female in a hole in a tree. In some cases it is possible to discern how instincts evolve. The three-spined stickleback has a complicated ritual of courtship behaviour, which resembles that of the ten-spined stickleback. The latter, however, utilizes simpler components of behaviour, demonstrating the evolutionary origins of the more complex acts performed by the three-spined stickleback.

Instinct is an inborn tendency (God-given sense) that impels each creature to behave in a way that is characteristic of its species. It is not surprising, then, that a thrush with "thrush sense" always would build a nest in the same way regardless of whether it were in Britain or South America.

Neither do the similarities and differences in the courtship behaviour of the three-spined sticklebacks and the ten-spined sticklebacks represent scientific proof of their instincts having evolved. Their different behaviour in courtship simply proves there is individuality within the species.

If instincts evolve from simpler forms to more complex ones, as scientists infer, then one should expect to see the pattern repeated in other places. If all mankind, for example, has evolved from a lower form of animal (which is what the evolutionists teach), one should see all men in a given time frame exhibiting the same behaviour in courtship. The fact that they behave differently indicates that each individual is able to respond in a unique way to the innate mating urge that God, the Creator, has placed within him.

The science of *Biochemistry* also is supposed to offer evidence for the theory of evolution, according to our source, *The New Encyclopedia Britannica*.

> The chemical characteristics of organisms are no less typical of their species than are their structures, embryonic development, or behaviour. Serology (the study of blood serum) provides evidence of the degree of divergence between the chemical composition of the blood of different animals. Human blood injected into a rabbit makes the latter produce antihuman serum, which, when mixed with human blood, causes clumping and settling (precipitation) of 100 percent of the blood protein. This antihuman serum precipitates blood of other species in the following percentages: gorilla, 64%; orangutan, 42%; baboon, 29%; ox, 10%, deer, 7%; horse, 2%; kangaroo, 0%. These figures serve as measures of chemical resemblance and affinity. It has been shown that seals resemble dogs, and whales resemble even-toed ungulates (e.g., cattle) - results that, expressed as relative degrees of affinity, agree with the evidence from comparative anatomy, embryology, and paleontology.

The only evidence these experiments provide is that human blood does not mix with animal blood. Chemical resemblances, similarities, and affinities merely confirm the common origin and the mutual parent of all creation—the LORD God. They are not evidences of evolution. As we have stated, it is very normal to see similarity in the Works of the same master Artist, the Creator.

The New Encyclopedia Britannica proceeded in its report on Biochemistry:

> Biochemistry provides countless further examples of similarities between species, of which one of the most instructive is the structure of the pancreatic enzyme insulin, which is made up of 51 amino acids, arranged in particular order that varies in details in different related species. At the site where the insulin of cattle has serine, that the sheep has clycine; where insulins of both these species have alanine and valine, insulins of horse and pig have threonine and isoleucine, respectively. The general resemblance of the molecules of insuline in all these species is explicable as due to their descent from a common ancestor; the differences between them are due to adaptation evolved by each species.

The biochemical similarities and differences between the species are not evidences of evolution. If all this fantastic chemical structure is due to evolution, it is even more miraculous than creation; and the supporters of the theory of evolution must, then, answer these questions: Who decided, then commanded, certain chemicals to evolve on the similarity side so organisms could "keep up with the Joneses"? Who decided and told other chemicals to be different?

Innate similarities and differences in creation point to a common ancestor, the Creator. Scientists have not *proven* otherwise; they have done studies from which they have drawn their own conclusions in the light of their belief in the evolutionary process, but what man believes is not the truth if it conflicts with God's Word.

IV. The Impossibility of Mutations Having Been Numerous Enough or Beneficial Enough to Have Produced Man

Calculations have proven that there has not been a sufficient amount of time in the history of the earth to allow for generations of gradual change to have taken place that would form all the different kinds of animals and plants we see today.

Dr. Satoko Yamada, a Japanese biochemist, graciously has translated some informative writings by Dr. Haruhiko Noda so they could be used in this book. Although the material was published more than a decade ago, the facts Dr. Noda recorded about the impossibility of creation having occurred through the process of a series of mutations are still valid. Dr. Noda's work shows the vast time frame that is needed for the necessary accumulation of mutations to occur in order for evolution to have taken place.

It is said that evolution is due to an accumulation of mutations that occur in the nucleic acid that had been fixed in the particular species after enduring selection. The way those mutations occurred can be assumed from the percentage of appearance of mutations in cultures of microorganisms, and also from the substitution of amino acid radicals in similar proteins of different species. Using either of the experimental measurements to base our calculus, we get the figure $5 \times 10(39)$ to $10(40)$ as the maximum number of mutations in one billion years.

In an earlier article written in *Kagaku Asahi*, September, 1971, Dr. Noda's work on the theory of mutations is quoted.

We tried to think on the simplest matter with the possibility of having the characteristics of a living organism. It would be made up of just one molecule of nucleic acid and one molecule of protein, and would be so small that each molecule would consist of only 100 units.

These figures are so small that this simple matter would be a lot smaller than any virus and the possibilities of its being alive would be very small, yet it might live if all things work very favorably.

To say that it is made, we will need each one of the 100 units that make up both of the molecules to be arranged in a sequence, not at random, but according to some sort of special plan.

When a parent gives birth to a child or if a chemist synthesizes something, it can be made according to that plan, but we cannot expect such a thing of the very first living organism.

So we have to wait until, in a place rich in organic matter such as a vast ocean where many molecules are formed at random, a molecule that exactly fits the plan would appear.

We can calculate under these conditions that we will get one molecule of what we desire after 4(100) x 20(100) - 10(190) (Nucleic acids are made of 4 classes of nucleotides, and proteins are built up of 20 amino acids. 10(190) means 10 followed by 190 zeros) trials.

Nevertheless, even if we dispose of all the existent material in the whole universe, we cannot make but a small portion of this amount which is 1/100,000,000 (one hundred millionth) of a one hundred millionth of a one hundred millionth and so on for ten times.

Moreover, even if we make many hundred millions of molecules every second, what we get in 10 billion years (that is about 10(18) sec.) is negligibly small.

Since it seems so difficult, from either the material viewpoint or timewise, for a thing with even such simple combination of molecules to have appeared by chance, it might not make sense to think that even the simplest of the known organisms came to existence by an accidental combination of substances.

Dr. Noda assumes that since 10(40) mutations are the maximum that can be produced in one billion years, they should be sufficient to produce a simple organism in the beginning that eventually, after "several" billions of years of exchanging amino acids at that same rate, will become the whole spectrum of living creatures we have now on the earth, including man.

Now let us assume we could produce a viable, really meaningful, progressive, sequential mutation every single second since the earth was formed, scientists say, 10 billion years ago (that is just 10(18) seconds ago), we would still need 10(22) seconds to get the 10(40) mutations needed.

10(22) seconds is about 10 quadrillion years (10 million billion years).

These scientific facts, 10,000,000,000,000,000 = 10 million billion years, negate the possibility of things coming into existence by the process of random selection and mutations.

The theory of evolution, when applied to plants and animals, basically says that life progressed from one-celled organisms to its highest form, the human being, by means of biological changes which took place over multiplied millions of years.

Dr. Noda's work proves that the earth has not had the time to accomplish such a miraculous feat, even if it had been granted the power to do so.

Dr. Gange agrees with Dr. Noda. In his book *Origins and Destiny*, Dr. Gange said, "Careful scientific calculations show that natural sources cannot produce the information we find in life's blueprint. The universe is simply too young and too small to have produced the information found in even a single bacterium."

Thus, we see that as scientific knowledge increases in the world, instead of more and more people being convinced that the process of evolution is a fact, they are finding that the world in its blindness has been accepting unproven theories.

In his book, *The Collapse of Evolution*, Scott M. Huse made this statement: ". . . it is impossible to prove scientifically any theory of origins."

V. The Immutableness of God's Creation Which Refutes Natural Selection and Adaptation as Being the Means of Developing a New Species

Evolutionists offer their suggestions, probabilities, and hypothetical theories as though they were tried and proven facts.

They theorize that through natural selection and adaptation apes experienced a change that enabled them to walk on two feet, use their hands, and descend from trees in order to find food and carry it back to home base. But apes still are leaving trees to obtain food and carry it back to home base. Why are their feet and brains not continuing to evolve, therefore, becoming more man-like? Where is the evidence, the proven facts to match the hypothetical theories of evolution?

Fossil records reveal that species remain basically the same throughout their existence and that, according to Secretary Adams' editorial in the September, 1978, issue of *Smithsonian Magazine*, ". . . 90 percent of identified bones represent extinct species." These high rates of extinction seem to coincide with the earliest arrival of mankind, scientists think. (This is additional corroboration from the scientific world that earlier creations were destroyed by God's catastrophic judgments on the sins of man.)

There are simple forms of life now existing which existed in prehistoric times, and they have remained the same through millennia. Present-day species reveal that they also have remained basically the same thoughout their existence on the present earth.

In his article "Life After Darwin," to which we have already referred, D. J. Tice, managing editor of the *TWA Ambassador Magazine*, dealt with several problems Darwinism faces. He quoted scientist Niles Eldredge, chairman and curator of invertebrates at American Museum of Natural History in New York, one of America's leading evolutionary theorists, who contends:

> . . . it is the appearance of a new species that triggers
> anatomical change, and not the accumulation of changes
> that produces a new species. . . . [Mr. Tice's conclusion was
> "(this) pretty much stands Darwin on his head."]

While Mr. Tice did not negate natural selection as a significant force, he also said it *has not been proven* that it is the pre-eminent force responsible for everything we see.

He also pointed out that "The very idea of 'fitness' is under attack in some quarters because the real issue in natural selection is not survival but reproduction."

"Survival," Mr. Tice maintains, "is relevant only to the extent that the organism must survive long enough to reproduce, and presumably the longer it survives, the more offspring it will leave." He then posed this question, "Why, then, has evolution moved with conviction from simple, abundant reproduction (the sort bacteria conduct) and toward complicated, sparse reproduction (typical of higher animals)?"

Posing more questions about Darwin's theory of selection and adaptation, Mr. Tice asked:

> But as we look out at nature, *what we see again and again,*
> *what biologists are forever describing* (and attributing to
> natural selection) *are organisms that are perfectly adapted*
> *to their environment.* Where are the creatures in need of
> adaption? And what should we suppose an animal will do as
> its habitat becomes less suitable to its lifestyle? In a 1974
> paper, Gould and Eldredge addressed the question: "Are we
> to believe that a species can exist for a million years
> gradually improving its adaptation . . .? Isn't it more likely

that, faced with a linear change in environment . . . a species
as a whole will change its area of residence, rather than sit
there, grin and bear it, and 'adapt'?"*

Darwin maintained that a species developed those characteristics which were the most advantageous for its survival. Yet Mr. Tice gave examples of plants and animals whose features, if supplied by natural selection, do not seem to be advantageous. The following are some examples he used:

- Flowers formed so that only one species of insect can
  pollinate them. (Certainly not an advantage.)
- Many varieties of bees who die after they sting
  (Would not the advantage be to grow a stinger
  which could be used over and over without
  destroying its owner?)
- Birds that cannot fly, although flying is an advantage.
- Bloodsucking mosquitos and non-bloodsucking
  mosquitos. (Which has the advantage since natural
  selection developed both?)
- Mammals who are supposed to have evolved from
  reptiles because being a mammal is advantageous.
  (Why, then, are there still reptiles?)

The examples could continue on and on. Then to cast further doubt on the Darwinian theory of natural selection, Mr. Tice referred to Francis Hitching's book, *The Neck of the Giraffe*, which tells of experiments that have been made with the fruit fly in which scientists have tried to create new species. However, the conclusion was: ". . . not a single clearly new species has been created, and there is barely a handful of even remotely plausible cases in which an 'advantaged' variety has appeared."

Mr. Tice's article further pointed out that dog breeding, horticulture—all selective breeding—tell the same story: there are limits to what can be produced through artificial selection, and that natural selection, without man's interference,

*Emphasis by Author

265

leads to uniformity—not diversity. Dogs the world over that mate freely across breed lines look the same. "As soon as the selective breeding ceases, so does the variation," Mr. Tice said.

More and more scientists are agreeing that natural selection and adaptation do not prove evolution, nor do a lot of other evolutionary ideas make sense; still scientists do not abandon their evolutionary beliefs and accept that matter came into being and developed according to God's master plan and purposive will.

Some of Dr. Gange's statements in his book *Origins and Destiny* that refer to the subject of natural selecton bear quoting. He said: "One reason that natural selection is an empty phrase is that we can create any story to defend it. . . . Biological miracles are everywhere, but natural selection provides no sober insight into their origin . . . Natural selection no more explains living systems than does natural affection explain the people who express it. . . . Everything we know tells us that machines are structures [that] intelligence designs, and that accidents destroy. Therefore, accidents do not design machines. Intellect does. And the myriad of biological wonders that sprinkle our world testify to the design ingenuity of a Supreme Intellect."

The uncertainties about their theories even cause struggles and emotional fights among scientists.

Their prejudiced reasoning and their immature behaviour reveal their emotional frustration which is, no doubt, a result of their lack of evidence to support their theories. Security, satisfaction, and quietness are the fruit of established truth. The joy of finding the truth in any field brings peace and satisfaction to the finder. The finding of truth is a sufficient reward to the seeker of truth. Hence, theories that first have been proven by facts always produce satisfactory and peaceable conclusions. But when one places preconceived and unproven conclusions, first, then one always is forced to use unproven theories to crown his unproven conclusions.

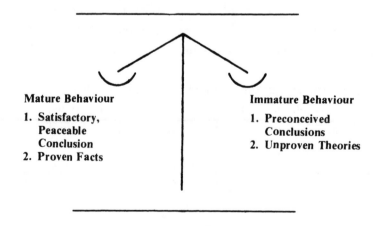

Mature Behaviour
1. Satisfactory,
   Peaceable
   Conclusion
2. Proven Facts

Immature Behaviour
1. Preconceived
   Conclusions
2. Unproven Theories

266

When we take up preconceived conclusions about anything, we find ourselves frantically looking for any kind of theory to support our conclusion, whether it be proven by facts or not. Then we find a great degree of hostility and animosity filling our minds when someone dares to suggest that our conclusion is supported by unproven theories. These feelings are displayed by evolutionists when their unproven theories are questioned. Without proof, they say evolution is a *fact!*

However, a true, sincere scientist analyzes all the available facts, first, and then draws his conclusions. This is how an unprejudiced and unbiased investigator works. He does not force a union between his unproven theories and his preconceived conclusions.

Since the unproven theory of evolution is not supported by natural selection and adaptation of the species, it does not support the satisfactory and peaceable conclusion that they are responsible for our present creation.

The immutableness of God's creation from one creation to another refutes all theories of an evolving creation by natural selection and adaptations.

The eternal, immutable God, His eternal Word, and His divine Works are everlasting witnesses against the theories that our earth and its world of inhabitants came into existence by evolution.

VI. The Complexity of Creation Which Argues Against Random Selection

The many infinite twinings and weavings of complicated, intricate, and interrelated parts in creation are sufficient reason *not to believe* that all creation had its origin from a beginning cell which evolved into billions of life forms. If the infinitude of elaborately interrelated and interconnected parts of creation are so complex and complicated that a collection of the most intelligent brains throughout history have been unable to understand all their intricate interweavings, how could one cell have had the infinite wisdom and knowledge needed to expand itself through millennia until it eventually evolved into nature's highest organized structure, the human body?

God's complex Work, manifested in all His created hosts, is sufficient reason to prove the theories of evolution untrue.

From Dr. Gange's book *Origins And Destiny* comes this enlightening bit of information about the complexity of living cells.

> Prior to the practical development of the electron micro-
> scope the true extent of the complexity of living cells was
> unknown. . . . The calculations show that the belief that

life arose accidentally is statistically impossible and intellectually outrageous.

Furthermore he added:

> . . . one thing is sure: Scientific data do not support the thesis that life arose by chance.

> . . . the information (complexity) found in even simple cells is so vast, that to suppose it was produced by natural processes in a universe as young as 13 billion years and as small as 30 billion light-years is to abdicate one's cognitive faculties. . . .

Evolution cannot account for the beginning of life nor for the complicated and complex wisdom that fills all creation, but God's Word does. The Bible's account reveals that God is the Source of all *begotten* and *creative* life.

The principle of biogenesis says that life comes from life. Therefore, the Bible is in agreement with the principle of biogenesis.

> For with thee *is the fountain of life*: in thy light shall we see light (Psalm 36:9).

God is the Source, the Fountain, of all life, both simple and complex life. He is the divine Intelligence Who is responsible for all wise design, the blueprint that is necessary to produce all life.

Dr. Gange referred to the development of the electron miscroscope in the 1950's and explained what has happened to scientific information since its use in research. He said: "Thus if we believed life was an accident, before 1960 no one could prove us wrong. Today that's changed. . . . The result is this: To get life, you need life. Nothing less will do. Anything else is wishful thinking."

Later in his book, he said, "Despite all one hears and reads, no one has ever produced life from nonlife. . . . No one anywhere has ever created life from chemicals. . . ."

Life exists because of information along the DNA. This information is in the form of groups of chemicals that are strategically positioned to create life's blueprint.

If one compares God's glorious, complex creation of plants, animals, and insects to man's simple, finite inventions, he discovers there is no comparison.

268

The earth is filled with multitudinous examples of complex life-forms in the lower realms of animal life. And the complexities within the cells of the higher realm of life, namely man, amaze the scientists who study them.

The following are some examples of the mysterious, wise designs and innate intelligence with which God has endowed His creatures.

Locomotion in Sea Creatures

Consider the squid who travels by jet propulsion, taking in water and squirting it out through a powerful syphon near the head. The squid can overtake nearly anything that swims.

Probably one of the most astounding navigational feats is performed by the porpoise. In *Origins And Destiny*, Dr. Gange referred to the porpoise as one of the most amazing biological miracles. He said:

> The reason that a porpoise can swim so fast (over forty miles
> per hour) is because spongy material within its loose, finely-
> laced, layered skin rhythmically vibrates with movements
> that virtually match laminar flow, and that reduce its drag
> by 90 percent.

With all his intelligence and planning, man has not been able to achieve laminar flow in the marine craft he has designed, yet he sees this capability working in lower forms of life. It is inconceivable that such knowledge could be acquired on its own by a lower form of animal life. That all animals develop according to their God-given blueprint is most believable.

Mimicry in the Insect World

God has designed insects to fool the eye of their predators. Since nontoxic insects and spiders have no means of protecting themselves in any other way, God placed within their design protective coloration and shapes. Everyone is familiar with the insects called "walking sticks." They resemble the twigs of trees to perfection. Treehoppers look like thorns. The sphinx moth's wings blend with tree bark. Harmless insects look like poisonous ones—all forms of mimicy to perpetuate the species.

Although evolutionists claim these creatures developed the art of mimicry by themselves, it is impossible to suppose that the egg of insects would have developed the intelligence to perform this creative feat. Surely such protective designing points to an Intelligence beyond that of the insects. Who would design His creation so that it had no chance for survival? Why create it in the first place?

The Complexity of Insects' Structures and Functions

According to an article by Alan Devoe, "The Marvel of an Insect,"* insects represent nearly 80 percent of all animals on earth. There are close to one million kinds of insects already classified, but entomologists predict the total may reach ten million.

An insect has no bones, but some can move around under a load of 850 times their own weight. Winged specimens perform extraordinary feats. A mosquito can fly carrying twice its own weight. A flea can leap 100 times its own height. Butterflies can survive atmospheric pressures that would crush an elephant.

Ears may be positioned anywhere on an insect. Katydids have supersonic hearing, detecting as many as 45,000 vibrations per second.

Insects see with eyes on top of their heads, by compound eyes at the sides, and by a kind of all-over light sense. The insect's sensory organs of taste and smell reach tremendous capacities. Butterflies and bees taste with their mouths and their feet! While human taste can detect sweetness in a solution of one part sugar to 200 parts water, some moths and butterflies detect one part in 300,000. Moths can catch scents nine miles downwind.

Mr. Devoe concluded his report on insects with this statement: "To know something of the wonder of insects is to contemplate a little of the miracle of life."

And who but God could have planned cross-pollination? The way insects and flowers combine to accomplish this is almost unbelievable—except for the fact that God planned it that way. Man may discover the way God planned all creation, but to ascribe *His* planning to the finite intelligence with which He endowed each creature is sheer unreasonableness. There is nothing wrong in searching for spiritual and natural laws and wanting to unravel their mysteries, but to say all planning and intelligence lies in what we, as finite creatures, can see and understand, makes man the most colossal, egotistical, conglomeration of confused cells in the universe.

An article, "The Marvels of Cross-Pollination" by Rutherford Platt,** described the intricacies of cross-pollination, and his report fills one with wonder at God's

---

*Alan Devoe *Our Amazing World of Nature* (Reader's Digest Assn., Inc., 1969).

**Rutherford Platt. *Our Amazing World of Nature* (Reader's Digest Assn., Inc., 1969).

270

meticulous plans. Mr. Platt tells us that if it were not for bees, half of our most beautiful flower species would disappear. His article gives us the following, astonishing information.

Usually a bee gathers pollen from only one kind of flower at a time, distinguishing between different flowers of the same color growing close together!

Only the bumblebee can pollinate red clover because the size of his head, his weight, and the pressure he exerts are all precisely balanced for this flower. The mechanism does not operate accurately for any other kind of insect.

The honeybee is *forced* to pollinate the flower, lady's slipper, because the entrance to its nectar chamber closes behind the bee, and the bee is then forced to exit under an arching stigma that scrapes pollen off its back; then it must squeeze its way past a mass of pollen which it takes to the next lady's slipper.

Mr. Platt concluded his article this way:

> You will find that each kind of flower has its own blueprints and schedules. And as you study them you cannot help feeling that sense of incredulous awe which prompted Jean Henri Fabre, the Homer of insects, to say of cross-pollination: 'Before these mysteries of life, reason bows and abandons itself to adoration of the Author of these miracles.'

To Jean Fabre's statement, we add a loud AMEN!

The Innate Intelligence in Animals

God's complex organization of His creation proves that He is a Master Organizer. God has endowed the animal world with a complex animal sense to practice the physical laws that He has established for them. (That animals respond to their God-given instincts is more than God can say for man, who, most of the time, refuses to practice the spiritual, moral laws that God has established for him.)

The innate, complex intelligence that God has placed within each animal so it can survive and fulfill its God-given role in life is truly amazing!

Observers see wild animals who seem to plan strategies to outwit their enemies, banding together to kill their prey; animals, who go outside their normal pattern of behaviour to help injured fellows, exhibit a brotherhood that puts man with his superior intelligence to shame. Who gave them this kind of intelligence?

Alan Devoe, in an article titled "How Animals Help Each Other," cited the example of the coatis of Central and South America, relatives of the raccoons, who band together to hunt food:

> One band goes aloft and scares dozing iguanas out of the branches. As the lizards fall, they are grabbed and overpowered by a contigent of coatis deployed on the ground.

Devoe cited other animals who exhibit the same co-effort in finding food—America's great white pelicans who fish together and coyotes who form relay teams to chase jackrabbits because jackrabbits run faster than the coyotes.

Everyone has heard stories about elephants helping an injured member of the herd, but birds do, too, and in unusual circumstances. Mr. Devoe told about watching in the dead of winter—not mating time, nor fledgling time—an adult bluejay feed another adult whose lower mandible had been broken off. Animal's God-given intelligence is truly uncanny in the way it exhibits what we would consider human-like behaviour.

If one looks to the present creation, he sees a complex, supernatural intelligence abiding in the most minute forms of created life. This proves a Master Architect with a master blueprint has been at work.

Every phase of nature bears witness to the Workings of the infinite intelligence of a Mastermind Who has had a master plan for every part of His creation, including man who is the most complex of all God's creation since man is made in the image and likeness of God Himself.

Complexity in Man

How sad that with such a glorious heritage man *wants* to put himself on a level with God's lesser creation! The Psalmist asked the question, "What is man that Thou art mindful of him?" (Psalm 8:4). How ungrateful of Charles Darwin not to give God praise for his life and his position on earth as a man—the highest of God's creation.

Darwins' studies should have made him exclaim with David, "O LORD our Lord, how excellent is thy name in all the earth!" (Psalm 8:9).

But Darwin looked at the creation, after sin had entered through man's choice, and he accused God of being unjust.

God made man the highest in the order of His creation—and the most complex.

To the student of life, today, nothing is more marvelous than the development of a single fertilized egg cell into a human being! How a single fertilized egg cell can multiply itself into 200 million cells that are organized into the complex machine called Homo sapiens is not comprehended by any man. No one ever has unlocked all the secrets of the human body.

Man has every reason to stand in awe and amazement at the remarkable piece of complex machinery called the human body.

The theory of evolution cannot explain God's complex intelligence in His purposive will in the amazingly complicated process of the birth of a human baby. However, the Bible explains this process by giving God the glory and honour as being the divine, omniscient, intelligent One with the master plan, and the One Who had the divine omnipotence to implement the intricate designs of His plan in everything.

King David prophetically described God's intricate designs for his body.

> Thine eyes did see my substance, yet being unperfect; and in thy
> book all *my members* were written, *which* in continuance were
> fashioned, when *as yet there was none of them* (Psalm 139:16).

All of God's creations and His roles for His creations were conceived in God's mind and written in His Book in advance of creation. His eyes were upon us when we were still a shapeless body. Likewise, in the beginning, all of our parts were written or *hidden* in the complex DNA by the Creator God.

Man of this present world did not have his origin in a less perfect form. In the beginning, God created present man in His image and likeness, and *all races* have descended from the first man and woman, Adam male and female, who after their sin became known as Adam and Eve. When primitive tribes have been found in our present world, their origin has been the same as all other men today. Their life-style shows the results of sin and separation from God, not a retarded development in their evolutionary line.

When man sinned, by rebelling against God's command at the tower of Babel, he was scattered abroad upon the face of the earth (Genesis 11:1-9). Mankind developed different cultures because God changed his language and his geographical locations, separating him into different races, according to His purposive will, not because of evolution.

Man, even in his present imperfect state, is still a complex creature, and he is a living witness of the Work of a Divine Designer and a Master Maker.

The sweet Psalmist of Israel bore witness to his Master Maker.

I will praise thee; for *I am fearfully and wonderfully made*: marvelous are thy works; and that my soul knoweth right well (Psalm 139:14).

Man does not need to study heaven and earth, first, in order to behold the wondrous greatness of God's divine Handiwork. Man needs only to look in the mirror at himself to see God's complex creation; yet of all His creatures, man, with the most intelligence, rebels against rendering the homage due to his eternal Creator, Owner, Master, Governor, and Redeemer.

VII. The Degenercy of Man and the Destruction of His Environment Which Argue Against the Final Outcome of Evolution

In addition to their unproven hypotheses, another fallacy evolutionists must deal with is the idea of the upward progression of organic life, especially when applied to the development of man. Science cannot prove from the history of man on this present earth that he is progressing to higher planes in his moral development, nor is he succeeding in preserving his environment.

Man's knowledge has increased, as the Bible said it would in the last days, but man's knowledge without God's wisdom leads only to problems and ultimately to death. The *fact* is that *man is degenerating* into a worse, demoralized state, both intellectually and spiritually.

These discoveries are only proofs that mankind as a whole has not ascended or evolved into something higher and better. On the contrary, man, in general, continually is descending downward in mental degeneration and moral degradation. God said that the end of this downward pathway is death. The destructive effects of Adam's disobedience still is being experienced by his descendants today. This destructive effect of Adam's sinful disobedience and death cannot be eliminated by man's knowledge and wisdom; it can be stopped only by God's redemptive wisdom and knowledge. This is an irrevocable law of God.

God's Word gives a most clear revelation of an individual's responsibility before God.

The soul that sinneth, it shall die. Thy son shall not bear the iniquity of the father, neither shall the father bear the iniquity of the son: the righteousness of the righteous shall be upon him, and the wickedness of the wicked shall be upon him (Ezekiel 18:20).

Evolutionists cannot explain the death they constantly encounter as evidenced by fossillized bones and the death of today's human bodies. Scientists cannot explain the aging factor or offer a solution for stopping it. But the Bible has the answer for the mystery of death. It tells us why man dies; it also tells man how he can overcome death and *live* again in a new, resurrected body through the sacrical death and resurrected life of the LORD Jesus Christ.

In referring to Astronaut Frank Bormann's remark, made in an interview after his return from the moon, Professor Rigutti, in his book *A Hundred Billion Stars*, quoted Mr. Bormann as having said, "'The earth, seen from lunar distances, is so beautiful, so quiet, so peaceful that if we had not known its problems, to tell you the truth, we would have believed it a small, silent, peaceful, and lonely world.'" Professor Rigutti added to Mr. Bormann's remarks: "But the truth is, the earth is neither peaceful nor silent. . . . People on earth are hungry, thirsty, and afraid." He then said that, of course, not all people are hungry and not all people are thirsty, but that ". . . Almost everybody is afraid. Some [like us again] live in fear as if in a new dimension—total fear, without hope. For violence, poverty, disease, intimidation, exploitation, cowardice, cynicism, and war are the threads that form the fabric of today's world. . . . It is all so hopeless that you feel like giving up and consigning the whole world to the devil."

How diametrically different is the life, hope, and faith in Christ that allows us to grow in His infinite grace and eternal knowledge. While tremendous strides have been made in some fields, the results of which help to alleviate man's problems, such as improved medical technology, mankind remains the same with his abnormalities, deficiencies, defects, diseases, sin, and death.

The wisdom of man is unable to negate God's law of ultimate death for sinful man.

> And as it *is appointed unto man once to die, but after this the judgment:* (Hebrews 9:27).

All that science has uncovered about man's destruction and death through fossil records simply verify the account of man's rebellion, disobedience, and death as outlined in the Holy Scriptures. Every graveyard is a veritable witness of the veracity of God's Word. The death of prehistoric men, and present man's 6,000 year-long decline morally and physically, plus his eventual visitation by death are all witnesses of the depths to which man has sunk.

The statistics of the declining morals of our society bear witness that man is not evolving into something better and better.

The following survey was made in 1980 by Morris Robertson, the Assistant Chief of Police in Winston-Salem, North Carolina.

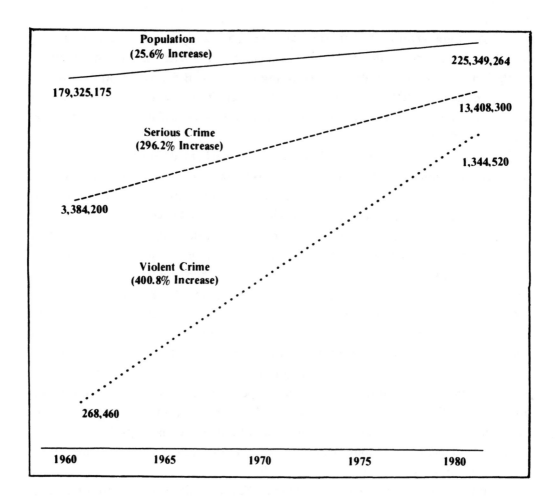

Population
(25.6% Increase)

225,349,264

179,325,175

Serious Crime
(296.2% Increase)

13,408,300

1,344,520

3,384,200

Violent Crime
(400.8% Increase)

268,460

| 1960 | 1965 | 1970 | 1975 | 1980 |

Based on statistics compiled by the Federal Bureau of Investigation through the Uniform Crime Reporting system. Chart prepared by Morris A. Robertson, Assistant Chief of Police, Winston-Salem Police Department, Winston-Salem, North Carolina.

Notice the *population increased* only 25.6%, but *serious crime* increased 296.8%, and *violent crime* increased 400.8%. This is incredible! Yet, it proves that mankind's *evolving degeneration* is rolling downward at a fast rate.

U.S. News & World Report, May 5, 1986, confirmed the increase of man's degeneration.

> . . . Also, some experts believe that many of today's criminals commit more offenses per capita than those of their parents' generation.

Prison populations nationwide reached about 500,000 by mid-1985, rising nearly 50 percent in five years.

'. . . We are incarcerating more people, but most get out before very long and many are worse than before' observes criminologist Lyle Shannon of the University of Iowa.

. . . two basic facts of life stand in the way of its bringing a marked decline in crime:

- Police fail to catch most violators. At best, they solve 1 in 7 burglaries and 1 in 4 robberies.
- Young people are constantly entering criminal careers. 'The imprisonment of one offender may simply provide opportunities for another,' says researcher Joseph Sheley of Tulane University. . . ."

It is impossible to look at our world situation today without seeing man's tremendous need of God.

Stephen A. Egger gave a report on man's increased lawlessness in *The Futurist* dated April, 1985:

Predator: One who lives by preying on others; addicted to or characterized by a tendency to victimize or destroy others for one's own gain.

In the past few years, there has been an increase in violent incidents resulting from discourtesy and people's perceived inability to control their immediate environment. The impression that some aspects of one's life are beyond one's control—or that no one cares, or that the quality of life is deteriorating—is resulting in increased incidents of violence over seemingly trivial matters. For example, three people were killed in a Houston bar in an argument over a locked rest room that was out of order.

Minor traffic accidents and driver impatience have resulted in assaults and killings on urban roadways. Neighbor has shot neighbor over parking problems. People want to have some control over their own lives. When they begin to feel out of control, violent and predatory acts sometimes result.

Many people now feel unsafe in their own neighborhoods and barricade their homes. A recent Gallup Poll found that 53% of the people surveyed were afraid to walk in certain areas located within one mile of their homes.

All of this violence and degeneracy presents a problem and a question. Since, in our evolutionary journey, we are *supposed* to have evolved from the uncivilized ape (which is a lower form of animal), why is it that higher, civilized man behaves worse than the poor ape? Should we, as civilized people, apologize to the poor ape for insulting him when we claim to be his "kinfolk"?

The condition of the declining morals of these last days also is recorded in God's Word.

> This know also, that in the last days perilous times shall come. For men shall be lovers of their own selves, covetous, boasters, proud, blasphemers, disobedient to parents, unthankful, unholy, Without natural affection, trucebreakers, false accusers, incontinent, fierce, despisers of those that are good, Traitors, heady, highminded, lovers of pleasures more than lovers of God; (II Timothy 3:1-4).

The Bible's description of the last days is confirmed in almost every newspaper and magazine. We have noted only a very few in this book.

In all honesty, we must ask, "Is mankind as a whole rolling upward with God and evolving into a more perfect man of love, joy, and peace? Or is mankind as a whole rolling downward in moral degeneration? Is man, apart from God, evolving into total disrespect for God's law and man's law and daily becoming more vicious, violent, and war-like?" The answer to the first question is unquestionably "NO!" The answer to the second and third questions is absolutely "YES!"

God has created man with freedom of choice. For a season, God has allowed man to take his own wicked way, which has produced misery, woe, affliction, and death. Thoughout man's history, he has taken his liberty and freedom of choice and used them to live immorally. He has tried to blot God out of his mind and negate God's eternal existence. But statistics constantly prove that miseries, woes, and afflictions have followed man as a result of his sinful, disobedient deeds!

The reports of today confirm that man is neither evolving upward by gradual change nor evolving upward by spurts. In fact, he is not even in a state of moral stasis.

Neither has man improved his environment. To the contrary, he has damaged and destroyed so much of his environment that he faces annihilation himself. A recent letter from the former Governor of Wisconsin on behalf of the Wilderness Society said: "At no time during my public life as Governor of Wisconsin, U. S. Senator, and now Counselor of the Wilderness Society have I have been so concerned about the state of America's natural resources and the quality of our environment. . . . In truth, I doubt there is any other single issue with a more compelling entitlement to our attention and our time."

Of course the state of the environment is compellingly important! There are balances in the way God has created the earth and its inhabitants that cannot be changed without life-threatening consequences.

Consider what scientists have recently discovered about the earth's delicate ozone layer. An article in the *Smithsonian* magazine of February, 1988, entitled "Solo Flights into the Ozone Hole Reveal Its Causes," by Ellen Ruppel Shell, apprised the public of the following startling information:

> Left alone, nature keeps the creation and destruction of ozone in careful balance. But it has been years since nature has held sole rein over this process.
>
> Man-made chemicals emitted freely into the atmosphere have disrupted the equilibrium. Some fear that the ozone hole above the South Pole is a consequence of this hapless process, the first physical sign that we are systematically destroying the very substance that made life as we know it possible in the first place.
>
> We are pushing chlorine levels in the stratosphere higher every year—eventually even the sturdiest slab of stratosphere will be altered by the chemical envasion.

At first scientists were not concerned about CFCs (chlorofluorocarbons) being emitted into the earth's atmosphere, but now they are sounding an alarm. According to the article, ". . . if CFC emission is not controlled, the ozone will deplete dramatrically by the middle of the 21st century, exposing Earth to untold levels of ultraviolet radiation."

A letter from the Nations' Wildlife Federation sounded the same alarm: "Toxic, poisonous wastes are released into the air every day, all across the country. You can read about it in the papers almost every day. It's a pollution problem which is silent and invisible. . . but the long term threat to America is very real, . . ."

Why are man and his environment becoming worse and worse? There seems little doubt that left to himself man will self-destruct. Why? Because man chose death in the Garden of Eden. The only way out is through the Creator. We still have a choice for life through God's gift to man, His Son.

Summary

We have the right and the moral obligation to weigh the evidence presented by the evolutionists against the evidence presented by believing scientists and the Word of God, and then to choose the answer we believe the facts show. The evidence for creation is more convincing than the unproven theories presented by evolutionists.

First of all scientists themselves are uncertain about what their findings reveal. Then there are the scientific and Biblical proofs that many ideas upon which the theory of evolution has been built are false: fossil records do not show transitional forms which would indicate there has been an evolution of the species; similarities are not proof of common ancestors; mutations or random selections do not account for new species.

The complexity of creation, the degeneracy of mankind, and the threat of death to his environment argue against evolution as the answer to the origin of living matter.

Conclusion

Chapter One

The Dark Stairway of the Atheistic View of the Origin of Living and Nonliving Matter

THE PURPOSE of all atheistic theories is to negate man's responsibility and accountability to a living God. If there is no God, there is no one to whom we have to give an account. The truth is God, the Creator, created man like unto Himself with freedom of moral choice between good and evil or right and wrong. Hence, man *is* responsible and accountable for his sinful deeds.

God's Word declares that a man is a fool or a degraded and withered man in his heart who says, in his heart, there is no God.

> *The fool hath said in his heart, There is no God.* Corrupt are they,
> and have done abominable iniquity: there is none that doeth good
> (Psalm 53:1).

When man's heart withers and decays with the spiritual disease of unbelief, he ultimately says, "There is no God." A person becomes a fool when God's wisdom withers and decays in his heart. A fool willfully rejects God, while at the same time he really knows that God exists.

It is unparalleled, ignorant conceit that makes a foolish heart turn to atheism after it has had the privilege of inquiring into the nature of God's Handiwork in His creation. Atheistic evolutionists endeavour to attribute God's creative natural effects to some other cause than God, the original Cause; then they attempt to convert all other hearts and minds to their own misleading philosophical ideas.

The atheistic concept of evolution never deals with the beginning or first cause of the existence of matter. According to atheistic scientists' assumption, matter always has existed. The atheistic concept of creation denies God as the beginning or the first Cause of all things. Denying God leaves the atheistic mind covered with the dark clouds of assumption concerning the beginning, the first cause of all things.

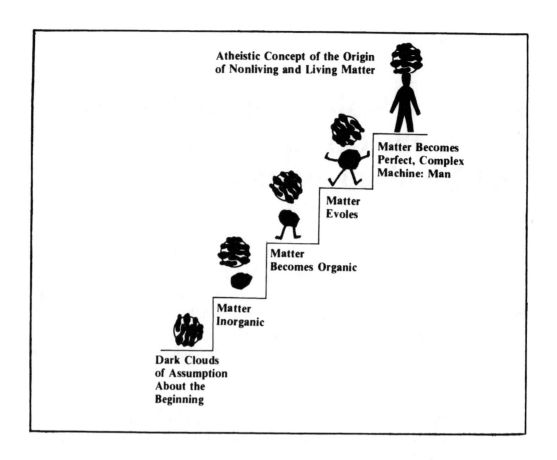

Atheistic Concept of the Origin of Nonliving and Living Matter

Matter Becomes Perfect, Complex Machine: Man

Matter Evoles

Matter Becomes Organic

Matter Inorganic

Dark Clouds of Assumption About the Beginning

It is an insult to the intelligence of a rational, thinking soul to be asked to believe that a small inorganic speck of matter could be so perfect and complete in its intelligence that while it was still in an immature and imperfect state it could, without the help of a Master Designer and the force of His omnipotent power, intelligently work its way upward into the perfect and orderly piece of complete, complex, and complicated machinery called man.

Because atheistic evolutionists never return to the true beginning, the *first cause* of existence of matter or the first cause of force, they never stop searching for that moment when a little inorganic speck of matter supposedly transformed itself into a speck of organic matter that was filled with wisdom and knowledge to increase itself until, ultimately, it fashioned and formed itself into a perfect, complicated machine called a man.

If all creation were indeed brought into existence by this evolutionary method, then we must ask *who* supplied the master plan and *who* furnished the powerful force to accomplish all this?

According to the scientific theory of biogensis and the First Law of Thermodynamics, Life had to be present to beget life and Intellect had to be present to form the life into all its myriad designs and functions. So scientists have proven the existence of God whether they admit it or not. God is Life and Light and Love!

> In the beginning was the Word, and the Word was with God, and the Word was God. The same was in the beginning with God. All things were made by him; and without him was not any thing made that was made. *In him was life; and the life was the light of men* (John 1:1-4).

> Jesus saith unto him, I am the way, the truth, and *the life*: no man cometh unto the Father, but by me (John 14:6).

And God has a mind—an Intelligence!

> For who hath known *the mind of the Lord?* or who hath been his counsellor? (Romans 11:34).

If, indeed, all existence came into being by itself, then the miracle of existence by evolution is even greater than the miracle of existence by creation. However, the Bible gives an accurate, sensible, and truthful account of the beginning and the first cause of existence. It reveals the omniscient Master Planner and the omnipotent Force Who implemented His master plan into all created existence.

God's Word does not allow the mind of any true seeker of truth to remain shrouded with dark clouds of confusion, mental chaos, or spiritual bewilderment which would prevent him from being able to distinguish between truth and error. The Word of God does not cause one's mind to be filled with the disorders and disarrays of the carnal, diseased perception of reality. God's Word does not create a disturbance in one's mind concerning the orderly arrangements of His master plan and the perfect organization of His omnipotent force that brought all things into visible existence.

However, fallen Lucifer, or the Devil as he is known today, has instilled his pernicious lie into heathen minds that *matter always has existed.* If matter always has existed, then it is infinite, omniscient and omnipotent. Matter, therefore, is a God of wisdom and power.

The Bible is either true, or it is not true. If it is false, and not true, then it is the biggest fraud in time. However, *the Bible is true*, and those who experience its illuminating light and its quickening life know the reality of its truth.

Although many atheists constantly try to destroy the power of the Bible, it continually remains the best seller, which confirms the fact that man has a spirit and soul which can be satisfied only with the spiritual meat and the spiritual drink from God's Holy Word.

Since true science and true revelation have their origin in the same Source, the one true God, they *cannot be* diametrically *different*. However, both *can be* greatly *misinterpreted*. God's "book of nature" has been greatly misinterpreted. Likewise, His Book of Truth, the Bible, has been greatly misinterpreted. When the "book of nature" and the Biblical Book of Truth are properly understood, one discovers a beautiful harmony and unity between the two.

Unbelieving scientists work from the light of their discoveries to the darkness of their ignorance. They trace backward to a point where there is no light (from light to darkness). The theories and interpretations that they then rely on are based on their lack of understanding. When they go beyond the light of their understandng, they are left with only the darkness of their ignorance with which to work.

But God's Working is diametrically opposite to that of the scientists. He works from Light to Light. God begins His Working with the Light of His understanding, and He finishes His Work with the Light of His understanding. The Bible begins with the sole existence of God, the Father of Light, and proceeds out to creation which is God's great tabernacle of Light. Thus, the Bible deals with Light from the beginning and progresses to the end of Light, manifested in all creation. But some scientists deal with only the creation, the Light manifested in the end. When they try to find the beginning, they end in a place of *darkness* because they try to negate God and His Light, the true beginning.

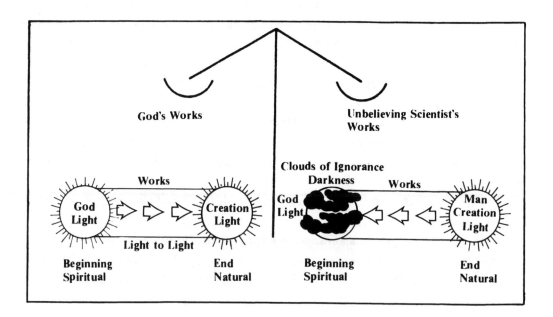

286

With his natural eyes of light or understanding, man can work in the end of God's creative Work or creation. To see God's spiritual Light in the beginning requires spiritual eyes of faith. We cannot understand the spiritual beginning Light with our natural eyes of light. If we work our way backward from the natural end of creation, we ultimately encounter our dark clouds of ignorance that prevent us from seeing the beginning Light of God.

When our spiritual eyes have been enlightened, we see the beginning "stone" of Light and Truth that deifies God as the infinite Creator of all finite matter. However, the atheistic scientists' beginning "stone" of darkness and deceit deifies finite matter as the infinite creator. If matter *always* has existed, then it has to be infinite, divine, and self-existent in its original form. On one side of the scales, the atheistic scientist confesses his beginning "stone" to be that matter always has existed. On the other side of the scales, he then has to be acknowledging that divinity exists in the form of matter. If matter always has existed, it must be divine. So while atheists willfully deify created matter on one side of the scales, they also willfully deny the existence of the infinite and divine Creator on the other side of the scales.

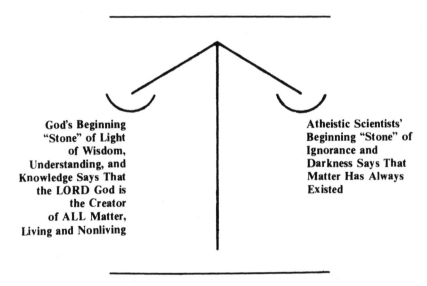

God's Beginning
"Stone" of Light
of Wisdom,
Understanding, and
Knowledge Says That
the LORD God is
the Creator
of ALL Matter,
Living and Nonliving

Atheistic Scientists'
Beginning "Stone" of
Ignorance and
Darkness Says That
Matter Has Always
Existed

According to their false theory, finite matter has the infinite wisdom to evolve itself into an infinitude of miraculous forms and shapes. This hypothesis deifies matter.

Such a concept is born out of fallen Lucifer's ignorance and darkness and is a metaphysical lie which robs people of the truth that God is the Originator, the first and the final Cause of all things that have come into existence.

The pernicious denial that God's eternal, creative power is the power responsible for finite existence is also a far-reaching, deleterious denial of God's free will and of man's free moral will. The denial of God's omnipotence undermines all morality. If there is no Creator with a free will, then there is no man who was created in the image and likeness of God with a free will; and there is no man with the power of choice which enables him to choose between right and wrong. Consequently, the atheists say, man has neither responsibility nor accountability for what he does wrongfully.

The real motive underlying the atheistic theories of evolution is not for true scientific research or for true scientific knowledge. The purpose in the atheistic mind, concerning his concept of creation, is a vain effort to discard God and to negate His moral truth.

If there is no God, there is *no Lawmaker*. If there is no Lawmaker, there is *no Lawgiver*. If there is no Lawgiver, there is *no Judge*. If there is no Judge, there is *no Punisher*. If there is no Punisher, then every man is free to live in the sensuality and licentiousness of his own carnal will. When people discard God, they also discard the holy standards of His moral law as accepted rules of conduct. Therefore, when people think that they have negated God's existence, they feel morally free and unrestrained to live according to their own sinful appetites.

The atheistic scientist experiences a paradoxical life between what he thinks in his heart, what he says with his mouth, and what he discovers in every law and force in nature. While man denies God's existence with his heart and mouth, he discovers, through science, the Works of God's master plan which confirm God's existence as a Master Mathematician, a Master Architect, a Divine Lawmaker, and an Almighty Judge.

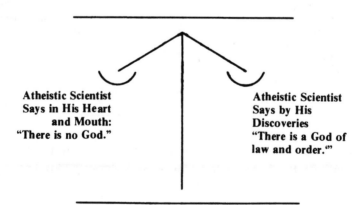

Atheistic Scientist Says in His Heart and Mouth: "There is no God."

Atheistic Scientist Says by His Discoveries "There is a God of law and order."

The atheistic scientist who denies God's existence confesses the very Works of God by his findings and investigations into the realms of nature. Scientific findings constantly confirm the existence of an infinite, omniscient God, although the atheistic scientist continually denies God's existence. How sad it is to see a person deny the existence of God's Person and His creative Works, while he finds supreme satisfaction and utmost joy in discovering God's Handiwork. His very discoveries of God's Works scream loudly, "There is a God of law and order."

God's divine laws and order in His universe constantly bear witness that He does exist. Therefore, man's reasons for believing in evolution are unfair to God and to himself.

Chapter Two

The Shining Stairway of the Believer's View of Creation

THE ATHEISTIC view of life's origin is in diametrical opposition to the truth. The truth is that the infinite, divine God descended with His life to bring all His creation to birth; and He crowned His creative Works with man, who is made in God's own image.

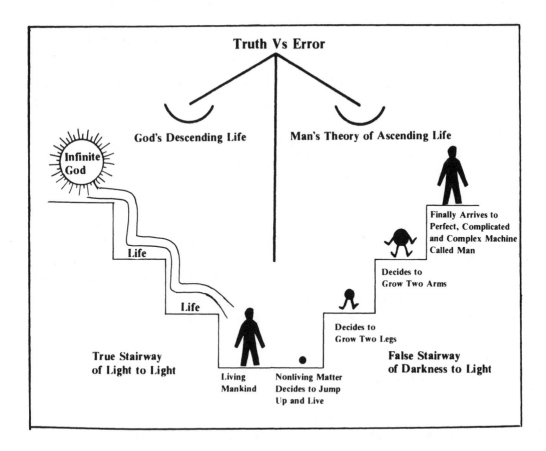

God, as the Framer of the world, selected and cut down perfect substance from His own invisible Word and brought it forth into visible forms of nonliving matter *and* living matter. Everything—all material, all shapes, patterns, molds, and everything in existence—has sprung from the infinite thoughts of God's free, almighty, creative will. The LORD God, the Creator, rules and reigns over all matter, forms, and life which He has brought into existence. God has established laws that are in operation which govern all the forces of nature. All matter, forms, and life are governed by God's fixed laws within nature.

Even atheistic evolutionists are forced to admit, on one hand, that there is a purpose, a reason, a pattern, and a design in both the structure and the behaviour of all forms of life. Who conceived the purpose and reason in nature? Who brought forth all these patterns and designs in nature? Atheistic evolutionists guess, assume, and speculate that the little original speck of matter with its infinite wisdom brought all the infinite amount of forms into existence. They expect others to accept with blind faith the pernicious lie that an original speck of matter is the original cause of all things. They want others to take for granted that their hypotheses are real and true. But God's beginning "stone" of Light and Truth teaches us that *He* is the primary Cause and Creator of all things.

The first reason man has for believing in God's creative power is because he can experience the creative power of God's Word and His Works within his own soul.

> Therefore *if any man be in Christ*, he is a new creature: old things are passed away; behold, *all things are become new* (II Corinthians 5:17).

Man first enters into Christ by faith; then Christ enters into his heart with His creative power, creating a new heart within him. Thus, Christ's creative power within revolutionizes one's whole manner of thought, and he enters into a new world of thought and life. God created the old worlds out of His Word, and He creates man's new heart out of His Word. The new creature receives new understanding, new enlightenment to see that which he never saw before. The new creature has a new will, a new purpose in life, which is to grow in his spiritual education and moral development.

The second reason man has for believing in God's creative power is because he can see the clear descriptions of it in God's infallible Word.

> Praise ye the LORD. Praise ye the LORD from the heavens: praise him in the heights. Praise ye him, all his angels: praise ye him, all

his hosts. Praise ye him, sun and moon: praise him, all ye stars of light. Praise him, ye heavens of heavens, and ye waters that be above the heavens. *Let them praise the name of the LORD: for he commanded and they were created* (Psalm 148:1-5).

The entire terrestrial world is filled with heights, depths, length, and breadth of God's creative Word, which man's mortal mind cannot conceive. For example, God's Word describes the vast host of His created luminaries in His super-celestial heavens. Yes, God's immutable Word reveals the excellent greatness of His creative power.

The third reason man has for believing in God's creative power is the magnificent display of God's infinite Word through His creative Works in the natural creation.

The heavens declare the glory of God; and the firmament sheweth his handywork. Day unto day uttereth speech, and night unto night sheweth knowledge. There is no speech nor language, where their voice is not heard. Their line is gone out through all the earth, and their words to the end of the world. In them hath he set a tabernacle for the sun (Psalm 19:1-4).

The creation everywhere bears witness to God's ineffable wisdom and power. What man's naked eye alone can see of God's creation is sufficient to proclaim a majestic, divine Creator. Moreover, man's invention of astronomical instruments gives him an infinitely greater witness of God's majestical Works and, therefore, greater cause for reverential wonder and awe.

The daily rising and the setting of the sun is a witness of God's wondrous might. The nightly shining of the moon and stars is a witness of God's majestical and almighty power.

The fourth reason man has for believing in God's creative power is the revelation of His master plan which is made known throughout His Word. God's infallible Word describes His creative Works in the prehistoric worlds, the present world, and what shall be in the future worlds. Scientists, by their discovery of bits and pieces from the prehistoric worlds, also have given man evidence that these worlds *did exist.* Man himself is a witness of the present, existing creation. Since there are witnesses concerning the *past* and *present* creations in God's Word, man surely can trust the veracity of God's Word concerning the *future* creations.

Chapter Three

God's Master Plan for Man's Future

GOD'S master plan for the future creations calls for a new heaven, a new earth, and a new city.

> For, behold, *I create new heavens and a new earth*: and the former shall not be remembered, nor come into mind (Isaiah 65:17).

> *For as the new heavens and the new earth, which I will make*, shall remain before me, saith the LORD, so shall your seed and your name remain (Isaiah 66:22).

> And I saw a new heaven and a new earth: for the first heaven and the first earth were passed away; and there was no more sea. And I John saw *the holy city, new Jerusalem*, coming down from God out of heaven, prepared as a bride adorned for her husband (Revelation 21:1,2).

How infinite and how inexhaustible is God's almighty, divine power! The same God, Who by His Word and Works created the heavens and the earth, also will create new heavens and a new earth. Therefore, when one understands God's master plan—past, present, and future—it chases away the overhanging clouds of deceit in one's mental sky, leaving the radiant rays of light and truth illuminating the mind and soul.

God's original, eternal master plan is a harmonious plan that calls for perfect unity and harmony between God and His creation. Because of God's immutable omnipotence and omniscience, He will not cease Working in His creation until He has accomplished the perfection of His master plan.

God has a creative master plan that He wrought through His Son, and He has a moral master plan in the spiritual realm that He must Work through His Son in the hearts and minds of His creatures. God *gave* His Son a mature perfect plan in the beginning for both the natural and the spiritual realms. Although the enemy, sin, has endeavoured to hinder God's master plan, God still is implementing His master plan.

God's moral master plan for fallen mankind is for him to grow in spiritual education and in moral development as he receives God's Word and obeys it.

God uses all of man's failures, mistakes, miseries, and wretchednesses of his own self-will as an educative, instructive lesson to show him the uselessness of his independent self-will. Hence, God uses the failure of man's self-will as a preparation for teaching him the fallacy and deceitfulness of his own independent way. Then God leads the believer to His perfect moral master plan which He has hidden for him in His mysterious, purposive will.

From the beginning, God's mysterious, purposive will has continued to Work in and through His creation; it will continue Working in the same manner until some day all things will be brought into perfect unity and harmony with God, His Spirit, and His Word, the Christ.

> Having made known unto us the mystery of his will, according to his good pleasure which he hath purposed in himself; That *in the dispensation of the fulness of times he might gather together in one all things in Christ,* both which are in heaven, and which are on earth; even in him: (Ephesians 1:9,10).

Our final joy and happiness will not consist in our solitary soul being in solitary communion with God; but we will joy and be happy in the joint fellowship and communion with God and all His creation. This final joy and lasting happiness will be experienced when God and all His creation are joined together into complete harmony and unity in the dispensation of the fullness of times, through His Son, the LORD Jesus Christ.

God's mysterious, eternal master plan is forever Working, and it will bring every knee to bow and every tongue to confess that Jesus Christ is LORD to the glory and honour of God the Father.

> That at the name of Jesus *every knee should bow,* of things in heaven, and things in earth, and things under the earth; And that every tongue should confess that Jesus Christ is Lord, to the glory of God the Father (Philippians 2:10,11).

The unified light in the starry heavens is a witness of the unity and harmony in God's creative Works that already exist and have existed *from the beginning.* No single light in the heavens ministers as a single, solitary light. Each joins its light to others, making one unified glorious, splendourous servant to the earth and its world of inhabitants. Thus, the unity and harmony of the lights of heaven are examples of the

296

unity and harmony that will ultimately exist in the dispensation of the fullness of times.

Because God is the Cause and Creator of all creation, He is worthy to receive the praise and respect from His creation and the acknowledgment from them of His right to govern and to guide them.

God's Word confirms His right, in His infinite excellencies, to receive glory and gratitude from His creatures.

> *Thou art worthy, O Lord, to receive glory and honour* and power:
> for thou hast created all things, and for thy pleasure they are and
> were created (Revelation 4:11).

God the Father is the first Cause of all things because all things first existed in His master plan before He gave it to His Son, the Christ, Who created all things at His pleasure and for His pleasure. Through His creative Works, the Son of God implemented the Father's master plan. Therefore, God is worthy to be acknowledged by His creation as the supreme Sovereign.

> That they may see, and know, and consider, and understand
> together, that the hand of *the LORD hath done this, and the Holy*
> *One of Israel hath created it* (Isaiah 41:20).

In the verses preceding this verse, the prophet described the great things that the hand of the LORD God (the Father) and the Holy One of Israel (the Son) will create for His people, Israel, during the millennial reign of Christ on earth. God promised to do a special creative Work in Israel's land during the Messiah's millennial reign, by opening special rivers and fountains which will turn her barren wilderness into a pool of water, and by planting special trees in her barren wilderness and desert. The hand of the LORD God (the Father) and the Holy One of Israel (the Son) will continue their unified creative Works during the millennial dispensation to come.

God, by the divine will and power of His Spirit, created all things at the first, and by His same Spirit, He preserves His creation. God has established His law of circularity in the earth. Man is born and dies; then he is succeeded by his living offspring. All creation, both on land and in the sea, are dependent on God for their existence, for food to bring them strength and satisfaction, and for the very continuation of their lives. Since sin has entered into mankind, all generations of the earth are born of earthly, mortal, physical bodies of dust; therefore, they are subject to decay. However, the Spirit of life from God continues to renew life upon the earth.

Thou sendest forth thy spirit, *they are created*: and thou renewest the face of the earth (Psalm 104:30).

Faith comes by hearing God's Word (Romans 10:17). Therefore, the more we learn of God's master plan as it is revealed in His Word, the greater is our faith in His creative Works.

Chapter Four

Which Do You Choose— Faith in God's Word, or Faith in the Unproven Theory of Evolution?

GOD has given man the power of choice in this life. All mankind has the power to choose between two or more things; he has the power of election and preference.

As a free moral agent, man has the freedom of choice as to the course pursued or as to the things chosen. Therefore, everyone should be very discriminating about his choices. Wise choices lead to God. Foolish choices lead away from God and to misery, woe, and death. God offers to every soul the choice between good and evil. Hence, let every one carefully consider his choice between God's eternal Word and the temporal words of earthly creatures.

It is obvious from the study of the many different theories that have existed in evolution, which have had to be changed because of scientific discoveries of the truth, that the theory of evolution is temporal and changeable. It is anything but immutable.

However, the immutability of God's Word continually is being proven by scientific discoveries.

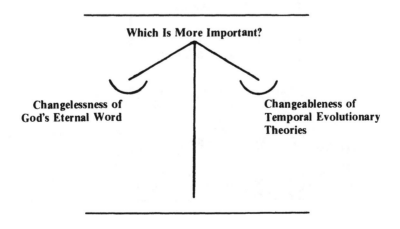

Which Is More Important?

Changelessness of
God's Eternal Word

Changeableness of
Temporal Evolutionary
Theories

God's Word is changeless. It remains the same. It never alters in its nature, will, and disposition. It is the same as it always has been and as it always will be. God's eternal Word is never changeable, fickle, or inconstant. It is immutable. It is changeless. It can be trusted both now and forever more.

God's Word is infinite and eternally permanent, and it remains a prominent pinnacle of Truth. The more that Satan tries to rub out God's ineffaceable, everlasting Word, the brighter its shines because it has been written with God's immortal pen.

What a contrast God's eternal Word is to the temporal theories of evolution which are variable, inconstant, and fickle. The discoveries of true science always are revealing the fickleness, inconstancy, and inconsistencies of the theories of evolution.

If we collect the real, scientific, established facts about evolution and then draw our conclusions, what do we find? To our utter amazement, we find a "dream house of conclusions" which evolutions have built upon the sinking sands of speculations, assumptions, interpretations, and hypotheses.

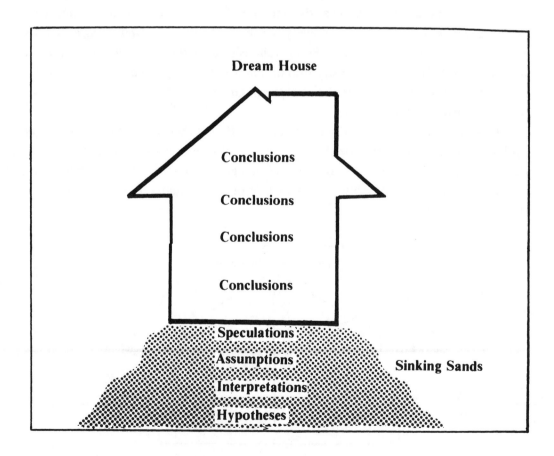

Evolutionists' "dream house of conclusions" is built upon erroneous sinking sands which, sooner or later, will allow the house to collapse.

It takes less faith to believe the changelessness of God's eternal Word and Power than to believe the changeableness of temporal theories of evolution.

Which do you, the reader, choose—truth or supposition?

Bibliography

(Quotes appear on
following pages
of text)

Adams, Robert. McC. "Smithsonian Horizons."
    Smithsonian Magazine. Sept., 1978.   263

Barnet, Lincoln. *The Universe and Dr. Einstein*.
    New York, NY.: William Morrow and Co., 1957.   228

Bethell, Tom. "Creationists and Authoritarians."
    The Wall Street Journal. 9 Dec., 1986.   246, 247

Bryan, Williams J. "The Bible or Evolution."
    Rpt. Murfreesboro, TN: Sword of the Lord Pub.   174

Cuvier, Georges. *Essay on the Theory of the Earth*. 1817.
    rpt. 3rd. ed. from rpt. 1978. New York. Arno Press.
    From a copy in the University of Wisconsin Library   198-209

Devoe, Alan. "The Marvel of an Insect." In *Our Amazing
    World of Nature: Its Marvels & Mysteries*. 3rd ed.
    Pleasantville, N.Y.: The Reader's Digest Assn.,
    Inc. 1969.   270, 272

Dorfman, Andrea. "Quest for the Missing Link." *Science
    Digest*. March, 1984, p. 24.   141

Egger, Stephen A. "The New Predators, Crime Enters the
    Future." *The Futurist*. April, 1985, p. 16.   277

Freeman, Ira M. "Light Travels in Straight Lines." *The New
    Book of Knowledge*. New York, NY.: Golier, Inc.,
    1972, Vol. 11, p. 260.   228

Galloway, Joseph L., Carla Anne Robbins, Stephen
    Budiansky, Erica E. Goode, and Gillian Sanford.
    "Currents." *U.S. News & World Report*.
    29 Feb., 1988, p. 9.   49

Gange, Dr. Robert A. *Origins and Destiny*. Waco, Texas.
    Word Book Publisher, 1986.   170, 179, 180, 183,
    186, 188, 232,
    263, 266-268

Gest, Ted. "Crime-rate Forecasts Go Awry:" *U.S. News & World Report.* 5 May, 1986, p. 24.   276

Gribbin, Dr. John. *Genesis.* New York, NY.: Delacorte Press/Eleanor Fried, 1981.   184, 185, 187, 188, 198

Hedgpeth, Joel W. "Ocean/How the Ocean Moves." *The World Book Encyclopedia.* Chicago, IL.: Field Enterprises. Educational Corp. 1974. Vol. 14, p. 498   225

Hunter, Robert, A.M., F.G.S., (English ed.) and Prof. Charles Morris (American ed). *Universal Dictionary of the English Language.* New York, NY.: Peter Fenelon Collier. 1897, Vol. 4, p. 4142.   9

Huse, Scott M. *The Collapse of Evolution.* Baker Book House Company. Grand Rapids, Michigan, 1986.   192, 243, 250, 263

Jastrow, Robert. "The Dinosaur Massacre, a Double-barrelled Mystery." *Science Digest*, Sept., 1983, p. 51.   24

Lamsa, Dr. George M. *Holy Bible, From Ancient Eastern Manuscripts.* Philadelphia, PA.: A. J. Holman Co., 1957, 19th print.   9

Leakey, Richard and Alan Walker. "Homo Erectus Unearthed." *National Geographic.* Nov., 1986, pp. 624-629.   196

Lister, Clive R.B. "Oceanography/Movement of Ocean Water." *The New Book of Knowledge.* New York NY.: Grolier, Inc., 1972, Vol. 14, pp. 32, 33.   224

Miller, James E. (Chairman of the Department of Meterology and Oceanography at New York University). "General Circulation of Air Around the Earth." *The World Book Encyclopedia.* Field Enterprises. Educational Corp. Chicago, IL.: 1974, Vol. 21, p. 278.   217, 218

Monmaney, Terence. "Complex Window on Life's Most Basic Molecules." *Smithsonian Magazine.* July, 1985, p. 114.   189

Morris, Henry M. *Science and the Bible.* Trinity Broadcasting Network Edition. 1988.   165

Muller, Richard A. *Reader's Digest*. Sept., 1985, p. 99.
    Condensed from *New York Times* magazine.
    March 24, 1985.   197

Newsweek. "Is Man a Subtle Accident?" 3 Nov., 1980.   249

Noda, Haruhiko. *Kagaku to Kogyo*. "Busshitsu to Beimei:
    Seibutsu Gakusha no Miru Uchu." Trans.
    Dr. Satoko Yamada. (Nihon Kagaku Kai
    [Publisher], Japan), 1975, Vol. 28, No. 10, p. 734.   261

Noda, Haruhiko. *"Hoshi No Shinka to Seibutsu No
    Shinka." Trans. Dr. Satoko Yamada.* Kagaku
    Asahi. (Asahi Shinbunsha. Japan.)
    Sept., 1971, Vol. 9., p. 127.   *262*

Pfeiffer, John E. "Cro-Magnon Hunters Were Really Us,
    Working Out Strategies for Survival."
    Smithsonian Magazine. Oct. 1986, pp. 75-84   194

Platt, Rutherford. "The Marvels of Cross-pollination."
    In *Our Amazing World of Nature: Its Marvels
    & Mysteries*. 3rd ed. Pleasantville, NY.:
    The Reader's Digest Assn., Inc., 1969, pp. 100-104   270, 271

Rigutti, Mario. *A Hundred Billion Stars*. Trans. Mirella
    Giacconi. Cambridge, Mass. The MIT Press,
    Eng. ed. 1984.   141, 178, 180, 275

Shell, Ellen Ruppel. "Solo Flights into the Ozone Hole
    Reveal Its Causes." *Smithsonian Magazine*.
    Feb., 1988.   279

Spar, Jerome. "Winds and Weather." *The New Book
    of Knowledge*. Grolier, Inc.: New York, NY.:
    1972, Vol. 20, pp. 184-186.   219-221

Stanley, Steven M. "Mass Extinctions in the Oceans."
    Scientific American. June, 1984, pp. 64, 65.   62, 63, 197

Tice, D. J. "Life After Darwin." *TWA Ambassador*.
    Aug., 1986, pp. 43, 45, 46, 47   243, 264, 266

The Academic American Encyclopedia, Danbury, Conn.:
    Grolier Inc., 1983. Vol. 19, p. 386.   34, 35

The New Book of Knowledge. Grolier, Inc.: New York,
    NY.: 1972, Vol. 17., P. 458.   215

The New Encyclopedia Britannica. 1980, Vol. 7.   141

The New Encyclopedia Britannica. 1980. 15th ed.
    Vol. 17, pp. 8, 9.   251, 253-255, 259, 260

The New International Encyclopedia. Dodd, Mead and
    Co., New York, NY. 1908, Vol. 5   238

The Universal Dictionary of the English Language.
    New York, NY.: Peter Fenelon Collier.
    1897, 15th ed., Vol. 2., p. 1858.   256

Trachtman, Paul. "The Search for Life's Origins—and a
    First 'Synthetic Cell.'" *Smithsonian Magazine.*
    June, 1984, p. 43.   56, 57, 247, 248

Trefil, Dr. James S. *Space Time Infinity.* 5th ed.
    Washington, D.C.: Smithsonian Books, 1985.   1, 2, 18, 42, 63, 129, 138, 141, 142 153, 159, 178, 182, 183, 194

Vidal, Gonzalo. *Scientific American.* Feb., 1984.   181

Weaver, Kenneth F. "The Search for Our Ancestors."
    National Geographic. Nov. 1985, pp. 561-623   195, 196

Wendt, Herbert. *Before the Deluge.* Trans. from German
    by Richard & Clara Winston. Doubleday, 1968;
    Original ed. 1965.   239, 240

Index